D0517448

Introduction

PETERSEN AUTOMOTIVE BOOKS

LEE KELLEY/Editorial Director
BRUCE CALDWELL/Editor
CRAIG CALDWELL/Contributing Editor
DAVID COHEN/Managing Editor
SPENCE MURRAY/Automotive Editor
SUSIE VOLKMANN/Art Director
LINNEA HUNT-STEWART/Copy Editor
RAYMOND HARPER/Copy Editor
LINDA SARGENT/Copy Editor
FERN CASON/Editorial Coordinator

Cover Photography
EDDIE PAUL

BASIC BODYWORK AND PAINTING

Copyright 1981 by Petersen Publishing Company, 8490 Sunset Blvd., Los Angeles, CA 90069. Phone: (213) 657-5100. All rights reserved. No part of this book may be reproduced without written permission. Printed in the U.S.A.

ISBN 0-8227-5057-0

Library of Congress Catalog Card Number: 81-81069

Bodywork and painting are rewarding activities either as vocation or avocation. Body repair and painting, as vocation, are usually based on a background of simple, backyard experiences. Although there are very good classes at technical and vocational schools, most bodymen and painters start out by reading books like Petersen's *BODYWORK & PAINTING*, and then experimenting on an old car.

We can't stress practice and experimentation enough. All bodywork and painting skills take time to refine. Sure, you can usually do passable work on your first try, but fine quality work takes lots of practice. Experience will help you over the rough spots and the times when something goes wrong. This is especially true in painting because any time chemicals are used, deviations in mixing, application, and atmospheric conditions can cause undesired results. The experienced painter will immediately know what went wrong and the best way to correct the situation. When you do encounter mistakes and problems, it is important to remain calm and remember that old painter's motto, "It will rub out." Almost any mistake can be corrected; panic will only compound the situation.

Every effort has been made to ensure that the information presented here is as accurate as possible, but you should always check out any new technique or product. Experiment on a piece of scrap metal or an out-of-the-way place. Pay strict attention to the manufacturer's directions—they know what they are talking about. Oftentimes you will encounter information that differs from the manufacturer's directions (this is not to say that more than one method won't work), but stick with the manufacturer's instructions until you feel confident enough in your own abilities to experiment.

Safety is a topic that should never be overlooked or understressed when discussing bodywork and painting. Both fields have lots of potential for accidents, especially fire and chemical accidents. Torches and welders are an obvious source of fire danger, and paint products are quite flammable. A lot of force is used in bodywork, so wear sturdy shoes, clothes, and safety goggles. Paint fumes (especially those from two-part paints) can be very dangerous, so get a top-quality respirator and wear it whenever painting. Pay attention to all safety regulations and precautions, and bodywork and painting will be enjoyable rather than hazardous.

A real sense of accomplishment can be gained by doing your own bodywork and painting, not to mention the benefit of saving the high cost of professional labor. We hope this book will help you achieve success in the field of bodywork and painting.

PETERSEN PUBLISHING COMPANY

R.E. PETERSEN/Chairman of the Board; **F.R. WAINGROW**/President; **ROBERT E. BROWN**/Sr. Vice President, Publisher; **DICK DAY**/Sr. Vice President; **JIM P. WALSH**/Sr. Vice President, National Advertising Director; **ROBERT MacLEOD**/Vice President, Publisher; **THOMAS J. SIATOS**/Vice President, Group Publisher; **PHILIP E. TRIMBACH**/Vice President, Financial Administration; **WILLIAM PORTER**/Vice President, Circulation Director; **JAMES J. KRENEK**/ Vice President, Manufacturing; **LEO D. La REW**/Treasurer; **DICK WATSON**/Controller; **LOU ABBOTT**/Director, Production; **JOHN CARRINGTON**/Director, Book Sales and Marketing; **MARIA COX**/ Director, Data Processing; **BOB D'OLIVO**/Director, Photography; **NIGEL P. HEATON**/Director, Circulation Marketing and Administration; **AL ISAACS**/Director, Corporate Art; **CAROL JOHNSON**/Director, Advertising Administration; **DON McGLATHERY**/Director, Advertising Research; **JACK THOMPSON**/Assistant Director, Circulation; **VERN BALL**/Director, Fulfillment Services

Contents

1
Metalwork Fundamentals

All damaged cars can be repaired; it's just a matter of economics. Because of high labor costs many cars are now considered "totalled" that were previously "repairable." It is amazing to see how mild some body damage is on supposedly totalled cars. Consequently, the current costs of professional body repair can often work to the advantage of the do-it-yourself bodyman. If you have more time than money, you can get some real deals on fixable cars.

A related area that affects the home repairman is the high cost of parts. Since labor is so expensive, many body shops will replace a fender rather than remove the dents. This trend has increased wrecking yard prices for sheetmetal close to factory prices and has created a lucrative market for "stolen to order" body parts. Since body shops often discard repairable fenders, a tour through body shop trash bins could turn up parts you need.

Also, learning to repair panels with the time-honored hammer and dolly methods is a valuable skill.

Even in this era of replacement and filler body shops, there is still a big demand for talented craftsmen who can transform metal with their hands and a few traditional tools. In the growing field of automobile restorations, metalworking craftsmen are highly sought after and handsomely rewarded.

When it comes to making body repairs, there are two methods: the quick way and the thinking man's way. The quick way is to rush into the job just removing the damaged parts without any thought as to how the damage was caused. The thinking man's way starts with a little consideration and inspection of the damage to determine how the dents were caused. When you realize how the damage was caused, it is easier to reverse it.

Know Your Work

It only stands to reason that the more you know about a subject, the better your chances of success in that field. Just as a butcher needs to know about the different cuts of meat before he can start hacking away at a side of beef, so must the body-man know about metal and the design of automobiles before he can start hacking away at the side of a damaged car.

Because of the requirements of forming and use, the sheetmetal used in a car body is of low-carbon steel. If a higher carbon metal were used, the parts might resist certain impacts better, but the panels would be very hard to form at the factory and extremely difficult to repair. Special car bodies have been made from rather exotic steel and other metals through the years, usually as a publicity stunt or part of a research program, but ordinary steel remains the leader in automotive body construction. Strength for mild steel body panels can be achieved with extra reinforcements, strong shape, or a little more thickness in the metal.

Sheetmetal plasticity permits a shape change when enough force is applied. In the beginning, the sheetmetal is a large flat sheet that becomes a fender or a hood or a top panel. When the flat sheet is modified by the press, the change is called plastic deformation. The amount of deformation possible without breaking is relative to the metal's hardness. Plastic deformation is achieved with both tension and compression. Deformation under tension is ductility; deformation under compressive force is malleability. The end result of tension deformation is stretching, and the result of pressure deformation is upsetting. The enthusiast is interested in both aspects of deformation since both stretching and upsetting take place in body panels during modifications and repair work.

When metal is bent, stretched, upset, or changed in shape at a temperature less than red heat, it has been cold worked. That is, plastic deformation has taken place without the use of heat. Of course, how much a piece of metal can be worked cold has a limit, beyond which it will break. As this limit is approached, the metal increases in strength and stiffness. This is called *work hardening*. A good example of work hardening is supplied by bending a flat piece of sheetmetal double without creasing the bend. When the metal is flattened out again, the original bend remains and two new ones are added, one on either side of the first. The metal at the first bend stretched and became work hardened, and so it is stronger than the rest of the metal.

Some work hardness will be found in all body panels, caused by the original press forming. When a panel has been damaged, additional hardness will

Repairing damaged cars can bring a real sense of accomplishment. This Camaro had enough types of sheetmetal damage to serve as a metalworking textbook.

Metalwork Fundamentals

occur and still more hardening will accompany the straightening process.

Elasticity is the ability of the metal to regain its original shape after deflection. Also, when a panel is warped slightly, it may spring back into its original shape when the restraining force is removed. Of course, the harder the steel the greater the elasticity which means elasticity will increase as work hardening increases.

When the metal will not spring back completely to the original shape, it has reached the elastic limit, or the yield point. When a damaged fender is removed from a car, both the fender and the inner splash panel will have a tendency to spring back toward original shape slightly. All sheet steel will retain some spring-back no matter how badly damaged. This is of significance to the body repairman since a badly "waved" panel may return to normal shape when a single, simple buckled spot is removed.

When a body panel is made in a press or die, residual stresses are left in the panel. That is, there will be areas of stress that remain in the panel. Cut through the edge of a hood panel and the two pieces will pull apart slightly; the residual stress from the original stamping causes this. Such stresses will usually be greater the more complicated the panel shape. Thus, when a panel is repaired it will probably also be restored to a state of minor tension.

Heat is a part of body repair, whether from the torch or from the grinder, and will have three separate effects: scaling, grain structure change, and expansion/contraction. The three effects happen at the same time during a repair operation.

When steel is heated to 430 degrees F., if the steel is clean and bright, the color will be a pale yellow. As the heat is increased, the color will change to straw, brown, purple, light blue, and dark blue, which is reached at around 600 degrees F. The color will then fade to a gray or greenish tone until the first reddish color comes at about 900 degrees F. Various colors of red are then apparent until approximately 1550 degrees F., when the red increases in brightness through orange and yellow to white. Steel melts at around 2600 degrees F.

Scale forms when the heated area is attacked by oxygen; therefore, this scale will form faster on the side away from the torch. When the torch is removed, however, scale will immediately form on the near side. This scale is not a major problem. A definite and progressive change in metal grain structure occurs when steel is heated toward the melting

Here is the same car after the body was massaged back to its original shape. The body was covered with an outstanding custom paint job by Bill Carter of Carter Pro Paint in Chatsworth, California.

point, with a consequent result in hardness and strength. There is not enough carbon in sheetmetal to harden from heating, but it can be annealed. When a piece of metal has been work hardened, it can be returned to the soft stage by rearranging the grain structure. If the metal is heated to the salmon color just above bright red (about 1600 degrees F.) the metal will reach the critical temperature where the grain structure is reformed.

When metal is heated it will expand a given amount; when it cools it will contract. The coefficient of expansion in automotive sheetmetal up to 1500 degrees F. is six-millionths of an inch per degree, which seems infinitesimal. But this is the reason metal will warp when heat is applied. There is a significant difference between heat distortion and stretching. There are four basic classifications to the crown of a particular panel. A ''crown'' is the curvature of a given panel. There is the low crown (low curvature), high crown (high curvature), combination high and low crown, and reverse crown.

Panels with low crowns have very little curvature, and consequently, very little load-carrying ability. The roof panel is a good example, with slight curves at the edges and a midsection that is nearly flat. At the extreme edges near the drip molding, the top panel will usually curve rapidly with a high crown.

A high crown is often considered a shape that

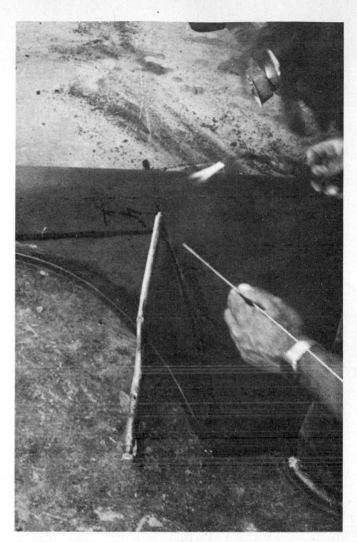

Creative metalmen like customizer Eddie Paul can do much more than repair a fender; they can change the whole look of the car with a torch. This new Mustang quarter panel was sectioned to form a wild fender flare.

curves rapidly in all directions. Such surfaces are quite common on older cars and will usually resist deformation due to damage. Such high crown areas would be the top and front portions of a Model A fender, the body roll at the rear of the top, and so on. The tendency has been away from this type of tight styling during recent times. The modern car is made up of very large low crown panels. Obviously, a high crown area is very strong in itself and will not need reinforcements as will the low crown panel.

The combination of high and low crown panels is very common to the modern car; fenders and door panels, for instance, provide a very strong structure. A door panel is usually much stronger than a roof panel.

The reverse crown shows up in the complicated areas of design, as an inside curve on a hood or fender. A typical example of an inside curve or reverse crown would be the taillight area of cars where the metal is ''pooched'' out to accept the taillight assembly. These areas have very high-strength concentrations, the reason damage to such an area is usually severe but localized. To the bodyman such damage usually means using some kind of body filler.

Grinding discs can be scalloped like this to make them ''floppy'' so the edges won't catch in a crevice or seam.

Metalwork Fundamentals

When the metal of a high crown area is struck, the metal can always be expected to push outward from the point of impact. When a low crown area is struck, the metal will tend to pull inward. A combination panel will include both outward and inward forces.

Types of Damage

When a collision occurs, damage will depend on the area affected and the force of the collision. Damage can be separated into five types: displaced areas, simple bends, rolled buckles, upsets, and stretches.

A displaced area is a part of the metal that has been moved but not damaged. If a door panel is smacked sharply, for instance, the entire panel may buckle inward. But the actual damage will be only around the edges of the larger buckle. If the panel is lightly pushed from the back it may snap back into place, and repair is needed only around the small buckles, or edges. If a fender is hit slightly near the headlight, it may cause slight waves down the side of the fender toward the door. There may be a small buckle in the fender somewhere that is holding the

metal down. If the fender is pushed or pulled in a reverse direction from the impact, the displaced metal reverts to orginal shape and only the small buckled places need repair.

Whenever collision occurs, there is usually some form of simple bending involved. In the above case, if the fender is struck hard enough, the small-buckled area may turn into a simple bend, where the metal makes a kind of S-shape as it is forced out of place. As the severity of the simple bend increases it becomes a rolled buckle. In the simple bend, the outside of the bend includes metal-under-tension and the inside of the bend under-compression. This is in a very small area as sheetmetal is so thin, but there is a distortion of the metal involved.

In the rolled buckle, the S-shape of the bend is pronounced, and the metal tucks under itself. Such damage is not unusual to front or rearend collisions and indicates a rather severe impact. For the enthusiast, such a buckle indicates a considerable amount of metalwork, starting with pulling or pushing the panel back into some semblance of shape and then working the buckled area carefully with hand tools.

An upset in metal happens when opposing forces push against an area of metal causing it to yield. Because of this yield, the surface area of the metal will be reduced and the thickness increased. An upset

Here is the fender flare in rough shape. You can still see where the quarter panel was sectioned.

area will tend to gather the surrounding metal and does not, to a large extent, occur in automotive bodies. However, a very small upset can cause the panel to react strangely, sometimes even as though the panel had been stretched. Unless the metal shows signs of having been worked before, chances are the panel has an upset area somewhere on its surface.

Stretching is the result of tension rather than pressure as in upsetting, with stretching typical of the gouge type of damage. When a car bumper rakes down a door panel, it will probably cause a gouge in the panel. This is stretched metal and the repair procedure is usually one of filling the gouge as there is seldom a raised bump anywhere near. A false stretch can result from a nearby upset, but it usually takes an expert to see this.

When making the decision about proper repair procedure, the bodyman must determine the angle of impact; speed of the impact object; size, rigidity, and weight of the impact object; and construction of the damaged panel. Trying to visualize how the metal folded during the impact is the first step to repair, since applying an opposite force will ordinarily pull much of the damage out.

The impact angle is determined by either a direct or glancing blow with a resulting effect on all other areas of the car. A big impact on the front end can cause misalignment at the rear of the body, and so on. If the impact angle is not too great, much of the impact force will be absorbed by the panel. If the angle is high, the impact energy may be diverted, leaving small damage. In some cases, the impact object may be sharp, driving some of the metal before it. This pushes the metal up in front of the object and stretches it behind. A typical sideswipe illustrates this possibility.

Taking the Body Apart for Repairs

It is important to understand that time spent trying to repair or modify a piece of sheetmetal is the same as spending money on the car since time is money. If an untrained metalman spends three hours repairing a 30-minute dent, the cost will likely be too high. Learning to assess the damage is important and not too difficult. A few minutes spent looking at a crumpled fender may save many hours of labor.

One typical consideration would be determining how much of the crumpled front end must be removed for a straightening operation, with the amount of time spent on the total project relative to the amount of body tear-down required. It is often easier to straighten a particular panel if it is removed from the vehicle, perhaps an inner splash

A tremendous amount of metal finishing is necessary to end up with a final product like this. When you realize the amount of work that goes into a set of metal fender flares, it is easy to see why flares cost so much.

Metalwork Fundamentals

Welding generates a lot of potentially damaging heat. To prevent warping, this custom front fender was packed with Moist Bastos.

or collapse of one section to slight misalignment. In all cases where frame damage is suspected, the enthusiast should entrust the vehicle to a frame shop for repair. Such shops are completely equipped with necessary gauges and equipment to check and repair the frame. Repair of the major frame is *not* a backyard project. It is possible to replace small front frame extensions, called frame horns, but nothing larger should be attempted in the home garage. Also, it is possible to save considerable money on a frame repair by removing all sheetmetal that might be in the way. The frame shop will have direct access to the job, so cost savings can be substantial.

Using Hydraulic Body Jacks

Hydraulic body jacks are specialized tools that not everyone owns, but they are readily available at tool rental outlets. These hydraulic body jacks are able to do a wide variety of repairs quickly and easily. If you plan to fix heavily damaged cars, a hydraulic body jack would be a good investment. Whether you buy or rent, a hydraulic body jack can restore buckled metal to near factory fresh shape quickly.

Pulling the wrinkles from a piece of sheetmetal is better than pushing. This is particularly true where the section features low crown construction, such

panel, and sometimes the removal of an adjacent panel makes repair of a specific panel easier and faster.

When body parts are being taken apart, save all the nuts and bolts, as well as small brackets. These parts are seldom included on replacement panels and, as a result, are difficult to obtain individually.

The front sheetmetal can sometimes be removed from the chassis as a unit, by removing bolts down either side of the cowl and one or two bolts holding the radiator core support to the frame. When the electrical wiring and radiator hoses have been disconnected, the front fenders, grille, radiator, and core support can be detached as a single piece. Nothing else on the body is so easily removed. The doors and deck lid are removable at the hinges.

Frame Damage

Any time a vehicle is damaged, it is possible that the frame or frame structure has also been damaged. While some of the damage may be obvious, misalignment can be involved to a great extent without being seen.

Frame damage can run the gamut from twisting

Hydraulic body jacks like this one made by the H.K. Porter company of Somerville, Massachusetts, are great for "pushing" out damaged sections.

as a top or quarter-panel. When tension is applied to a panel, the dented area is pulled back to shape rather than pushed. Pushing or driving a dent tends to concentrate the force in small areas which upsets the metal. This means the upset areas must then be taken out if the final job is to be a success. By pulling the metal straight, there are no upset areas, thus less work. In areas where the primary concern is alignment, such as door posts, pushing with the jack is acceptable if done correctly.

Learning where to attach hydraulic body jack points is a matter of recognizing the proper leverage angles, lift reaction, work hardening of the damaged place, variations of the surface crown, and alignment with the panel crown. Attachment of the jack ends should be done so that the most leverage is applied directly to the bent area. It helps to use a hydraulic body jack with a lot of versatile attachments like the body jacks made by H.K. Porter, Inc., 74 Foley St., Somerville, MA 02143. They make the P-F line of body tools which includes the P-F all angle pull clamp. This versatile clamp allows force to be applied in the most ideal areas.

Lift reaction should be considered when using hydraulic body jacks. When a jack is attached on either side of a dent, there is an action to pull the dent up and a reaction through the jack to force the metal downward at the attachment points. This reaction force will cease when the dent is pulled out, although the jack can still be bumped to increase tension on the metal being straightened. When looking for attachment points for securing a jack in tension-straightening, these points should be strong. The edges of the door or fender would be

Even very tight areas can be spread back to their normal shape with P-F's hydraulic spreader.

Body jacks are also designed to "pull" out damaged areas. Jacks like the P-F Speed-Master are available with a large selection of accessories to make it possible to pull from almost any angle. P-F's unique BU0285 pull clamp is extremely versatile.

good examples.

When a panel has been crumpled, the area most affected will be work hardened due to upset of the metal. When tension is applied to pull the metal back into a rough shape, as much of the area as possible should be worked out with hand tools before the tension is released. The reason is simple enough, since any work done to the metal will tend to stretch it back to the original shape.

Repairing areas of high crown or combination crown design will take more time than simple low crown repair, but the jacks can still be used effectively. However, go slowly at first. In fact, the maxim for any hydraulic jack work, "Proceed with caution."

Metalworking Techniques

The initial step after disassembly of destroyed pieces is roughing the metal into shape. This first step will be followed by bumping (hammer and dolly work) and finishing (filling and grinding). Align-

Metalwork Fundamentals

The correct use of a hammer and dolly is one of the most important bodywork skills anyone can learn. A tremendous variety of shapes can be handled due to the many different surfaces on a set of body hammers and dollies.

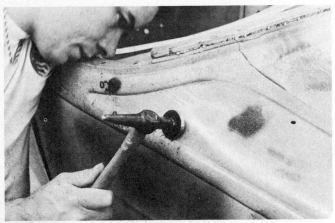

An experienced bodyman knows when to use the hammer on the outside of the dent and when to use it from the backside.

ing is also part of the repair and is usually included with roughing, but it is so full of tricks that we have treated it separately in a chapter called ''Panel Alignment.''

Sheetmetal repair is like building a house, in that each step builds upon those taken previously, and a mistake made at first will likely be magnified at the finish. Roughing generally means bringing a piece of sheetmetal back into general contour, including supporting members and reinforcements. When a panel is being roughed into shape, it may have force applied by using a hammer and dolly, by pushing with a body jack, or pulling with a body jack. Sometimes a combination of these methods will be required, or all three may be involved.

The importance of initial roughing is emphasized since the newcomer to bodywork will make fewer mistakes in the later stages if the roughing is reasonably successful. The cardinal rule is to always pull if possible, and never push or hammer major damage unless absolutely necessary.

Once the rough shape has been attained and the panel at least looks like part of an automobile, the second and third phases of repair start. This begins with the hammer and dolly, two hand tools that can easily be misused if the workman is not careful. While the dolly can be used as a hammer, it is primarily used in conjunction with a hammer in both the hammer-on and hammer-off methods.

Hammer-on Technique

When the neophyte begins to learn metalwork, the hammer-on method seems the most difficult. This entails placing the dolly behind the panel and striking it through the metal. It is very difficult at first, but can be mastered with minimal experience. It is advisable to practice hammer and dolly coordination on a discarded piece of metal before attempting an actual repair.

At first, the force of the hammer blow on the dolly is not nearly so important as hitting the dolly at all. It is important to learn a technique wherein the hammer hits with just the right amount of force, time after time. Further, the hammer is allowed to bounce back. That is, the dolly should remain in constant contact with the metal, with the hammer rebounding from the blow. Improper use of the hammer and dolly can be expected at first, with the hammer striking the metal, causing the dolly to bounce away and restrike the backside of the metal. The dolly will bounce away slightly when the hammer is used

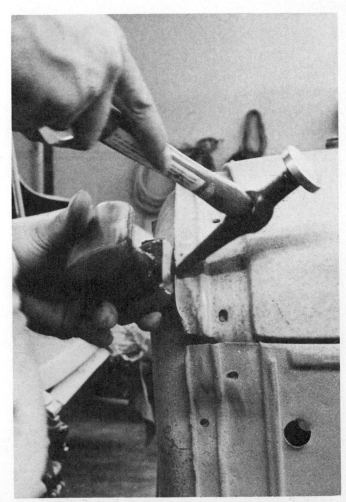

Straightening a wavy lip is one of the easiest tasks you can perform with a hammer and dolly. The dolly serves as an anvil for the hammer.

properly, or snapped with a definite wrist action, but it will not be a pronounced "limp-wrist" bounce.

The hammer-on technique is especially effective for raising a low point in metal as the hammer first tends to flatten the metal being struck. This is followed by the reaction of the dolly as it rebounds slightly from the hammer blow. If the hand holding the dolly increases its pressure, then the tendency of the dolly to raise the low spot also increases.

Hammer-off Technique

In the hammer-off technique the dolly is placed adjacent to the hammer blow, but not directly under it. Learning the hammer-off style is easy after learning the hammer-on technique. The spot struck by the hammer drives the metal down since it is not being supported by the dolly. Movement of the metal transfers the hammer-blow force to the dolly making it rebound the same as with the hammer-on technique. The effect is to drive the low spot up (from dolly force) and the high spot down (from hammer force) with a single hammer blow.

When using the hammer-off technique, the hammer blow should always be on the high metal adjacent to the low spot, never anywhere else. Learning to "see" with the hand is part of metalwork experience, and feeling to locate the low and high parts of the damage becomes a natural reaction. The dolly should be the high crown type, or the portion used should have minimum contact with the metal, and hammer blows should be just enough. Too much hammer effort will cause extra damage. Normally the dolly would be about ¼ inch away from the hammer blow depending upon the metal "springiness."

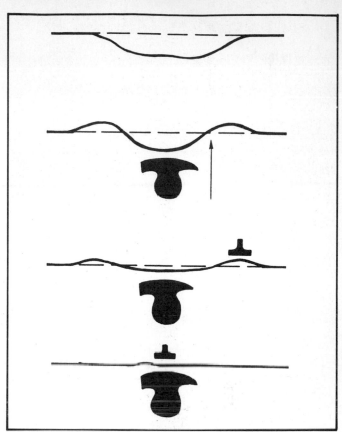

Shrinking a low spot starts with heat, then a blow from behind with a dolly. High spots are worked "off-dolly" as shown, then "on-dolly."

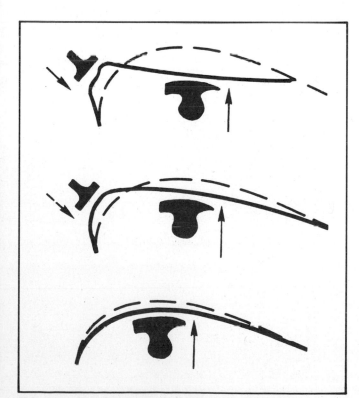

This illustration shows how "off-dolly" work straightens a damaged high crown fender.

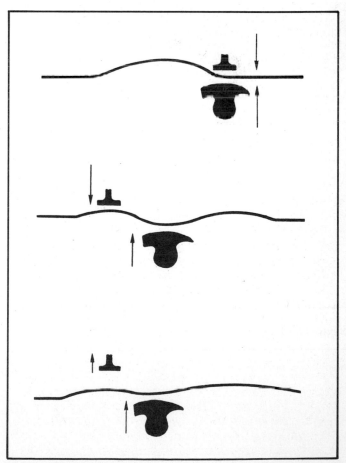

This illustration shows the "hammer-on" versus "hammer-off" dolly techniques.

Metalwork Fundamentals

This pick hammer is going to be used from behind a series of very small dents. The dents were marked with a marking pen for the purpose of this photo. Experienced bodymen know instinctively where to place hammer blows.

Using Pick Hammers

It is very difficult to "hit where you look" when learning to pick up low spots. Since the pick hammer is being driven toward the user and is out of sight behind the panel, the normal reaction is to hit below the desired spot and often off to the left side. Learning to use a pick hammer is a matter of practice, but the way to begin is to bring the hammer into view at first, then move it up to about where the low spot should be. A good guide to keep the hammer working in the same spot is to rest the arm on an available piece of metal which will keep the hammer from wandering during use.

Start with a gentle tap on the metal and see where the blow lands. It may be difficult to locate this spot at first so lay the flattened hand against the metal as a guide. The small bump can usually be felt and the pick adjusted to hit the low spots. Low spots will feel like high spots on the inside of the panel, so the pick head can be rubbed against the metal to locate the spot if the touch is sensitive. Go easy and slow with the pick hammer as too much metal can be hammered up.

Finishing Metalwork

After the hand tools have been used to straighten a damaged section, the metal must be finished before painting. In bodywork, metal finishing means restoration of final surface smoothness after straightening. This means that areas which are still too low or too high can be picked up or lowered, whichever is necessary.

The file and disc sander are two prime tools of metal finishing. The beginner should become thoroughly familiar with the file first since it works slower than the sander and consequently will make only minor mistakes.

Body Files

Body files are usually fitted with flat, 14-inch blades. Holders are available in either wood or metal. Metal ones are usually adjustable.

When a file is used correctly, the many cutting blades will remove minor surface irregularities. When a file is drawn over a freshly straightened surface, the blades will cut on the high or level spots and leave the low spots untouched. So the file becomes a sort of tattle-tale straightedge.

The file should always be moved in the direction of the flattest crown of the panel in order to show up the greatest imperfection in the panel. At the same time the file must be shifted slightly to one side during the stroke for maximum coverage.

After the file has been passed over a straightened

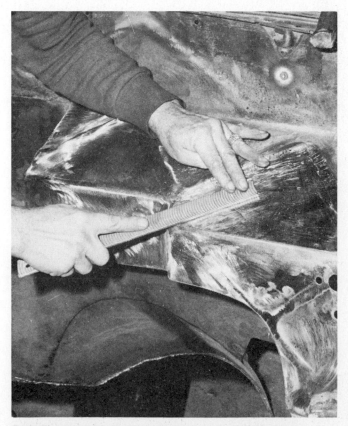

Body files are very useful tools for both preliminary and finishing stages of bodywork. Early in a repair the body file will show where the high and low spots are. In the final stages, the file will smooth the area.

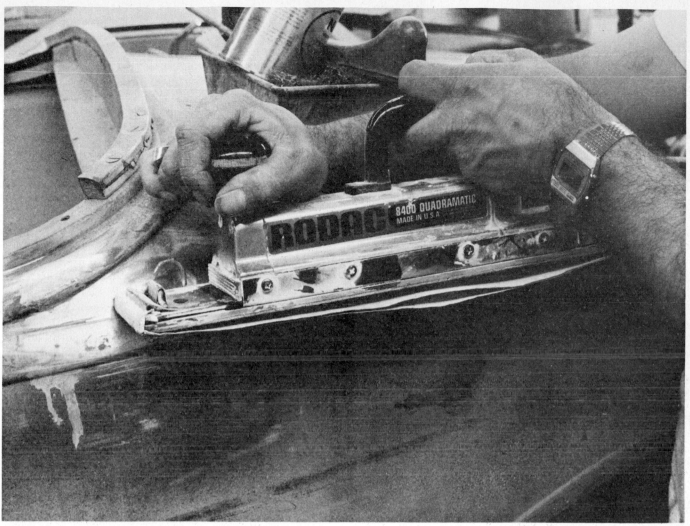

Air files are useful for both preliminary and final finishing. Their sharp edge works well on creases like this. Air files are used mostly for getting large panels smooth and wrinkle-free.

area, any excessively high spots will show up as sharp cuts. Usually very low spots will show up. These spots can be lifted with a pick hammer. Besides the traditional metal files, there are air-powered files that can be used with very coarse grit sand paper to achieve results similar to those reached with metal body files. Since the air files are so powerful, exercise caution when using one.

Disc Sanders

The disc sander is a versatile power tool that can perform a variety of bodywork chores. Most disc sanders are electric, but there are also air powered models. The sanding discs commonly come in 7 and 9-inch diameter sizes.

The grit size of the sanding disc is designated by a number such as #34 or #36 and refers to the size of screen which the grit will pass through. These discs are available in open or closed coat types with the open coat discs commonly used as paint removers. The closed coat discs have a heavier layer of abrasive for heavy-duty use in metal grinding.

Grit size determines how the disc will be used, with the coarse #16 selected for paint removal and

coarse cutting. A #24-disc is most commonly used as an all-around grit since it will cut paint and finish off the metal smoothly. However, a #36-grit is better for finishing.

When using the sander rather than a file, the disc is run across the surface at such an angle that the grit swirl marks will bridge across the low spots. This is done by moving the sander back and forth following the flat direction of the panel as with the file. Also, pressure is applied to cause the disc pad to flex slightly. This will produce the best cutting action, but the sander motor will not be so loaded it will slow down. During the side-to-side strokes, the sander is tilted first to one side and then to the other. That is, when going toward the right, the left side of the disc is working; when moving back to the left the sander is twisted slightly and the right side of the disc is working. Moving the sander this way will cause a crisscross pattern which will show the low spots better.

If there has been considerable metalwork, it is advisable to go over the area with a file after the sander has been used. This is a final check for low spots and is particularly suited to the beginner.

After the area is smooth, a #50 or #60-grit disc can be used to buff the metal. While the sander fol-

Metalwork Fundamentals

Disc sanders or grinders are among the most useful of all body tools. Their high speeds create a lot of friction when used with coarse sanding discs. This type of energy is necessary to remove welding slag.

A panel can have a false stretch which is easily confused with a true stretch because the false stretch will tend to "oil can" or have a raised hump. A false stretch will always be smooth and unworked and next to an area that has been upset; the raises are being caused by the gathering effect of the upset. A false stretch is usually found around the reinforced edge of doors, hoods, and deck lids where there has been a rolled buckle, and the upset has not been relieved completely. Beating out a stiff buckle which should be straightened under tension is a typical cause of false stretch.

When an area of sheetmetal is shrunk, the high crown or bulge must be upset to bring the bulge

lows the flattest plane of the panel, the buffing is done across the greatest crown, usually up and down. The sander is not tilted on the edge quite so much, so that a much larger part of the pad contacts the metal surface during a stroke. The final buffing cuts down the deeper scratches of coarse discs or a file and is a preliminary to the painting operations.

When using the sander around a reverse crown area, it is advisable to cut the disc in a "star" shape. The round disc edge will have a tendency to dig into the reverse crown, while the floppier corners of a star-shaped disc will follow the crown contour. A disc may have any number of points, depending on how severe the reverse crown is, but as a guide, the more severe the crown, the more points on the disc.

Never use a disc sander without some kind of eye protection. Be careful how the sander is handled, as the disc can cut a nasty wound in a leg or arm.

Metal Shrinking

As far as the bodyman is concerned, shrinking really means the use of heat from an oxygen-acetylene torch to soften metal for a specified upset. A propane tank without oxygen will not give enough heat. When an area is being shrunk, a spot or group of spots is heated and worked with a dolly and hammer, then cooled. While shrinking looks easy, it is a precision job and requires more "feel" than ordinary bodywork.

Stretched metal will have an increase in surface area, either in length, width, or both. In collision damage, the stretched area may be confined to a rather small section, and may show as either a depression or bulge in the panel. If a large section of the panel is stretched, it is usually advisable to replace the entire panel.

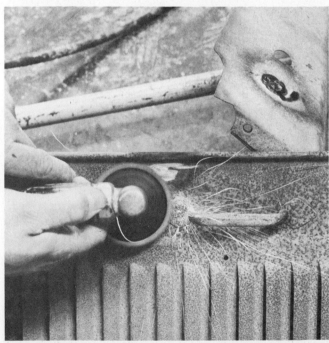

Most grinders are rather big, but you can also get a very compact, right-angle die grinder, which is ideal for getting into areas that would otherwise have to be hand sanded.

back down to its original contour. If a bulge is struck cold, the hammer force is transmitted through the metal toward the edges and little or no effect is usually noted. However, as the bulge is heated the metal at the hot spot will tend to upset readily. When the heat is first applied, the bulge will grow noticeably, but will return to the bulge shape as the metal cools. If the metal is upset while the spot is still hot, the metal will shrink to a state smaller than the bulge. Of course, the hot spot will begin to cool as soon as the torch is removed so hammer and dolly application must be immediate. The hammer does not drive the bulge completely away, leaving a perfectly level surface while the metal is still hot. If this were to happen, the metal would be over-shrunk as it cooled.

The rate at which the metal cools will have an effect on the total shrink; therefore it is possible to use a sponge or wet rag as part of the shrinking procedure. If the heated spot is cooled faster than normal, more of the upset can be retained. That is, shrinking can be more effective if the metal is quenched immediately after working with hammer and dolly. The rapid cooling stops the yield of the heated area to contraction-tension, but must be done while the metal is still quite hot. It will take a little experience to learn when and when not to use quenching. If the metal resembles original contour during the hammer and dolly work, chances are that little or no quenching will be necessary. If the area receives too much quenching, buckles will often appear in the surrounding panel and must be worked out with the hammer.

A gouge in a door or quarter panel is typical of the type of shrinking job the metalman will encoun-

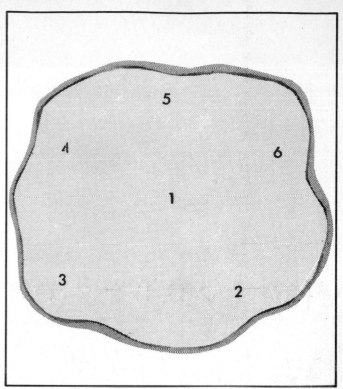

This is the sequence for a heated high spot to be struck with the hammer, using light blows. Work around the edges more than the middle.

ter frequently. Shrinking a gouge is similar to shrinking raised metal, but it is done from the back side.

When shrinking a gouge, the dolly must supply the force to upset the metal from the back side. A small gouge can be bumped out from the back and then shrunk as a raised bulge, but this method is limited to very small damages. The more common gouge requires heating to above 1400 degrees F., or good and red, which will deepen the gouge. The dolly is used as a hammer from the back side, knocking the gouge outward at the deepest point and driving the metal adjacent to the gouge higher than the original contour. The dolly is then held hard against the low point and the hammer used in a hammer-off technique to drive down the surrounding high metal. When the gouge is very close to the original contour, the hammer should then be used directly against the dolly to relieve some of the stress that might cause overshrinking.

A small gouge is usually removed with one or two heatings; a long gouge may require a number of heatings down its length as the hammer and dolly work progresses. Usually, quenching is not needed for a gouge shrink.

Learning to get the proper heat application will be the hardest part of shrinking for the novice, as heat requirements will differ with each type of shrink. The problem is getting just the right amount of heat in just the right size and spot.

Shrinking is not difficult to master, but it definitely requires patience and practice. After a few gouges have been attempted with success, the beginner will learn to remove much of the gouge with one heat application and rapid use of hammer and dolly.

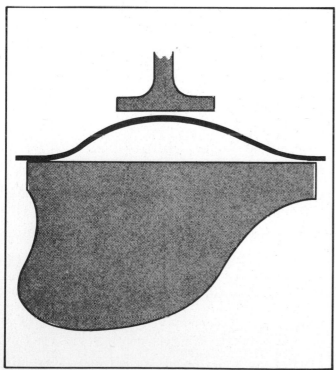

Shrinking with heat is an essential aspect of bodywork. For shrinking a high spot, metal is heated, backed with a dolly, and the hammer applied directly on the high spot.

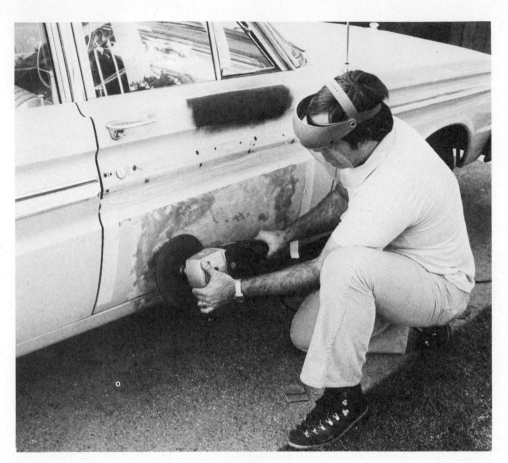

2
Bodywork Tools

It takes more than a sledge hammer to pound out dents. To do a really first class job of bodywork, it takes quality tools, many of them unique to auto body repair. These tools range from a simple body hammer to elaborate frame machines. The basic tools are all hand-powered and will fix almost any damage. Since time is money in a body shop, manufacturers came up with a wide array of pneumatic, hydraulic, and electric body tools that are tremendous time savers. The power tools also save a lot of your energy and/or multiply your energy so much that you can do jobs that would be impossible with only muscle power.

As always, your best bet is to start with basic tools and expand your selection as your needs and talents change. If you have more time than money, stick with the hand sanders, but if saving time and energy is important, get some power tools. Always buy quality tools because they will last decades or longer.

Hammers and Dollies

The two basic tools of bodywork are the body hammer and the steel dolly. The hammer is used to pound on the damaged area while the dolly acts as an anvil to back up the blows. The dolly keeps you from pounding the metal too far in the opposite direction. There are easily a dozen different body hammers, but four or five basic ones will handle the majority of dents. The different hammers have different heads, each designed to work best on a certain type of dent. There is some duplication in head styles since some hammers are available in large and small versions. Most body hammers have wooden handles although there are some models with fiberglass handles. If you get hammers with a flat face, a curved face, and a pointed end you should be able to handle most common dents.

You will seldom find a hammer being used without a dolly. Like body hammers, dollies come in a variety of shapes to best fit each dent. Each dolly has several different shaped surfaces to increase its versatility. The best dollies to start with are a universal dolly, an all-purpose dolly, and a heel dolly.

Closely related to dollies are spoons. Spoons are like long, stretched-out dollies or dollies with handles. Spoons can be used to reach areas not accessible to dollies. Since spoons have a greater surface area than dollies, they can be used to distribute the hammer blows over a greater area. Besides being a back-up tool like dollies, spoons can be used like a hammer to slap out dents. Spoons come in about a half dozen different styles. A good first choice for a spoon would be a surfacing spoon or a dinging spoon.

Dent Pullers

Many dents can't be reached from behind for proper hammer and dolly work so a dent puller is necessary in these cases. There are several different types of dent pullers including slide hammers, suction cups, and pull rods. Pry bars are similar in that they are used from only one side of the dent.

Slide hammers are basically a long bar or rod with a handle and a movable weight (weights vary from one to five pounds in most cases). The end opposite the handle has either a hook or a screw to attach to the body. The action of slamming the weight back against the handle forces out the dent. The best slide hammers have interchangeable screw tips and "L" hooks for better access to more types of dents. Unless there is some opening in the body panel or a lip to hook onto, a series of holes must be drilled in the damaged area. The screw end of the dent puller is twisted into the hole and the area is pulled out. The holes are later filled with some body filler.

Pull rods work in the same way as a screw-in slide hammer except that the pull rods are just inserted into the holes rather than screwed in. Pull rods don't remove dents as easily as a slide hammer since pull rods only use the pulling power of your hand. All rod pulls are very similar except that some

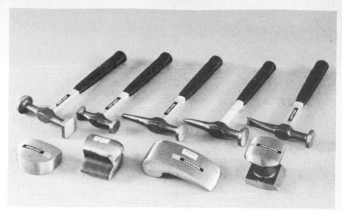

The foundation of any collection of bodywork equipment should be an assortment of hammers and dollies. A nine-piece set like this Craftsman auto body repair set should take care of most dents.

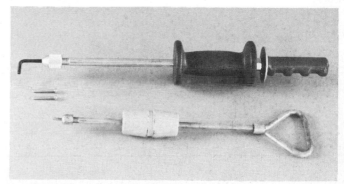

Dent pullers or slide hammers can be used to pull out dents when there is no access to the back side of the panel. The dent pullers come with either screws or "L" hooks for attachment to the panels. The better models have interchangeable end pieces.

have hooked ends and others have "L" shaped ends.

Mild dents that haven't creased or stretched the metal can sometimes be popped out so that the previous damage is hardly noticeable. Suction cups are handy for this type of dent. Suction cups come in various diameters and there are single and double cup models.

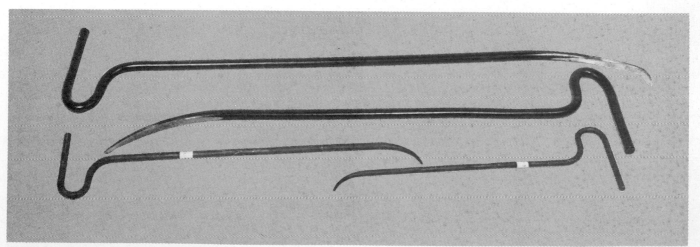

Pry bars can be invaluable in performing body repairs as they allow leverage to be applied to crunched-in panels. Their size is just right for reaching inside crowded access holes.

Bodywork Tools

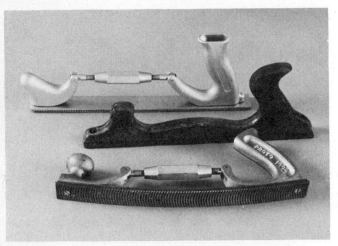

An inexpensive rubber sanding block is one of the best bodyworking tools around when it comes to getting a car straight and smooth enough for paint. Wet sanding makes the paper last longer and the sanding easier.

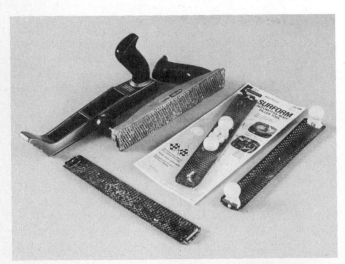

Metal files are used to shave metal off high spots. The holders are available in either wood or metal. The metal file holders can be adjusted for flat or curved surfaces.

Hand Powered Sanding Tools

When it comes to really fine bodywork, it is tough to beat simple hand tools. A lot of patience, a lot of sandpaper, and a rubber sanding block can produce a flawless finish. Long before there were power tools, craftsmen were turning out beautiful work with hand tools, so there is no reason it can't be done today.

The two basic types of sanding tools are sanding blocks and sanding boards. Sanding blocks are usually about 2¾ inches wide and 5 inches long although there are some that are 9 inches long. The blocks are mostly made out of hard rubber; some blocks are made of plastic. The sanding blocks have a flat and a curved surface. Depending on which side the sandpaper is fastened either flat or curved surfaces can be sanded. A sanding block should be considered mandatory equipment for any bodyman or painter.

Sanding boards are, essentially, long sanding blocks. The boards are the same width as the blocks, but much longer (usually 16 inches although there are shorter models), and they are designed for only one type of surface. Sanding boards are used to keep waves out of long flat surfaces. Most sanding boards are made out of wood, but there are also plastic models. The longer sanding boards have two handles, but the shorter ones usually have only one handle.

Before sanding, some type of file is often used to get the material into rough form. There are two main types of files used in bodywork, the curved tooth metal file and the cheesegrater or Surform file. The metal files are used to lower high spots or to shape lead when lead was used for filling work. The metal files are usually held in adjustable holders which can be adjusted so the file is either flat or curved. There are also wooden file holders, but they aren't as popular as the adjustable holders.

The cheesegrater files have dozens of sharp little teeth that cut through body filler like a cheesegrater, hence the name. The Stanley tool company is the best known maker of cheesegrater files and they call their products Surform files. Cheesegrater files are used almost exclusively on plastic body fill-

Air-powered sanders are real work savers. The most common types are, from left to right, a dual action sander, a jitterbug sander, and an air file. The dual action and the air file are more commonly used than the jitterbug sander.

Cheesegrater files are great for shaping plastic body filler. The blades are either flat or half-round. A variety of holders are available, although many bodymen use the files without any holder.

Air chisels or air hammers are very powerful tools that can cut through panels with ease. This front fender is being cut apart in preparation for some radical customizing.

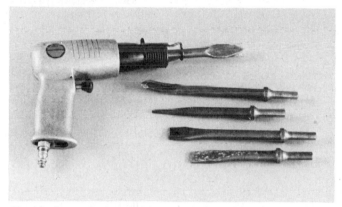

Air chisels can be used with many different bits and chisels to cut panels, break rivets, free frozen bolts, and many other tough tasks. This is a Craftsman air chisel kit.

er. The most popular model is the half-round model which is usually used without a holder. There are a variety of holders for cheesegrater files and the files come in many different sizes and shapes. A cheesegrater file should be considered standard equipment for any bodywork.

Air Tools

One of the biggest aids to ever hit the auto body business was the invention of air-powered tools. In the hands of an experienced pro, air sanders, grinders, and chisels can be a super time and labor saver. Air tools should be used with reservations, however, because improperly used they can cause more damage than good. Power tools use their force to create a lot of friction which makes sanding virtually effortless and very quick. This same friction, if left in one place too long, can actually create enough heat to damage the metal or leave difficult to remove gouges and sanding scratches. Air tools can be handy but only when used with discretion.

The most useful air tools are the sanders which come in three basic styles: straight line sander, orbital or jitterbug sander, and dual-action sander.

The straight line sander is nothing but an air-powered sanding board. Straight line sanders are good for working on big expanses of metal. Orbital sanders most closely resemble the standard rubber sanding block. The action of orbital sanders isn't straight back and forth hence the nickname "jitterbug sander." Orbital sanders are used on flat surfaces. The most common and most often used air sander is the dual-action sander (often known as a D-A). Dual-action sanders can be used either as a rotary grinder or an oscillating sander which reduces sanding marks. Dual-action sanders are good for feather-edging the paint around damaged areas. Most quality air sanders have built-in air regulators to control speed.

A very handy air tool for bodymen is the air hammer or air chisel. Air hammers look like a pistol with a spring on the end of the barrel. Air hammers can be used with a wide variety of attachments to cut rivets, punch holes, and cut sheetmetal. The main use of air hammers is to cut away damaged body sections that aren't bolted in place. This is the method to replace a rear quarter panel. There are long and short barrel air hammers. The former have a longer stroke for more powerful blows.

Electric grinders can be used as buffers by changing from the grinding discs to a buffing pad. This Craftsman grinder has two speeds; the slow speed should be used for buffing.

Air-powered grinders are popular with many bodymen because they are considerably lighter than the bulky electric grinders. The grinding discs are quite stiff, but if the edges are cut, the disc will conform better in concave areas.

Bodywork Tools

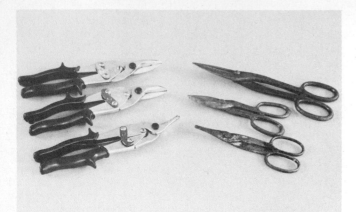

An assortment of metal snips is useful for fabricating patch panels or cutting away damaged areas. The compound leverage snips on the left are used for straight, left, or right cuts. Those on the right are straight cut and duckbill snips.

Vise Grip Pliers come in many different sizes and styles. They are very useful for clamping during welding operations.

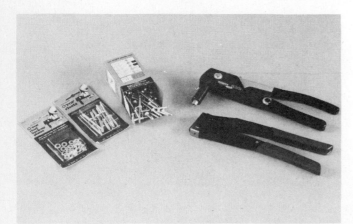

Rivet tools should be included in the average bodyman's tool kit for use when installing patch panels or temporarily holding panels prior to welding.

Air-powered grinders are another very popular type of air tool. The grinders come in a wide range of sizes from palm size to big two-handed models. The small grinders which are usually known as die grinders are great for reaching tight, difficult-access areas. The die grinders come with either a straight chuck or a right angle head. The larger grinders are used to remove all the paint around a dent so the filler will stick. Another use for air-powered grinders is for dressing welds.

Besides air-powered grinders, there are also electric grinders. These grinders are very common in body shops because they can also be used as buffers. For this reason the electric grinders are often known as grinder/buffers, or disc grinders. Some models have two speeds which make them better for buffing work. Electric grinders are usually labeled by the size of the grinding disc and the horsepower of the electric motor. The most common disc sizes are 4½, 7, and 9 inches. Electric grinders are super time savers when it comes to removing paint, rust, or welding slag, but care must be exercised so as not to damage the grinding surface.

There are several other types of air powered tools that are frequently used by bodymen. Most of these tools fall into the convenience group because they are used to perform tasks that could be handled by standard wrenches, but are quicker and easier. Air ratchets are useful when a lot of body panels need to be removed. Impact wrenches are real muscle savers when suspension or other hard-to-remove parts must be disassembled. There are air-powered shears and nibblers for cutting and trimming sheetmetal and there are air-powered drills. The number of air tools is surpassed only by their countless uses.

Hydraulic Power Units

Hydraulic power units or body jacks are special body tools that can turn an ordinary bodyman into a superman. Hydraulic body jacks use the power of 4 to 10-ton hydraulic jacks to push, pull, and spread body damage that would be virtually impossible without the benefit of hydraulic power. There are a tremendous variety of attachments that allow body jacks to undo almost any type of damage. Body jacks are super versatile tools that can

Many specialized tools can be used to make working on cars easier. Many newer cars use Torx fasteners which need either a Torx socket or Torx driver for removal and installation. The tools on the right are door handle tools which make working on interior door handles a snap.

A full face shield, or at least a pair of safety glasses, should always be worn when using tools like disc grinders. Bodywork can be dangerous, so never overlook safety.

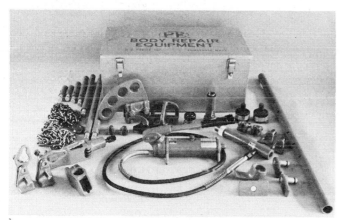

A hydraulic body jack set like this P-F Speed-Master is the type of equipment that can put you into the big leagues. A body jack with the right assortment of accessories can make quick work of otherwise difficult body damage.

handle any damage short of work performed by a full-size frame machine. Body jacks can handle certain types of frame damage, but their biggest asset is the ability to quickly push, pull, or spread damaged areas back into shape for final metal finishing. Body jacks are a necessity for commerical shops and even though they are expensive, many do-it-yourselfers also own body jacks. You can buy a body jack starter set that will do all the basic jobs and add the specialized equipment as the need arises. A home bodyman can justify the cost of a body jack based on the money saved by repairing a badly damaged vehicle at home instead of paying a shop to do the work.

The most important part of a body jack is the hydraulic power unit. This is the heart of the unit and a top quality jack is a must. Just as there is a tremendous price and quality differential among hydraulic automobile lifting jacks, the same difference exists among body jacks. Inferior hydraulic tools can be very dangerous so there is no reason to skimp on quality. Respected body tool companies like P-F Body Tools (H.K. Porter, Inc., 74 Foley St., Somerville, MA 02143) have strict standards to ensure the utmost quality of their tools. In the long

run, if you want to save money, buy a good starter set, not a poorly made ''bargain'' body jack.

The best body jacks like the P-F Speed-Master, Speed-Midget, and Hydro-Chief also have the best accessories for doing the most thorough work. For example, the P-F all-angle pull clamp is a multi-purpose clamp that can do the work of eight ordinary clamps.

Although pulling a dent out is preferable, there are many instances where pushing is a necessity. There are also many types of damage where access is very difficult. At these times, a tool like the P-F hydraulic spreader is very handy. The hydraulic spreader is a wedge-shaped attachment for the P-F body jack that can fit into a ¾-inch space and then spread to 3¼ inches. The pushing action of body jacks works well in areas like damaged door openings, i.e., fitting a new door into the old opening. The pushing function is also used to repair caved-in roofs.

A hydraulic body jack is equivalent to having several very strong men, yet the body jack is easily contained in a modest-sized toolbox. Besides the tremendous work-saving abilities of body jacks, they enable you to do jobs that previously would have scared you away.

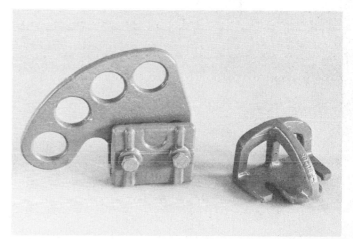

One key to the great efficiency of P-F body jacks is the unique pull clamp and adapter which allows pulls from a wide range of angles.

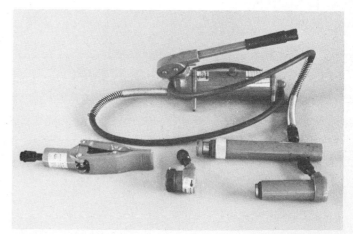

The ram units that do the expansion in a hydraulic body jack come in a variety of sizes so they will fit in almost any area. P-F even makes a hydraulic spreader for very tight situations.

3
Welding and Brazing

Welding is one of the most useful skills an automotive enthusiast can learn. Whether you are building a street rod from the ground up or fabricating a wild street custom or just doing bodywork on a transportation car, welding will help you do the job better, quicker, and cheaper.

There are many ways to learn welding, and one way is through a school. The best place for a do-it-yourselfer to learn is at a high school or junior college evening class. Most school districts offer adult education classes with several automotive courses like welding, bodywork and painting, and auto mechanics. These classes are usually inexpensive and truly great educational bargains.

A person can also learn to weld at home by reading books and articles and practicing a lot. Practice is the key ingredient to welding. Welding is a precision craft when practiced correctly. Sloppy welding can get the job done, but professional quality welding takes lots of practice.

The two main types of welding the home welder uses are gas welding and arc welding. Gas welding or oxyacetylene welding is used most often for bodywork. Arc welding is used for things like chassis fabrication. Each type of welding has its place in the overall scheme of bodywork.

Gas Welding Equipment

If you are interested primarily in bodywork rather than fabrication, and you can afford only one type of welding equipment, get a gas welding set. Oxyacetylene torches can be used for cutting, brazing, and welding, operations used in bodywork.

There are a variety of torch sets available, but the price range between the top-of-the-line models and the less expensive ones isn't too great. Therefore, we recommend buying the best torch set. The price difference between the best set and a lesser one over the torch's lifespan, usually decades, makes the cost differential almost inconsequential. Torches are generally divided into two categories: two-stage and single-stage.

Two-stage regulators are far better than single-stage outfits because the two-stage units maintain constant pressure to the torch. As the pressure in the oxygen and acetylene tanks on single-stage regulators is reduced, the torch must be readjusted. Single-stage regulators have another disadvantage since they can freeze in cold weather.

Sears offers a good selection of torch sets and other welding supplies that are perfectly suited for bodywork. Their best torch is a two-stage outfit that has a unique new feature: a thumbwheel control knob that saves fuel when not welding. The thumbwheel control allows the welder to switch to a pilot light when the torch isn't used, yet the torch doesn't have to be reset when it is taken off the pilot light setting. The outfit includes two-stage regulators, a welding torch with tips, a cutting torch, 20 feet of hose, a spark lighter, goggles, a wrench, and an instruction manual. An outfit like this Sears Craftsman 9KT5442C is an excellent investment for anyone who is serious about bodywork.

Besides the torch outfit, the other important ingredient for gas welding is the supply of oxygen and acetylene which comes in large cylinders that can either be bought, leased, or rented. Like most business deals, the cost will be about the same no matter which method you choose. There is, however, a dilemma when the choice comes to buying or renting your gas cylinders. A pair of cylinders can cost as much or more than the torch set. Yet, unless you use large quantities of gas like a professional body shop, the minimum cost of a monthly rental or lease

There is a lot of information available on welding from various manufacturers and vocational schools. This information is a valuable reference source for all welders.

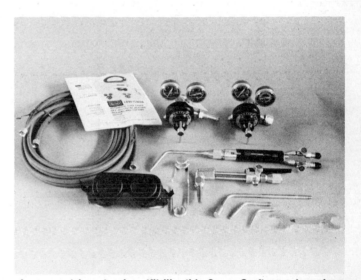

An oxyacetylene torch outfit like this Sears Craftsman two-stage set is the ideal welding equipment for either a home or professional bodyman. The #9KT5442C outfit includes the regulators, hoses, a welding torch with several different tips, a cutting torch, and safety goggles.

Knowledge of welding really expands the scope of possible body repairs. If you ever hope to call yourself a professional bodyman, this ability is mandatory. Here, a rusted door edge is being replaced with new metal. Without welding, the repair would have to be a temporary one using plastic body filler.

agreement can quickly add up to the cost of a set of tanks. If you decide to lease or rent, consult your local welding supply company for details.

Like everything else, the cost of welding tanks is constantly rising so a set of tanks can be an inflation hedge. Our advice, then, is to buy a set of tanks if you can afford the initial investment because welding supply shops will re-purchase your tanks for about half price. Even better, individuals usually are willing to pay about what you paid, especially if the market price has risen.

Oxygen and acetylene tanks come in several different sizes. The sizes are measured by the number of cubic feet of oxygen or acetylene that the cylinders hold. Common sizes for oxygen tanks are 244, 122, and 80 cubic feet. The common sizes for acetylene are 300, 100, and 60 cubic feet. Oxygen tanks

Welding and Brazing

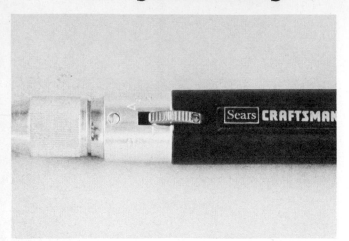

A handy feature of the Craftsman welding torch is this thumbwheel which saves fuel by putting the torch on pilot light when you're not welding. This means that the flame only has to be adjusted once.

Tip cleaners should be used to clean the torch tips. Sears sells this set of 12 cleaners that come in a handy case.

and regulators use right-hand threads while acetylene tanks and regulators use left-hand threads. Also, acetylene tanks have a safety plug (usually located at the top of the cylinder) which is designed to melt at 212 degrees F. in case of fire. The large or medium size tanks are best because the small ones need constant refilling if you do a lot of welding. Nothing is more frustrating than to run out of gas in the middle of a project, especially on a weekend when the welding supply store is closed.

There are many useful welding accessories that you should consider adding to your tool collection. Since gas tanks are heavy and must be stored in an upright position, some type of welding cart is useful. Sears makes a good welding cart, part number 9KT5429N, which has easy to maneuver 10-inch wheels and a sturdy steel frame. The cart has retainer chains to secure the gas tanks and a tray on the back of the cart for carrying the welding rod. Some type of welding cart is virtually a must if you want any versatility with your torch setup.

Good safety welder's goggles are a must as are heavy duty welding gloves; a lot of heat is generated with welding, so don't take chances. An assortment of locking pliers and clamps are handy for positioning work. Tip cleaners will keep the torch tips

free of debris, although the proper size drill bit will also accomplish this task.

Using Gas Torches

A high degree of heat is needed to melt or cut steel, or even metals with a lower melting point. A needle-like flame is needed which will burn consistently with its maximum heat concentrated at the tip. Therefore, acetylene is used as fuel with pure oxygen to "feed" it. When acetylene is combined with oxygen it will burn the hottest of all gases (approximately 6000 degrees F.). Acetylene gas is highly flammable but it is perfectly safe if used with reasonable care. Never apply heat to the cylinder or drop it. Always keep the cylinder upright.

Oxygen isn't harmful but it can puff a tiny spark into a roaring flame. Never oil or grease any part of the equipment, the cylinders, or the valves under any circumstances.

The gas cylinders should be stored and used in the upright position. They can be transported in a horizontal position. When lifting the cylinders to their upright position lift by the protective caps that

A set of oxygen and acetylene tanks is quite heavy, so some type of cart is necessary if you plan to weld in more than one location. This heavy duty Sears welding truck has 10-inch wheels, a shelf for an extra welding rod, and chains to secure the tanks.

encase the fittings on the top of the cylinders. To use the gases, remove the protective caps, examine the cylinder valve threads and wipe them clean with a *clean* cloth. Next, slightly open ("crack"), then close, both the oxygen and acetylene cylinder valves to make sure they do not stick and also to blow out any dirt or moisture that may have lodged in the valves.

Loosen both regulator adjusting screws until they turn freely, then install the regulators on their appropriate cylinders, tightening firmly but without force. Stand to one side of the oxygen regulator and open the cylinder valve very slowly so the high pressure gauge needle will move up slowly until full pressure is registered. Now the valve should be opened completely. The acetylene cylinder valve should be opened slowly a *maximum* of one complete turn. This is so you can turn it off rapidly in the event of any mishap.

Connect the green (oxygen) hose to the outlet of the oxygen regulator. This hose has a right-hand thread connector. Connect the fuel hose, which is red, to the acetylene regulator outlet. This hose has left-hand thread connections. Next, connect the welding torch to the hoses. Select the welding tip size that is recommended for the job. Now you can install the tip in the torch, snugly, but not too tightly.

Let's assume for the sake of illustration that you wish to weld sheetmetal 1/32-inch thick. Your welding manual states a size "0" tip is required and maximum oxygen and acetylene pressure should be at 3 psi. Now partially open the torch oxygen valve and adjust the oxygen regulator until the pressure rises to 3 psi. Close the torch oxygen valve. After being careful that no flame is about, partially open the torch acetylene valve and adjust the regulator pressure to 3 psi; then close the valve. All pressures in welding and cutting charts are flowing pressures with the torch valves open. If you change tip sizes in the middle of a job and must change pressures, do so with the torch valves open.

To light the torch, open the torch acetylene valve approximately one-half turn and ignite the acetylene with a striker; pointing the flame away from people, pets, the gas cylinders, or any flammable

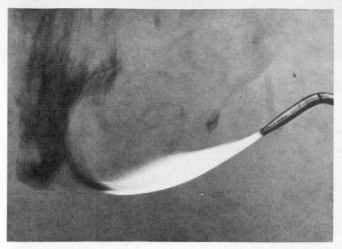

When an acetylene valve is first opened and the flame lit, heavy soot will pour out. Continue opening the valve until the soot stops, then start feeding oxygen into the flame for a proper mix.

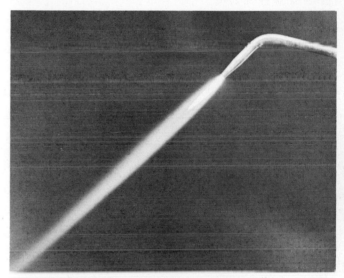

Some oxygen has been added here, but the flame is still acetylene-rich. Note the flame's long central cone.

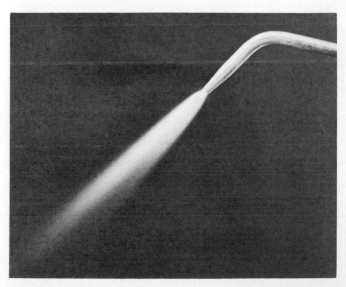

A neutral flame is achieved when the center flame is about ¼ inch to ⅜ inch long. Introduce oxygen until the inner cone just starts to become needle-sharp, then back off until it is the desired size.

Safety goggles are mandatory for any type of welding. The large welding helmet is for arc welding.

Welding and Brazing

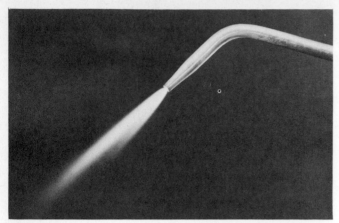

If you bring the inner cone out to a needle-like point and leave it there, you will have an oxidizing flame which will weaken the weld. Note how the outer flame is ragged.

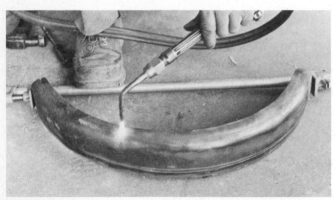

The heat from a torch can be used for work other than welding. Here, heat is being applied to help shrink a metal fender flare. Along with heat, pressure is being applied with a pipe clamp.

materials. Keep opening the torch valve until the flame stops excessive smoking and leaves the end of the tip about ⅛ inch; then reduce slightly to bring the flame back to the tip.

Open the torch oxygen valve now until a bright inner cone appears on the flame. The point at which the feathery edges of the flame disappear and a sharp inner cone is visible is called the "neutral flame." Adjust the torch oxygen valve back and forth until you are sure you have a neutral flame. If too much oxygen is flowing, you'll have an "oxidizing" flame that will burn the metal you're trying to weld, making it brittle and weak. This flame is pale blue without the clearly defined inner cone of the "neutral" flame. Should you attempt to weld with too little oxygen, you will get a flame that is acetylene-rich, which will have a "carburizing" flame, distinguished by its long carburizing feather.

There are two methods one may employ in oxy-acetylene welding: forehand and backhand welding. The forehand method is ordinarily used for welding material under ⅛-inch thickness. This method works by pointing the torch down at an angle, toward direction that you plan to lay the bead, with the rod preceding the torch. The flame tip preheats the edge of the joint; and the oscillating

motion you use with both rod and torch, moving them in semi-circular paths along the joint, will distribute the heat and molten metal uniformly.

In backhand welding, the torch is moved along in front of the rod in the direction of welding, with the flame pointed back toward the molten puddle and completed weld. The end of the welding rod is placed in the flame between the tip and the weld. The torch needs to be moved slowly along the joint in front of the weld puddle while the rod may be simply rolled from side to side in the puddle. Better fusion between the metals at the root of the weld is normally achieved with this method.

Enough emphasis cannot be placed on the importance of full penetration of the materials being joined and complete fusion along the sides of the joint. Where two pieces are being joined and the joint is quite long, you must consider the expansion of metals in heating, and contraction on cooling. For steel plate being welded, you should tack the pieces lightly at the edge and then tack the pieces along the joint about ¼ inch per foot. This will hold them in alignment but still allow joint closure.

In the long run you're going to have to practice a lot, if you're going to learn how to gas weld. Get some old pieces of scrap metal and practice, practice, practice.

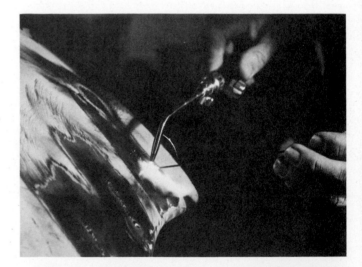

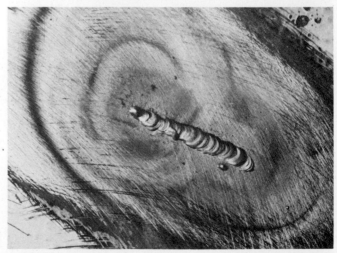

A forehand weld is being applied on this fender. The flame is neutral, with the proper mix of oxygen and acetylene for welding mild steel. The puddles should be uniform.

Brazing and Braze Welding

Learning to braze is easier than welding, but the beginner should learn fusion welding first before attempting brazing. There is a difference between braze welding and brazing although both use nonferrous filler rod that will melt above 800 degrees F. In braze welding the filler rod of brass or bronze fills an open-groove joint or makes a definite bead. In brazing, a closely fitted joint is filled by capillary action of the filler material (as in furnace brazing). Such a connection is really just a thin film of filler metal between the two surfaces, but it can be extremely strong. Furnace brazing is necessary when outstanding strength of precision parts is required.

Around a body shop the term brazing is used to mean braze welding and is used primarily in repairing a joint that was originally spot welded. Brazing of such joints may not be as strong as perfect braze welding or fusion welding, but the joint's strength is usually sufficient. It also requires less heat which means less heat distortion. For this reason most bodymen will steel-weld body panels together, so that the joint is strong even after grinding. Braze welding is done mostly on panels where you can't get at the back side to hammer and dolly it after welding.

Brazing is possible because many nonferrous metals will diffuse and/or penetrate into other metals when temperatures and surface conditions are right. This means the copper base filler material must be melted while the parent metal must be kept at the same temperature. This permits the filler metal to flow over the joint being brazed.

The parent metal must be clean, which can be accomplished by grinding, scraping, or using a wire brush. An easier chemical method is to use a strong flux, but it leaves a residue that is difficult to remove. The bodyman may use a combination of the two, cleaning the joint to be brazed and then using a flux with a low chemical residue.

Flux is both a chemical cleaner and a protective shield for the heated metal surface which allows the molten brazing material to moisten and to diffuse into the parent surfaces. Such a flux can be a powder or a paste, or you can buy flux-coated rods. The coated rods are more expensive than the plain ones but they are much handier to use.

On a good brazed joint, the penetration is called diffusion since the two metals intermix to cause an alloying action at the joint's interface. Such an alloy is sometimes stronger than the parent metal, especially with the newer high-strength brazing rods. The strongest brazed joints are made when the parent metal surfaces are between .003 and .005 inch apart. For the bodyman this means flush.

A good brazed joint should be smooth and bright, with edges that blend smoothly into the parent metal. A pitted or blistery surface or an edge that seems to stand on top of the parent metal means an unsatisfactory job. This doesn't mean the joint won't hold, it just means you need more practice. A very common mistake is to overheat the surface as shown by a fine white powdery material left on both sides of the joint.

Brazing is particularly applicable to sheetmetal

An oxygen-rich flame is used here. Such a flame is noted for the sparks it puts out, but the resulting weld is burned, pitted, and weak.

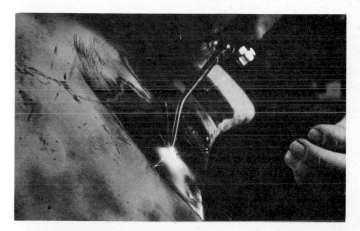

An acetylene-rich flame is used here, which introduces excess carbon into the weld. This is a carburizing flame, which produces a weak weld. This type of flame is preferred when brazing, instead of welding.

Welding and Brazing

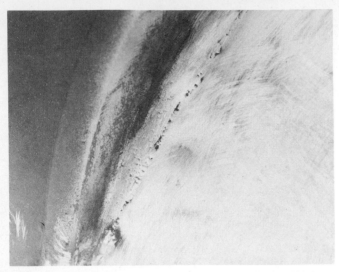

Here is a typical butt-joint of two pieces of sheetmetal which has been hammer welded. A few passes of the grinder and this undistorted seam is almost ready for primer and a few dabs of glaze. A normal overlap seam would have been quicker but would have required lots of filler.

A typical hammer weld operation is this repair of the lower rear corner of a '32 Ford. The original body and the patch piece were cut to fit, and the area surrounding the weld was cleaned of paint. Vise Grip pliers were used to hold things together for welding.

work where you wish to keep excess heat to a minimum, thereby preventing warped panels. But it should not be used for critical suspension parts, not even with a high-strength brazing rod.

Hammer Welding

A very useful type of welding in bodywork is hammer welding. Hammer welding is especially useful in custom work such as chopping tops or in restoration of older cars where pieces from several different cars may have to be joined to make one good body. Hammer welding is basically ordinary gas welding followed by hammer and dolly

work on the welded joint to provide as smooth and distortion-free a seam as possible. Hammer welding is desired when maximum strength and a minimum amount of filler are desired. It also allows the metal-man to gain better control over the panel, to shape and mold it the way he wants it with stress in the right place.

Hammer welding is usually employed in three situations: repair of a tear, replacement of a panel, or modification of a panel. In all three the emphasis is upon quality and metal control.

A quarter panel with a tear can be roughed into shape until the torn metal edges can be aligned carefully and then the rip can be closed by hammer-welding. With such a situation the area adjacent to the tear will probably be stretched, but when the metal is welded and hammered, a natural shrinking force is introduced that tends to reduce the stretch. After the initial hammer welding, the area may be treated as a gouge. Keep on shrinking and working the panel until it assumes its original shape.

It is in panel replacement and modification that hammer welding takes on such importance. Unless the panel is pre-shaped to the new contour it is entering (with seams hammer welded), there will be a need for an excessive amount of filler material.

This is not to say that every seam should be hammer welded; far from it. When a panel can be replaced and the joint made by spot welding, riveting, or even ordinary fusion welding—and the joint will not show—fine. But if the seam is in the open and

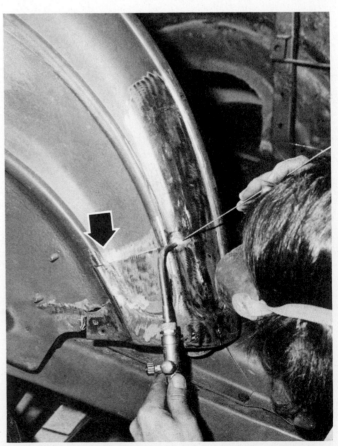

A thin strip was trimmed from the left corner piece so that the center bead would line up on the body, and this was hammer welded in place. The fit of the fenderwell bead (arrow) was accomplished by using the wedge end of a finishing hammer.

affects the panel's strength, hammer welding must be considered.

Take the situation where the bottom edge of an exterior panel has rusted away. Only about 2 inches of the metal is really cancerous, but the replacement strip will be from 3 to 4 inches wide. This strip will usually have very little (or no) crown and will generally include a folded lip of 90 degrees or more. Whether the panel is on a door, cowl, or quarter area doesn't matter. The metalman will be working directly in the middle of a nearly flat surface with heat. That means a high distortion possibility, which requires torch control.

It is absolutely imperative that all hammer welding include the smallest possible weld bead. To accomplish this, the panels to be mated must fit as closely as they can. The replacement panel should be shaped and trimmed first, then held over the area to be replaced and well marked. The bad metal should be cut out with as little distortion as possible. A saber saw or nibbler works well for cutting out the bad sheetmetal.

After the initial rough cut, try the replacement panel on for size. It will generally be off just a whisker because there is usually too much metal remaining on the parent panel. This thin strip may be trimmed off with a good pair of aviation tin snips. The two panel edges should fit flush along the full length with no more than 1/16-inch gap at any part. A gap requires too much filler rod, resulting in a larger bead which isn't desired.

Clamp the pieces together and tack weld the edges. Use very little or no filler rod and make the tack tiny. Speed is important here as well as a very small flame. A correct hammer weld cannot be made if the metal edges lap.

Make sure the edges are level during and after the tack weld. If not, heat the tack in a restricted area and use the hammer and dolly to level the edges. This means a few light taps when the metal is hot.

After the panels are tacked start at one end with the hammer welding process. Be prepared to travel rapidly not so much with the torch as with the hammer and dolly. The railroad dolly is well suited to hammer welding, since it has a number of conven-

Another typical problem that is best solved by hammer welding is replacing a lower, rusted-out area on an early car like this Model A. Here, the rusted section is cut off and the trim line ground straight. Flush fit of the panels to be welded is critical for a good hammer weld.

Vise Grip pliers will keep the panel in place during tack welding; mating surfaces should be hammered up or down to flush exactly during tacking.

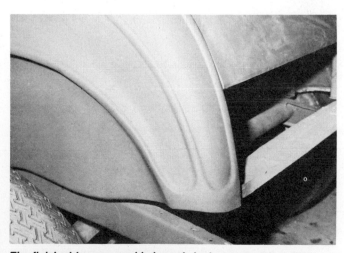

The finished hammer welded repair looks great after a little filling, sanding, and priming.

Any time a butt weld is being made, it can distort nearby low crown panels. The torch should have a very small flame; the tip may be laid flatter to direct the flame at the area just welded.

Welding and Brazing

Hammer each tack immediately, as this will tend to shrink the area and eliminate any distortion caused by the heat. It also keeps the edges flush. Don't worry about distortion in the larger panel at this time.

This is how a good fusion weld will look, with a little bead buildup. Such a weld is possible because panels grow together when heated edges melt and form a bond without filler rod drops.

ient crowns and is easy to hold. The hammer face should be nearly flat.

Hammer welding can be done in either of two ways. The simplest method is to weld the entire seam at once then follow with spot heat and the hammer and dolly. A better way is to weld a short 2-inch section, then use the hammer, then weld again. This way the area is still hot from welding and does not need reheating, allowing better control of the metal.

Lay the torch tip more parallel with the plane of travel than with normal fusion welding, thus reducing the heat to the metal. The filler rod can also be held at an opposite low angle to shield the edges. Although the two metal pieces touch, they will tend to grow toward each other even more when heat is applied, allowing the edges to melt and flow together without the necessity of the filler rod. Such flowing may be difficult at first, but can be accomplished easily with experience. An occasional hole will develop which must be filled by a drop from the filler rod.

Immediately upon setting the torch aside, place the dolly against the underside and hold it firmly to the weld. Slap the bead rapidly with the dinging hammer, working back and forth from one end of the seam to the other. This will cause the bead to flatten out and have a shrinking effect on the panel. Continue across the entire joint, alternating between torch and hammer/dolly.

Arc Welding

While an oxyacetylene outfit makes it possible to weld, braze, cut, and heat metal, an AC arc welder does these same things, but in a grander style. An arc welder can build a chassis or engine stand, install a rearend, engine mount, or front axle, or you name it. It's an indispensible item, and used with your acetylene torch, there is little this team can't do.

Arc welders come in a wide array of models. The models range from tiny hobby units to huge commercial welders. The do-it-yourself bodyman should consider an intermediate size arc welder. Typical of the types of arc welders well-suited for the enthusi-

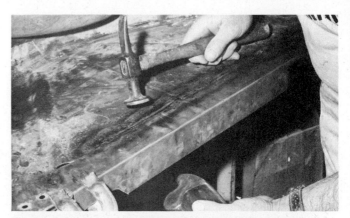

Continue the alternate welding/hammering schedule until the entire joint is closed. Keep the dolly firmly against the underside of the panel to reduce rebound; use hammer smartly.

A pick hammer is used to raise the low spots, but the dolly is kept on top to keep from raising spots too high. This is where experience with the hammer will pay off.

ast are those carried by Sears. The arc welders are rated according to their maximum amperage settings. The higher the amperage the thicker the steel that can be welded. Most arc welders have the capacity to vary their amperage rate. As an example, Sears' best AC arc welder has a range from 30 to 295 amps. The number 9KT20139N arc welder is a dual-range model with a low range for maximum arc stability and a high range for minimum current draw. As with gas torches, the price difference between the top of the line arc welders and the other models isn't very much when you consider the long life span of the welder and the increased versatility of the better units. The arc welders to avoid are the inexpensive little units known as "buzz boxes." These units have such a limited capacity that they aren't good for much automotive work, and they are prone to overheating.

The most poweful home arc welders may require some additional wiring for the average garage since the welders run on 230 volt, 60-Hz. AC power. It is best to wire the system with a 60 amp circuit breaker and direct wiring.

Arc Welding Basics

The keys to successful arc welding are to select the right electrode for the material to be welded and to set the welder at the right heat range for the gauge of metal involved. Practice will teach you how fast to move the electrode, how high to hold it above the work, and which angle is best.

After the welder is connected, connect the

Although it usually isn't to be found in the average bodyman's tool kit, the shrinking dolly is a handy item. It is grooved to "grip" metal and is used in conjunction with an aluminum hammer.

This is the panel as it appears in nearly finished condition. Some tiny low areas remain to be picked up and filed, then the panel will be primed.

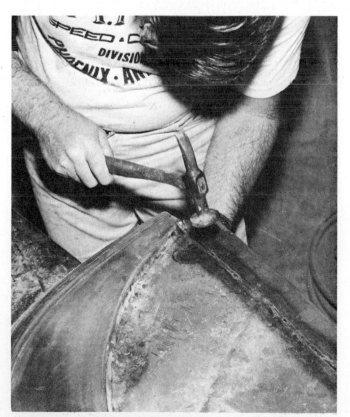

After the new section is hammer welded, the surrounding panel may be worked as necessary since "growth" through heat of welding may cause distortion. In this case, original parts of the weld needed several shrinks to remove "oil-canning."

ground clamp to the work to be welded. Make sure the connection is good, or you'll waste power and heat up the ground clamp. Use clean dry welding rods (electrodes) and be sure of a positive grip on the electrode by the electrode holder. The thickness of the metal to be welded and the diameter of the electrode determine the amount of heat required for welding. In general, the heavier and thicker a piece of metal is, the larger the electrode and the more heat (amps) it requires. Many welders have guides that indicate what diameter of electrode to use for specific metals. Follow the guidelines, at first, and then use your experience to judge if more or less heat is needed.

If you use too much heat you will burn holes in light metals, or the bead will be flat and porous. Also, the bead will likely "undercut" the work (caused by rapid movement of the rod along its surface, or due to the high heat and insufficient time for the

Welding and Brazing

Arc welders come with a variety of capacities, but only the bigger, heavy-duty units are well-suited for a variety of repair jobs. A perfect welder for the do-it-yourselfer would be a unit like this Sears Craftsman AC dual-range arc welder.

A heavy-duty electrical power source and hookup are necessary for arc welding. This receptical was mounted directly below the fuse box. A 60-amp circuit and direct wiring were employed.

crater to be filled).

Too little heat will result in beads that are too high, as though they lay on top of the work. The bead will also be irregular because of difficulty in holding an arc. With the amperage too low, it is difficult to strike an arc; the electrode will stick to the work and the arc will frequently disappear.

When the right heat is used the bead will lay smoothly over the work without ragged edges. The "puddle" will be at least as deep in the base metal as the rod that lies above it. The sound of the welding operation "crackles," like frying eggs.

The rate of travel affects the weld as much as the heat setting. Move the arc slowly to ensure proper penetration and enough weld metal deposit. Also, rod movement must be at a consistent speed.

The purpose of the arc is to create an intense heat between the end of the electrode and the surface of the metal to be welded (called the work or base metal). The heat energy generated by the arc is so great that the base metal almost immediately is heated to a liquid state at the point where the arc is directed. This creates a molten pool (puddle) of metal which is always present on the base metal during the welding process.

Making a Bead

The heat that melts the base metal also melts the electrode. As the electrode melts, the metal from it falls through the arc into the molten pool or puddle. This adds additional molten metal, which mixes thoroughly in the puddle, resulting in complete fusion of the two metals. As more metal from the electrode is added and the electrode is moved forward, the material added from the electrode forms a uniform pile of metal known as the "bead."

The first step to arc welding is to strike an arc. This is accomplished by scratching the end of the electrode across the surface to be welded. With a short stroke, scratch the rod end across the base metal close to where you want to weld. You will hear a sputter and see an arc.

As soon as an arc begins burning between the electrode and the base metal, raise the electrode about ⅛ inch above the work. If you don't, it will stick to the work. If it does stick, rock the electrode back and forth until it breaks loose. Keep practicing the art of striking an arc, using different gauges of metal and at different amperages too.

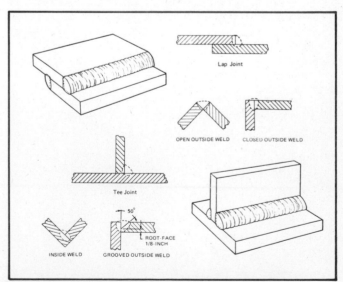

A fillet-weld joint forms a right angle pocket for weld metal deposit. Squaring of edges is usually all the preparation needed. Lap joints are formed by overlapping edges that must touch surface-to-surface on the entire joint for best results. Corner joints are formed by two pieces perpendicular to each other at the edges. On heavy material, the corners must be open or grooved as shown. Tee joints are similar, usually requiring welding on both sides of heavy material.

To lay a bead, first strike an arc and hold it at the starting point for a short time before moving the electrode forward. This ensures good fusion and allows the bead to build up slightly. Bear in mind that the electrode continues to melt off as you move across the work, so you must move the electrode down into the puddle as well as along the path you are following. The electrode should be held at an angle with the end held at a maintained height above the work surface. To ensure proper penetration and evenness, learn to watch the molten pool of metal forming just behind the arc.

The easiest bead to lay is called a stinger bead. It is made by making one continuous pass over the work metal, without any weaving or oscillating movements. If you are right-handed, move from left to right. If left-handed, reverse the movement. With the electrode tipped back toward the direction of travel (about 15 degrees), the arc will throw the molten metal of the puddle away from itself, ensuring good penetration. The average bead, when using a ⅛-inch electrode will be about ⅛ inch high and ¼ inch wide.

Another bead that is commonly used is known as the weave bead. Its purpose is to deposit metal in a wider space than would be possible with the stinger bead. It is accomplished by weaving from one edge of the space to be filled to the other edge and continuing this motion, along with the most satisfactory forward speed of travel. It is a good idea to hesitate momentarily at each edge of the weave so you will provide the same heat at the edges as that in the middle.

Any time two pieces of metal, 3/16 inch or thicker, are butt-welded together the edges should be beveled by grinding. Beveling makes a much better weld, since complete penetration is ensured. Where necessary, a second or third pass over an initial weld can even be made as long as the slag from all previous beads is removed.

An arc welder can be used to weld aluminum, stainless steel, cast iron, and galvanized steel, and for heating, burning holes, brazing, soldering, and so forth, in addition to welding mild steel. While the electrode holder and various types of electrodes will take care of most of these jobs, a convenient accessory is a carbon arc torch. The carbon arc torch is used with an arc welder to braze, solder, heat, bend, and weld aluminum and copper alloys.

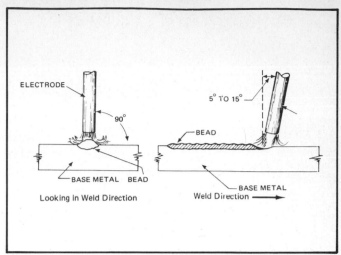

When arc welding, hold electrode perpendicular, but tilt the top or holder end in the direction it is moving (weld direction). Feed your electrode at a uniform rate down to the plate as it melts and forms a bead.

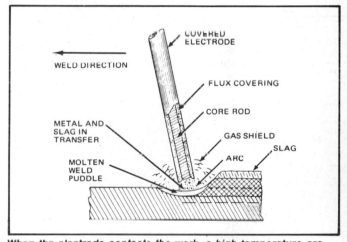

When the electrode contacts the work, a high-temperature arc forms. The heat is controlled by current and space between the rod and the work. The flux coating provides a gas shield against contamination from the air.

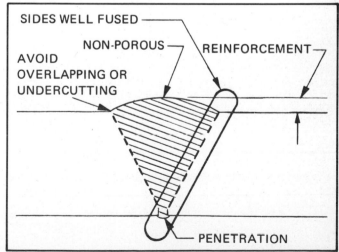

The completed weld should be thoroughly fused to the base metal throughout the groove area. The weld metal should penetrate to the root of the joint with a small amount extending below the surface to ensure a full section weld. At the face of the weld, there is usually a buildup known as "reinforcement."

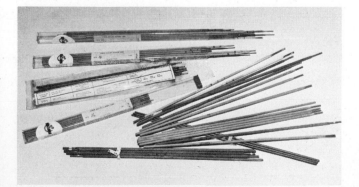

There is a wide choice of arc welding electrodes on the market for every type of material, including cast iron. Match the electrode to the specific job.

4
Replacing Panels

Let's face it, nobody really likes dents (except maybe body shop operators). If they did, dents would be offered as optional equipment on new cars. But accidents do happen, giving us the dents the original equipment manufacturers so kindly leave out, and there's really nothing you can do about them except get them fixed.

The economics of dent removal and repair is a complicated matter. Estimating body repair costs takes training and practice. But one fact is very clear: it is often cheaper and easier to replace a body panel completely than to try to hammer and dolly out all the kinks and bends. This is especially true if it is a fairly sizeable body piece, such as a door, fender, or quarter panel. Though replacement sheetmetal, whether purchased from a dealer or an auto salvage yard, can be very expensive, that cost is often less than the labor costs involved in repairing the damaged original. If you decide that replacement is the way to restore an entire or partial panel, this is how to go about it.

Removing Old Panels

Practically every portion of a car's body is available in replacement form from the manufacturer, but exterior panels are normally the only units replaced. Such external pieces include fenders, hoods, rocker panels, and the like.

Before you can replace a damaged panel, you must remove the old one. The method of removal depends largely on how the factory attached the panel in the first place. As a rule, large panels that can be easily distorted by heat are spot welded. Areas that are not easily distorted, or where stress may be concentrated (such as quarter panels), are usually fusion welded in several related seams. Fender panels are usually bolted on and require no welding. If a panel is to be replaced, the general area must be roughed into alignment before the panel is removed.

Panels may be removed in several different ways. If spot welding is involved, each spot weld may be

In some cases there is no question whether to replace or repair. This front fender is definitely beyond saving. It must be replaced.

Before installing the new fender, the inner fender panels must be jacked out. Check measurements from the new fender bolt holes on inner panels so they won't be stretched too far.

drilled using a ¼-inch drill bit. Areas near a fusion weld may be cut away with a torch if distortion can be limited and there is no danger of setting the interior on fire. Probably the best all-around tool for removing panels is the air chisel. Air chisels are great time savers in addition to their advantage of producing very little panel distortion when properly used. Other popular tools include the old standby metal snips or cutters, and electric saber saws.

When a fusion weld is to be parted, it is wise to cut below the weld (toward the damaged panel) about 1 inch. This is particularly true if a torch is used. The final trim up to the original weld should be made with a pair of aircraft-type tin snips.

Once a panel has been removed, take time to repair or treat the structure underneath as needed. In the case of replacing a panel to repair rust damage, you must remove any inner rust before reskinning or the rust will return immediately.

Partial Panel Replacement

It is not always necessary to replace an entire panel when only a portion of it is damaged. To replace a partial panel, first mark off the area that must be cut out and carefully inspect the remaining part of the panel for damage or distortion. Measure the exact location of the marked off area and transfer these measurements to the replacement panel (obtained from an auto dismantler, parts car, or factory parts outlet).

Cut the replacement section from the second panel, making the edges as straight as possible. Place this piece against the original panel and scribe a mark around the edge. Cut away the original panel along the scribe lines. Straighten the edges to be matched (body edge and replacement panel edges); then butt weld the new panel into place. Tack weld the section every 3 or 4 inches to avoid heat distortion before finish welding. Finish off as a normal repair.

From here it's a matter of bolting on new pieces and rechecking the fit. While this repair used an NOS factory fender, sheetmetal from a wrecking yard, if straight, works just as well.

When replacing panels, you'll usually need some minor, or sometimes major, adjustment of the bolts that hold the sheetmetal in order to get the gaps between the panels even.

Replacing Panels

This is another example of a good candidate for panel replacement. The rear panel is caved in, and the quarter panel is badly wrinkled.

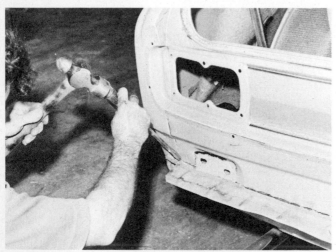

After removing the bumper and trim pieces, a chisel and torch are used to free the tack welded panels from the main body.

After all the tack welds are cut, the entire corner of the body is removed. A torch was used to remove the major portion of the rear quarter panel.

Quarter Panel Replacement

Replacement, rather than repair, of a quarter panel may often be easier, especially for beginning bodymen. Quarter panels are usually riveted along the door post and at the deck opening flange, with fusion welds where it mates to the top. A typical removal would be accomplished by drilling the spot welds and chiseling, torching, or snipping just below the fusion welds. The replacement panel should be trimmed a little long so it can be slid under the original body. Align the new panel with the body and drill holes down the overlap seam, using rivets to hold the panel in place. The replacement panel should be tacked and finish welded and the rivets ground smooth. Finish the repair as normal.

Door Panel Replacement

Other than the front fenders and quarter panels, the doors are replaced more often than any other part of cars. Replacement is usually due to excessive damage or rust that occurs when the door's water drain holes have become plugged. A door can be fully or partially replaced, depending on the damage.

Late-model cars usually have a window opening structure separate from the door panel, which means replacement panels come only to the window. Earlier model cars have panels that carry through to the window opening edges. This means earlier doors will need to be cut and welded somewhere near the top of the door panel, usually just below the window. (Deck lid and hood panels are crimped to the substructure much the same as doors, so replacement is similar.) Again, as with all panel replacement, be careful when welding not to distort the sheetmetal with the heat from the welder.

One consideration when replacing a door, hood, or trunk panel is that often the cost of a good used item is less than the replacement panel plus the cost of repair.

Replacing Top Panels

It is possible for even the beginner to replace a top panel without too much trouble. It is necessary to check the alignment of the roof substructure be-

When cutting a major body panel, have the replacement panel on hand so you'll know where to cut.

Grind off all paint where the new quarter panel will join the main body structure so the pieces can be tack welded together.

fore replacement, using a tape measure to check it corner to corner, side to side, and front to back. When the substructure has been pushed out and aligned with the doors, remove the front and rear windows. Remove the damaged top, using an air chisel, saber saw, or torch to cut about 1 inch in from the drip rail. After the major panel has been removed, the small remaining strip can be rolled off like a sardine can lid. An alternative method is to drill out all the spot welds.

After the panel is removed, dress down the sharp edges left by the spot welder and try the new panel for fit. It should drop right into place. If it doesn't, the substructure probably isn't aligned correctly. The top panel is then welded into position (use metal screws to hold it in place while the welds are being made) by either spot welding or spot brazing. Finish the repair as normal.

Panel Joints

There are four basic types of joints involved in panel replacement: butt welds, rivet laps, recessed lap joints, and the flange joint. Butt welds (butting two pieces of metal together and welding the seam), and the rivet lap (over-lapping two pieces of metal and using rivets to hold them in place while welding) are the quickest ways to join panels together. More involved are the recessed lap joints, where a recess is placed into the edge of the upper or lower panel so the mating panel will be flush in contour, and the flange joint, where both panels have a 90 degree approximate flange at the mating edge so that they can be joined by rivets or welds.

A recessed lap joint is usually made on the original panel in a high crown area, such as a door. Sheetmetal screws are used in the recess to keep everything aligned while the lap ends are welded; then the screws are removed and the holes filled.

A flange joint is used after the contours of the body and replacement panel are matched perfectly. A clamp is used to hold the flanges together while they are mated together with sheetmetal screws or rivets. The tiny crack that remains on the exterior is filled with body filler or lead.

Which joint you use is usually determined by the location and size of the panel being replaced. Always make sure the welds are secure and properly ground down before finishing your repair; also be careful to avoid heat damaging the new panels.

The inner fender edge must be drilled every few inches where it rests against the wheelwell. Then it is tack welded into place.

The upper edge of the quarter panel is likewise welded to the body panel. Then the rear panel is tack welded at intervals and all visible seams filled.

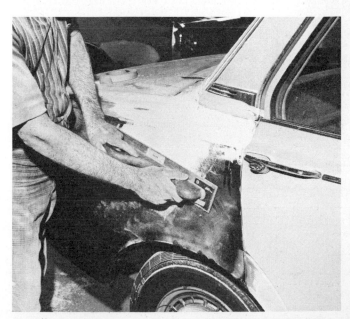

After the welds are ground smooth, the repair is finished with body filler to smooth the joints.

5
Plastic Fillers

There was a time, not so long ago, when plastic was an evil word around most reputable body shops. Plastic body fillers, with all their strange names and colors, were considered cheaters. Real bodymen used only lead, a substance that took some real skill to master. Plastic filler, on the other hand, could be mixed and slapped on a dent by anyone. Initially it was misused, often piled 2-3 inches deep as a shortcut way to fill, rather than straighten, a dent or body crease. But with experience, the limits of plastic fillers became known, as did the advantages. And today, these fillers are considered invaluable by both beginning and professional body repairmen.

Preparing the Body

Body "filler" is really a misnomer for the various plastic compounds available today. Anyone who tries to use plastic to fill holes or dents is going to have, at best, only a temporary repair. Instead, plastic should be thought of, and used, as a "finisher." Because sheetmetal cannot be worked after a plastic filler has been used, it is imperative that all bodywork be completed before the plastic is applied.

After getting the repair as straight as you can, grind the metal down with a medium weight sanding disc. Clean the repair as thoroughly as possible, removing the surrounding paint so that there is a good 3-4 inches of bare metal feather-edged around the repair. This allows the filler to be spread into the surrounding metal to ensure the necessary buildup. Do not spread the filler over paint as it does not adhere well to painted surfaces and will eventually crack or peel. Besides removing the paint and roughing the surface of the sheetmetal, this final sanding should reveal any high or low spots left by your repair work. Low spots are less of a concern because they will be filled, but a high spot on the metal will become even higher when covered with filler. Once you are satisfied with the metal preparation, wipe down the surface with degreaser to get rid of any waxes or oils that might prevent a good plastic-to-metal bond.

Mixing and Applying

Plastic fillers are made up of a resin base and a catalyst. Unmixed, the two agents remain pliable over a long period of time. But once the catalyst is added to the resin, it will harden in a matter of minutes. It is possible to control the hardening time somewhat by the amount of catalyst (hardener) that is added, but the best method is to follow the exact mixing instructions on the containers. Normally only a little catalyst is needed for a lot of resin.

Mixing of the two ingredients should be done on a clean, flat surface such as a piece of glass or cardboard. After reading the mixing instructions carefully, use a paint paddle to put an appropriate amount of resin on the mixing board. Experience will help you judge how much resin you will need for a particular job. Never mix more plastic than immediately needed, even if the fill will require several coats. Apply the correct amount of hardener and mix thoroughly. Be careful when using hardener. With too little catalyst, the mixture will be pale and won't dry properly. Too much catalyst will make the filler dry too fast and crack after application.

Once the plastic is mixed, apply it to the work area with a large plastic squeegee. Apply the mixture using a downward-sideways motion to force out any air bubbles. These bubbles must not be left in the mixture as they will shrink or burst later after the paint is applied. At the same time these pressure strokes will cause the plastic to achieve a maximum bond with the roughened metal. Don't apply more filler than needed as it will just have to be sanded off when dry. Work slowly and smoothly, using a minimum number of strokes. If too much hardener was used or if the mixture was left too long before it was applied, it will tend to roll up and pull loose from the metal. If this happens, don't bother going any further. Mix a new batch and start again.

The reaction time of a filler is controlled by the catalyst or hardener. Drying can be speeded up by the application of external heat, such as from a heat lamp.

Finishing and Sanding

Finishing plastic can be either very easy or extremely difficult, depending on how long it is allowed to set before the finishing process is started. After you have applied a smooth, even coat of filler, let it dry. Monitor the plastic carefully. When it has hardened to the consistency of soft rubber, cut down the high spots with a cheesegrater file. Pull the file diagonally to expose the greatest area of the file to the greatest area of the filler. Go lightly with this file; then let the filler dry for a while longer.

After about a half hour, the filler should be ready for sanding. Use a long sanding board or dual action pneumatic sander with about a 180-grit paper to sand the area smooth. Watch that you don't sand too much or you will get the area too low. Keep cleaning the sandpaper so it doesn't become clogged. Use your hand to gauge the smoothness of the finish. Switch to a higher (finer) grit sandpaper and continue to sand until the filler is smooth and blends into the body without leaving an edge. Often, especially with deeper repairs, it is necessary to apply a second coat of filler following the same procedures as with the first coat. The second coat should be easier to apply and work, and you shouldn't need nearly as much.

Spot Putty

After the filler has been finished to your satisfaction, wipe the area clean and apply a medium coat of primer. As the primer dries, tiny pinholes and scratches will appear. These imperfections should be filled with a light coat of spot putty. Spot putty should be applied straight from the tube or can with a small rubber squeegee. Spread it lightly over the entire area, making many passes to speed drying time. Let the putty, which serves much like a very thick primer, dry thoroughly before block sanding it carefully with a very fine grit sandpaper. There should not be very much putty left after sanding. It is meant to fill minute imperfections, not serve as filler for low spots.

Apply a finish coat of primer, inspect the surface and reputty or prepare it for final painting, as necessary.

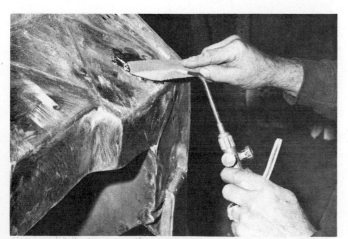

Before plastic fillers came into wide use, lead was the only way to go. While not exactly a lost art, it is getting harder to find someone who can still do the involved lead melting and mixing procedure.

Plastic Filler Application

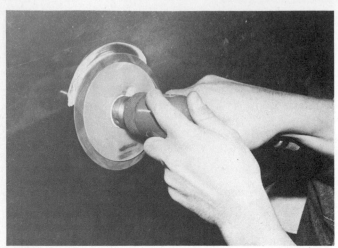

1. The first step in applying plastic filler is to prepare the surface so the plastic can make a good bond. After removing dirt and impurities with a degreaser, grind off all traces of paint and primer.

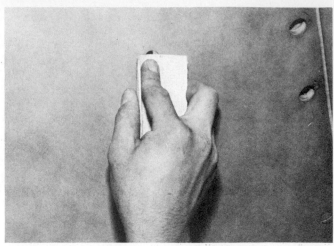

2. When you are applying filler around small holes, make sure the edges of the hole are well prepped. Take a piece of coarse sandpaper and rout the hole to remove paint or dirt.

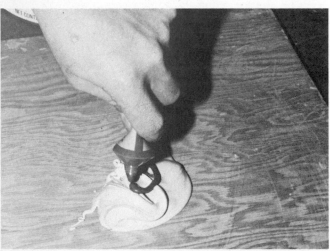

3. Now mix the filler, adding catalyst according to directions. Mix only as much filler as you'll need for the job. A piece of cardboard or a plastic mixing plate will work well for this process.

4. When mixing filler and catalyst, work quickly but thoroughly. Like most paints, the drying time of filler is affected by temperature and humidity. On cold or wet days, more catalyst may be needed to achieve proper results.

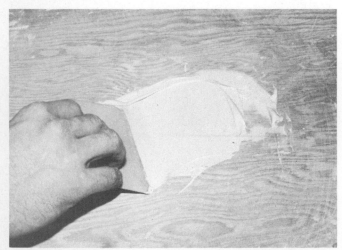

5. Most catalysts are a brighter color than the filler, which simplifies the mixing process. When the two are thoroughly mixed, the filler should be a uniform color, with no streaks, as shown here. Improperly mixed filler, when applied to a repair, will dry at uneven rates and eventually crack or chip off.

6. Filler should be spread with a plastic squeegee or spreader in long, broad strokes. You don't want to work the filler back and forth. Keep all strokes flowing in one direction so as not to lift the filler that is already laid down.

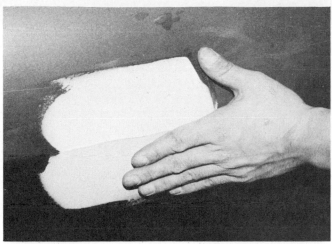

7. After allowing the filler to cure for a few minutes, lightly check it with your fingers. When it is ready for filing, it should feel firm and have the consistency of rubber.

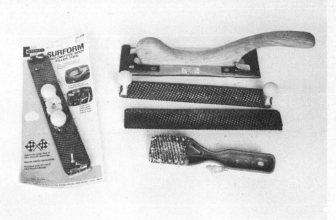

8. Cheesegrater files are recommended for use with plastic fillers because they can work down the excess filler without clogging or damaging the filler you want to leave on the repair. Use one that fits the size of the repair.

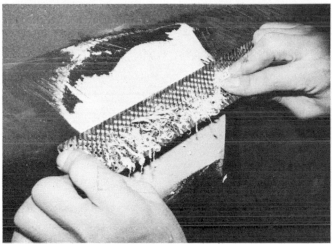

9. The cheesegrater file should be pulled across the repair in long strokes. If the filler is filed at the right stage of drying, the excess should come off in long, thin curls as shown.

10. Low spots in the repair will show up as dark spots in the filler after it has been filed and sanded. These areas should be filled with another very thin coat of plastic.

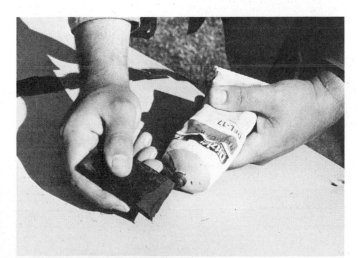

11. Spot putties are related to fillers in that they serve the same purpose—fill holes and leave a smooth, paintable surface. Putties come in either tubes or cans, and are premixed so you don't have to add catalysts.

12. Putty can be applied straight from the tube using a small squeegee. Keep the coats thin and smooth. When the putty has dried, it can be sanded lightly for a perfect finish.

6
Rust Repair

Rust—it's that flaky orange stuff you see on so many vehicles. It's a great color for autumn leaves and good exterior paint color, but when it appears on a vehicle's sheetmetal, rust is trouble. Rust destroys more vehicles each year than accidents. It never sleeps or takes a holiday. Though winter is the season when the worst vehicle corrosion occurs (especially in areas of heavy rain and snow, and where salt is used to de-ice the roads), a vehicle can rust anywhere, any time. Domestic and foreign vehicle manufacturers have increased the use of "anti-rust" galvanized steel, undercoatings, and zinc-rich primers in recent years, but any vehicle built is going to start rusting the first time it gets wet.

What can be done about rust? Quite a lot, but how much depends entirely on the severity of the problem. Within the broad spectrum of rust types are several different categories, a sort of the good, the bad, and the ugly of corrosion.

The good (only comparatively) is what is commonly called *surface* rust. Surface rust is the first stage of exterior sheetmetal corrosion; it is the light flaking you see on a pickup bed wall, around wheel-wells, on wheels and accessories, or around places where the paint has been chipped or scratched. Surface rust is the easiest to repair.

The bad category of rust is *hidden* rust. Hidden rust often goes undetected for months or even years, camouflaged by bodywork or paint. It starts out like surface rust, as a light flaking, but because it is inside the door panels or covered with paint or accessories, you can't find it or stop it from spreading. There's little you can do about hidden rust short of tearing apart the door panels, inner fender liners, or tailgates every few months. Under poorly prepared exterior sheetmetal, hidden rust shows up as bubbles or blisters in the paint. When you do find hidden rust you should fix it immediately.

The ugly category is the so-called *major* rust that

can turn a door or fender into sheetmetal lace. Once a car body starts to look more like Swiss cheese than an automobile, it's time for major surgery. The more advanced major rust is, in terms of total surface area, the more difficult and expensive the repair will be. With major body rust, it is often cheaper to replace a whole door or fender than to patch the existing sheetmetal.

There are three basic steps to busting any kind of rust. Remove the rust, repair the metal, and recover the repair. But before you can start putting the cuffs on corrosion, it's a good idea to figure out why the rust appeared or you may be starting the rust and repair cycle all over again. The most obvious reason a vehicle rusts is that it gets wet and doesn't dry out. But getting wet is not the problem— staying wet is. Moisture traps include the following areas:

Inner doors—Most vehicle doors have built-in drain holes. If the lower edge of your car's door has rusted out, chances are good that the drain hole has become plugged. Unplug it while making the repair or the rust will come right back.

Fenders—Moisture and mud often get trapped between fender and fenderwell, keeping the metal wet and promoting early rusting. While making the repair, be sure to seal cracks or openings in this area.

Under bumpers or other bolt-ons— Any place where accessories have been attached to bare metal, such as mirrors, hitches, or light brackets, are potential moisture trapping areas. After repairing rust in these areas, be sure to prime, paint, and protect the surfaces being mated.

Removing Rust

Once you've figured out the severity of the rust, the repair can begin. The first step is to remove the rust. This is the most important

One method of removing all rust is to have the metal dipped in a chemical stripping tank. Due to the complete disassembly required, dipping the vehicle is usually reserved for complete restoration jobs or for from-scratch street rod buildups.

step because if you don't remove all the rust, it will come right back. There are several ways to remove rust; all have their advantages and disadvantages.

One of the easiest methods is to remove the rust chemically. There are a wide variety of chemical rust removers, from naval jellies to sprays. When using chemical rust removers, the best advice is to use moderation. Follow the instructions of the specific product exactly, and avoid getting the chemicals in your eyes or on your skin. Some of these chemicals are very strong and can damage good sheetmetal if not carefully controlled. Be sure to remove all traces of the chemicals before priming or repainting the vehicle. Paint and primer won't adhere well to chemically coated metal, and that can cause more problems, including additional rusting. Chemical stripping is relatively expensive and is most suitable for small jobs. The exception is a professional chemical dipping, available in most major cities, which is often more economical for removing rust from an entire frame or body during a complete restoration or rebuild.

Another method of rust removal is sanding. Just as a little steel wool and elbow grease will clean up a rusty chromed wheel, some sandpaper and a lot of elbow grease will get rid of all but the worst rust. Sanding is safe and leaves a good, well-prepped surface for painting. For repairs of large areas you should invest in a few basic air tools, such as a dual-action or orbital sander. Many companies offer quality air tools that pay for themselves many times over in saved labor in just one job. When sanding, whether by hand or with power tools, take the rusted area down to bare metal to ensure that all traces

Rust—it doesn't take a genius to spot it in this advanced state. Major rust like this can be repaired, though it is often cheaper to replace the whole panel.

Rust Repair

Chemical rust removers, such as naval jelly, are much easier than dipping for small areas of rust.

of rust are removed. The disadvantages of sanding are that it's time consuming, strenuous, and only usable on rusted areas that have a solid metal base. Areas that have rusted completely through are not suitable for this method of rust removal.

Another method that works very well on major rust is sandblasting. Not only does it eliminate the rust by beating it away with high-powered blasts of abrasive sand particles, but sandblasting also reveals weak spots in the metal as well as lightly etching the surface for a good adhesion of primer and paint. While sandblasting equipment is available for sale or rent from many sources, a check of the Yellow Pages will usually locate a commercial sandblaster who can get rid of your rust very cheaply. The disadvantage of sandblasting is that you run the risk of stressing the remaining metal while removing the rust. If attempting to do your own blasting, be sure to check with an expert for advice on picking the right grit sand and the right air pressure for your specific repair.

The final method of rust removal is the most severe, cutting out the affected metal. This method allows you to discard whole body panels or just a section, using a hacksaw or air chisel. This method should be used only for completely rusted out areas, because the rest of the repair procedure is time consuming and expensive.

Repairing the Metal

Once the rust is removed, it is necessary to repair the remaining metal. Areas that were only lightly rusted should be sanded smooth or filled with spot putty or body filler, as needed. When sanding or removing paint to reveal bare metal, the

metal should be carefully conditioned with a chemical surface prep to prevent re-rusting and provide a good, etched surface for the primer to bond to.

Rusted areas that have been cut out will need to be patched. This involves cutting sections of sheetmetal (22-gauge is recommended to match most vehicle bodies) to fit the area removed and welding these patches into place. The patches should be clamped into position and carefully tack welded (alternating areas of tacking so as to avoid any heat warping of the body panel) before they are finish welded. The welds should be ground smooth and the surface finished with body filler and spot putty before priming and painting.

Recovering Repaired Areas

The final step in busting rust is to keep it from coming back. Repaired exterior sheetmetal should be properly primed and then painted immediately, if possible, on the day of the repair. Primer will not totally seal an exposed area; moisture can get underneath it and start attacking the metal again. A good paint coat is the best sealant against the elements and can protect your vehicle from renewed rusting. Underbody areas should be sealed with silicone sealant, undercoating, or body tar, all of which are available at automotive paint supply outlets. Never leave bare metal exposed for any length of time.

Once the repair is covered, you should use a few preventative measures to keep rust from coming back. Get your vehicle professionally undercoated if it isn't already. Thoroughly wash your car after driving in mud or over salted roads, rinsing the vehicle's underside well. Let the vehicle dry completely before putting it into a heated (humid) garage. In winter, don't park a snowy or icy vehicle in a heated garage. The snow or ice will melt, but not dry up, and the rust cycle will start again. Keep the exterior waxed year round, and touch up nicks and scrapes as they happen before rust gets a foothold.

Automobiles aren't meant to last forever, but with a little luck and an aggressive anti-rust attitude, you can keep your precious metal for a long, long time.

An ounce of prevention goes a long way where rust is concerned. A well-waxed and often-washed vehicle is less likely to suffer from the harmful oxidation caused by chemical, salt, or dirt deposits.

Common Rust Removal and Repair

1. This is a good example of surface rust on a primed pickup bed. Surface rust is easy to repair if caught in time. Left unchecked, it will rust right through the metal very shortly.

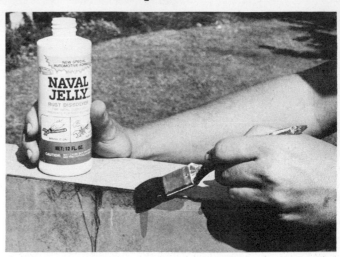

2. When using chemical rust removers such as naval jelly, always follow the directions on the label and protect your eyes and skin from the fumes or direct contact. Naval jelly is brushed on, and the rust washed off.

3. Another method of rust removal that works well on minor rust spots is sanding. When hand sanding, make sure you sand all the way to bare metal to remove all traces of rust.

4. Air tools, such as this orbital sander, take the trouble out of lengthy hand sanding. Again, make sure you remove all traces of rust. Any rust that is not eliminated will seed the rust cycle from underneath.

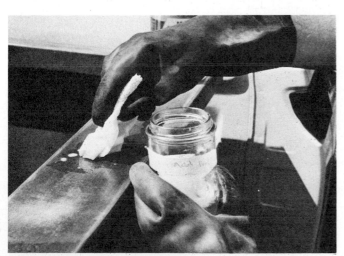

5. After sanding, wipe the metal down with a degreaser to remove residue and rust flakes. Then use a chemical surface prep solution to etch the metal for a good primer bond.

6. Spray the bare metal immediately after sanding and prepping with a heavy coat of primer. Apply the finish coat of paint as soon as possible, as primer alone will not seal out rust-causing moisture.

7. Sandblasting is an excellent method of rust removal. Commercial sandblasters can be located by checking the telephone directory, or you can rent a small sandblasting machine and do the job at home.

8. Major rustouts commonly occur where water becomes trapped, as it was inside this door. Rustouts like this should be cut out and patched.

9. For ease of repair, the door was taken off the car and placed on a workbench. The first step in the repair was to grind off all paint surrounding the rusted area to determine how far the rust had spread.

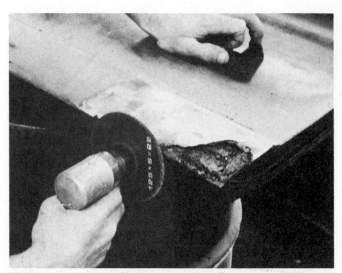

10. A body grinder was used to break the lower seam of the door. This step was made much easier due to the extensive metal decay.

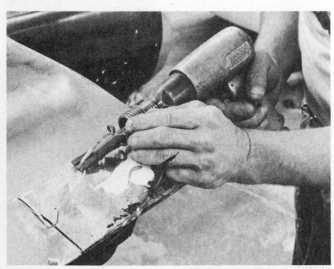

11. Once the door's outer skin was separated at the bottom edge, the entire rusted area was cut out with the help of an air chisel. Note the body filler indicating previous stopgap repairs.

12. This door had more rust and a few small holes under the outer skin. The rust was ground out and the holes brazed.

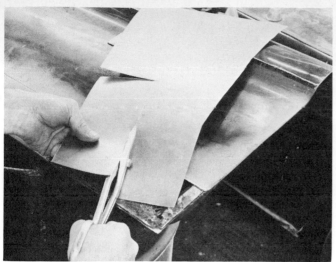

13. Next, a patch was carefully measured and cut from a piece of 22-gauge sheetmetal.

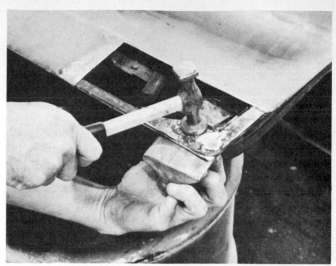

14. After the holes under the outer skin were brazed with a welding rod, the area was flattened with a hammer and dolly and the excess welding material ground smooth.

15. The patch panel was slowly and carefully tack-welded into place, with efforts taken to minimize warpage. The welds were worked over with a hammer and dolly to make the door smooth and flat. Then they were ground smooth with a disc sander.

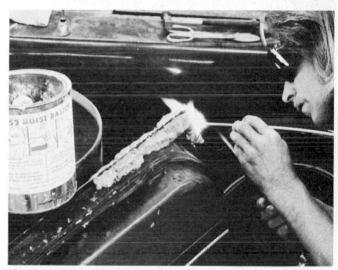

16. The bottom seam of the door was gas-welded shut. Both sides of the seam were packed with Moist Bastos to prevent heat warpage. The excess welding material left on the door seam was ground off.

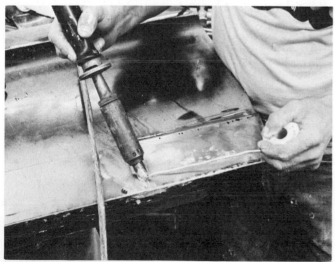

17. A heavy-duty soldering iron and acid-core solder were used to fill the tiny imperfections left after the welds were ground down. Then the whole area was covered with body filler and finished in the normal fashion.

18. The completed repair brought an old, rusty door back to life. The same techniques can be used to repair rust on almost any part of a vehicle.

7
Panel Alignment

Many times a car can be in an accident and superficially not be damaged. That is, the fender may not be buckled, yet something just isn't right. What usually isn't right is the fit of the panels. For example, a fender can be moved back against the front of the door edge so that the door can't be opened. The force of a collision can bend hinges and braces without actually denting the body. This kind of damage means that the pieces no longer fit properly—a frustrating kind of damage. Fortunately, the alignment of panels is relatively simple as long as you know how to tackle the problem without making the alignment worse.

Checking the Problem

There are two kinds of alignment involved in automotive bodywork: alignment of the basic substructure and alignment of the various panels, both stationary and opening. When repairs are made, if the reinforcement structure is not exactly perfect, the external panels will not align. The keys to repairing panel alignment problems are to accurately determine where the damage is and to locate the correct position of the panel. Thoroughly measuring and checking the problem before any work is done is a must.

It is possible for a panel to be completely out of alignment without a visible sign of damage. Consequently, you must look for hidden damage. A slight unnatural kink somewhere in the frame may lead to an entire unaligned front or rear body section. The best way to check for this misalignment is with a measuring tape.

Measurements are used for comparison since cars are basically symmetrical. These comparisons are usually diagonal, and are known as X-checks. The checks include four general body sections: the front section, from the front door forward; the center section, which includes the small area from the front door to the rear door; the rear section, from the rear door to the trunk; and the trunk, or deck section of the vehicle. Measurements are taken in the same places for all types of vehicles.

The same kind of diagonal measurement can be used for X-checking all aspects of the car: from frame to body substructure to individual panel openings. Once a starting point has been established, and all other sections have been checked for alignment, then each section can also be checked against the other. This type of checking is just an extended version of the individual section checking, since a specific point is selected on opposite sides. All measurements must coincide with their opposite measurements and will normally align if the individual sections are all right. When measurements are taken between sections, it is wise to double-check your work by taking measurements from several different reference points.

Alignment of the vehicle extremities, the front and rear ends, is usually a matter of making the hood and deck lid fit. Before these panels can be tried for a fitting, the openings must be aligned as closely as possible. The deck area is harder to align than the front end because the quarter panels are welded to the mating panels. When there is major rear end damage it is necessary first to straighten the frame. Once the frame is straight, it is possible to push or pull the crumpled metal back into place until the trunk flooring again aligns with the frame.

Working from frame/flooring reference points, the inner body structures are straightened until the deck lid opening checks out perfectly according to the X-reference. If the deck lid has not been damaged, it should then fit the opening. If the lid must be straightened, it can now be repaired to fit the opening. Finally, when the panels surrounding the opening are straightened, the damaged rear end can be reshaped, but a considerable amount of measuring will be required.

Even if the door wasn't hit directly, it is still a good idea to check all openings after an accident. Tolerances should be within 1/8 inch.

Diagonal checks can be made on all openings: doors, trunk, and hood. Be sure you know where the problem is before attempting to solve it. Double check your measurements.

The gap between the hood and fenders should be checked with a measuring tape. Check all around the hood's perimeter.

Front End and Hood Alignment

The big advantage to aligning front sheetmetal is that the entire front end assembly is bolted on. The fenders are attached with several bolts into the cowl structure and the radiator-core support bolts to the frame. If these bolts are removed, all the sheetmetal ahead of the cowl, except the hood, can be lifted off. Cars with unit body construction do not disassemble in this manner, since the front fenders

Diagonal measurements, also known as X-checks, are necessary to determine if part of a damaged vehicle is out of alignment. This Camaro was hit hard in the side, so metalman Eddie Paul made many comparison checks during the straightening process.

Panel Alignment

Sometimes hoods and trunk lids can be muscled back into alignment. Only pull a little at a time and then carefully compare measurements.

Whenever the front end of a car is hit hard like this, you can be pretty sure there will be alignment adjustments needed. Any time the front end is hit, the frame and suspension should be checked by a competent frame shop before trying to align the body panels.

and inner fender panels form part of the frame/body unit. However, some cars use unit construction for the main body with a subframe bolting to the firewall. This is common to Chrysler Corporation products and some GM products like Camaros and Firebirds.

Since front end pieces are so easy to remove and replace, it is possible that replacement with used parts will be the most economical. In any case, when a front end is being worked on, it must be returned to perfect alignment or the hood will never fit properly.

There often is room for a very slight change in hood opening size since the grillework and inner panel bolt holes are elongated, but this is minor and should not be considered a substitute for proper repair. As a rule, if the core supported panels and the grille assembly do not fit well, realignment is in order. As with most other parts of the body, the flooring or frame provides the basis for most X-checking measurements in the front sheetmetal section.

Any damage to a hood that is repairable will require constant checking, both of itself and against the fender/grille opening. The hood can be checked for correct dimensions with the same X-check procedure or diagonal measurements, but twist or contour damage can only be checked

against the fenders. At the same time, a new or replacement hood may need minor tweaking to fit either a repaired or undamaged front end.

Hoods are normally held in place by spring loaded hinges. The hinges hold the hood in an open position but can also be designed to pull the rear of the hood downward when the hood is closed. Small rubber buttons along the fenders, cowl, and grille rest form vibration dampeners between the hood and surrounding panels. There is a considerable amount of built-in adjustment in the hinges but only one or two are generally needed during the fitting process.

It is often necessary to shift the fenders to get the right hood opening. If a particular fender is too high, too low, too far aft, or too far forward, all the attaching bolts should be loosened and the fender shifted by use of a long lever such as a 2x4. In the case of fore/aft movement, a hydraulic jack will do the trick.

The proper use of shims and washers can solve many front end alignment problems. The rubber stoppers on many cars are adjustable by screwing them further in or out. If you are unsure about any changes, scribe the original location before loosening any bolts. This way you will at least be able to return to your starting point.

This repaired Mustang illustrates a common source of alignment problems. Original, new, and used parts, plus some repaired sections, now make up the front end. Careful assembly and alignment is necessary to obtain a proper fit from such a variety of parts.

An assortment of wood blocks can be quite handy in solving minor alignment problems. The left side of this trunk lid was a little high, so the block was placed on the right side and pressure exerted on the left corner.

Deck Lid and Rear Panel Repair

As with doors and hoods, deck lids should fit closely and securely. The problem of providing and maintaining deck lid alignment is intensified by the fact that there are only three points of minor adjustment—the two hinges and the latch.

The deck lid is aligned when it fits the body all the way around. Usually the lid is in alignment if the gap between the lid and body/fender panels is the same circumferentially; but this doesn't mean the lid is sealing. The seal can be checked by putting chalk on the body flange edge and then closing the lid. The chalk will be transferred to the weather strip at the points of contact. If the lid is not sealing along most of the bottom edge, it can be sealed either by drawing tighter with the latch or by loosening the hinge bolts and sliding it forward or lowering it slightly.

If the deck lid seems to be twisted on the hinges, the lid can probably be twisted by hand to fit. Open the lid and place something like a rubber mallet between the body and the lid on the side that is sealing correctly. Push downward on the opposite side, but do not use excessive force. After a few test "heaves" check the lid for a fit, then repeat if necessary.

Along the quarter panels/fenders, chances are that the body flange will be too high. If so, tap with a mallet on or very near the flange to bring it into alignment. If this area is too low, use the hydraulic jack. Making the lower edge of the lid fit is a matter of either hammering the lower body panel out or bending the lid. If the lid is not sealing tightly at the latch, adjust the latch. If the center part still does not seal, place two equal pieces of 2x4 (or two rubber mallets) at either side and push forward along the lid center. If one corner is high, place the mallet under the opposite corner and push down on the offending corner. If both corners are high, place the mallet under the middle and apply equal pressure to both corners.

If both corners of a deck lid are sealing poorly, it may be necessary to place a block in the center of the trunk and press evenly on both corners. On larger trunk lids it helps to have one person on each corner.

Whenever a hood or trunk lid is removed or adjusted, make a scribe mark around the hinge flange as a reference; make small movements and check, then retighten the bolts.

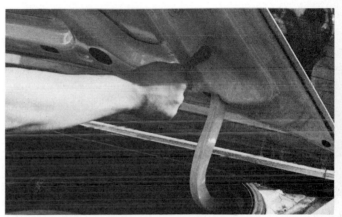

When adjusting hinges, it is only necessary to loosen the bolts slightly. You want to pull the panel into position rather than have it fall or come off the hinges. Remember, these panels are heavy and can easily pinch fingers.

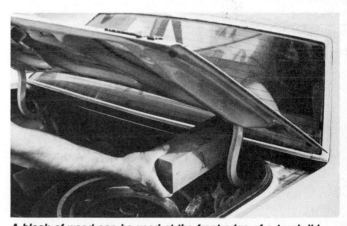

A block of wood can be used at the front edge of a trunk lid to raise or lower it depending on whether you lift on the back edge of the lid or push down on it.

Door Repair and Alignment

Perhaps the most perplexing panels to keep in alignment are the doors, since they can become misaligned through use, age, and damage. A door will be out of alignment when the contours do not match the surrounding panels and when the door itself is not exactly centered in the door opening.

Panel Alignment

When trying to make a trunk or hood seal properly, be sure the rubber cushions are intact, in good shape, and properly adjusted if the cushion is on threaded stock. Also check the condition of the weather stripping.

To check how a door is sealing, place a strip of paper in it and close. If the paper slips out of the closed door anywhere in the opening, that point isn't sealing.

The ever-popular 2x4 piece of wood can be used on door hinges, but try the hinge adjustments before using force.

A long piece of wood will work as a lever to lift a sagging door. It also works to have a helper lift up on the door handle while you adjust the hinge bolts.

If there has been extensive damage to a door or door frame, chances are the opening itself will have sustained some damage and must be carefully X-checked. At the same time, distortion of the door opening can be caused by frame misalignment, body twist, and other seemingly unrelated factors. If damage is involved, the opening must be X-checked to make sure it is ready for door alignment.

The surface contour of the door in all directions must match that of the surrounding panels. When checking for misalignment, the opening gap around the door perimeter should be uniform. There may be a slightly larger gap on one side, but this should remain uniform along its length.

While making the visual alignment check, look at the scuff plate to see if the door is dragging (sagging). Open and close the door slowly and note whether the door raises or lowers as it latches. If there is an up or down movement, the door is out of alignment vertically and is being centered by the dovetail.

There are two specific controls that keep a door in position when closed: the striker plate and the dovetail. The striker plate is the latch and the dovetail limits up-and-down movement of the closed door. The dovetail's function may be integrated with the latch mechanism, but sometimes it is included separately to keep the door from jiggling up and down on the hinges.

Striker plates can be adjusted over a relatively wide range, but before any adjustments are made the striker should be replaced if worn. A little wear is no problem, but excessive wear, which is visually apparent, or sloppiness in parts (such as a rotary latch) dictates replacement. If the door won't close or fits too loosely, the striker needs adjustment.

Spacers may be required to make strikers fit properly. If spacers are required, first add some caulking compound to the striker where the lock extension engages. Close the door to make an impression in the compound, then measure this compound thickness. If the distance from the striker teeth to the rear edge of the clay depression is less than 11/32 inch, spacers and different length attaching screws will be needed, as follows:

Dimension	No. of spacers	Spacer thickness	Striker screws
11/32-9/32 in.	1	1/16 in.	original
9/32-7/32 in.	1	⅛ in.	⅛ in.
7/32-5/32 in.	1 each	1/16 & ⅛ in.	⅛ in.
5/32-3/32 in.	2 (⅛ in.)	¼ in.	¼ in.

The dovetail does not correct door sag, but it will allow slight movement of the door up or down for adjustment. The dovetail on older cars will probably be very worn and should be replaced.

There is considerable adjustment available at the hinges, but no hinge work should be attempted without making sure this is where the problem lies. This is especially important on older cars that do not have hinge adjustment in the fore/aft plane. Such hinges must be spread or closed. If the door sags, the usual remedy is to spread the lower hinge slightly, which moves the door bottom closer to the pillar. Sometimes, the upper hinge must also be closed to correct sag.

A hinge can be spread by placing some kind of interference between the leaves. Most bodymen rely on a hammer or screwdriver handle. First the handle is placed between the opened hinge leaves, then the door is partially closed. When the handle is tight in the hinge, the door is forced toward the car. Sometimes it will close if the interference is slight. Make all force spreading adjustments in small increments to keep from spreading the hinge too far. After each force session, check the door for proper fit. Proceed slowly!

If the top hinge must be closed, the hinge has to be removed. If the door has been damaged and the hinge bent, the distortion will be apparent. Repair is a matter of squeezing the hinge leaves together in a large vise.

If the car has adjustable hinges, as most modern cars do, close alignment is possible with very little labor. Remove the striker and dovetail assembly so they do not interfere with the way the door actually hangs in the opening. The major difference among makes of cars is whether the hinge adjustment is made at the door or at the pillar. All types of adjustable hinges are adjusted by loosening the bolts and forcing the door to a new position. Loosen the bolts a little bit at a time only.

If the door alignment cannot be corrected by adjustments to the hinges or the striker plate assembly, the trouble lies in either door body opening or door contour. If the door contour is not correct, it could require special tools in severe cases or nothing more than a knee and two hands. If the door is not contoured (bowed) enough, the top and bottom must be bent inward while the middle is kept stationary. Any time you apply force to a door, do it slowly and carefully.

Door contour work can be especially difficult on very old cars that used wood as the major substructure (early Chevys are a prime example). If the substructure is wood, all rotten sections should be replaced and all joints glued and fitted with wood dowels or new screws.

Making body parts fit properly is one of those time consuming tasks, but it is the kind of attention to detail that separates the really good bodymen from the rest of the crowd.

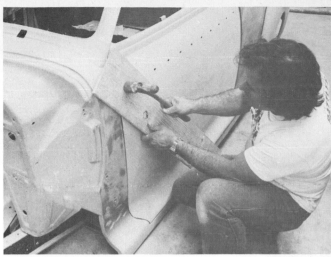

Using a block of wood and a big hammer to make minute alignment adjustments to a door isn't for the faint of heart. Take care to use a large enough piece of wood to disperse the blow. Centering the blow will cause a dent.

Most older cars rely on shims between the body and the frame to solve alignment problems. If the body is correctly shimmed, the doors will fit properly.

Whenever you encounter a damaged bumper, you should check the bumper braces for alignment if you expect the new bumper to fit correctly.

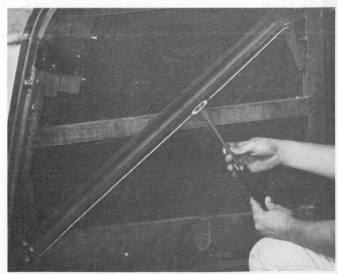

The doors on vintage cars are prone to sagging. Doors that use wood in their frames can be helped by the installation of a tension strap with a turnbuckle as shown here.

8
Fiberglass Fundamentals

Fiberglass is a material that's well known, popular, and almost universally accepted as the major alternative to steel in the construction and customizing of cars, trucks, and related vehicles. Yet it remains one of the most little understood substances in the entire body and paint industry. While there are many body shops around the country that specialize in fiberglass repairs, they make up only a very small percentage of all professional body shops. Chances of finding qualified, experienced fiberglass repairmen at a regular shop are not good. There is virtually no similarity between metal and fiberglass when it comes to repairs. Given the shortage of fiberglass repairmen and the ever increasing number of 'glass-bodied Corvettes, street rods, kit cars, and special interest vehicles, it's no surprise that more and more car owners are turning to doing their own fiberglass repairs.

Fortunately, even though fiberglass tends to be used most commonly on exotic-type cars, there is really nothing exotic about working with fiberglass. But before you can work with it successfully, it helps to know a little about the chemistry behind fiberglass-reinforced plastic. Unlike sheetmetal, fiberglass, with its plastic "skin," does not stretch or compress; it rips, tears, and melts when heated. Even the simplest fiberglass repair involves a complicated chemical bonding of fibers and resins. Although a metal repair can be pounded smooth and filled, a similar plastic repair must be patched from the outer and undersides, sanded, filled, sanded, and filled again as many as three times. And because the chemicals in the resins used must cure between steps, a typical fiberglass repair will take twice as long as a metal repair.

Fiberglass is a combination of three elements: glass fiber, polyester resins, and catalysts. By itself, resin is easily formed but has little strength. This is the job of the glass fiber reinforcements, which are available as either interwoven or matted blankets.

The resins themselves come in a number of forms, including phenolics, acrylics, epoxies, ureas, and polyesters. Polyesters are used because they are inexpensive and easy to control. Resin works well with glass fibers because, though it is manufactured in heavy liquid form, it cures or hardens as a solid. However, the hardening process requires heat in the range of 200 degrees F. That's where the catalyst or activators come in. The catalyst "kicks" the resin into an exothermic (outside heat) reaction. The amount of catalyst added to a batch of resin will control the drying or curing time of the fiberglass. When using catalysts, remember that shop temperature will also affect curing, with the time speeded up on a hot day and slowed down on a cold day.

Of the two types of fiberglass material, the woven cloth is the strongest. It is used for the base material of many fiberglass pieces such as kit car bodies, street rod fenders and sports car flares, and spoilers. Mat, on the other hand, is designed to give thickness and strength to a laminate. The glass fibers in the mat are laid so they run in one direction. The next sheet is then laid with the fibers going in the opposite direction; thus a kind of plywood effect is obtained, ensuring strength.

When working with fiberglass, remember that it can irritate the skin. This irritation can be avoided by using a protective cream on the hands or by wearing rubber gloves. Also, wear long sleeved shirts, button your shirt collar and use a respirator if necessary. Fiberglass dust kicked up by a disc grinder may irritate the nostrils.

Resins should be used in well ventilated areas, since toxic fumes are involved. These same resins accumulate on tools, shoes, clothing, practically everything. Everything should be cleaned with lacquer thinner, which is an excellent cleaning agent, while the resin is still soft.

Fiberglass on Fiberglass

The use of fiberglass in the automotive industry increases every year. There are three general kinds of fiberglass parts being used: matched metal molds, spray lay-ups, and hand lay-ups. With matched metal molds, chopped fiber and polyester resins are mixed, the catalyst is added, and the combination is placed in a male/female mold. Heat and pressure are applied and the finished product is ready in a few minutes. This method of making parts is fast and inexpensive, although not always strong.

With spray lay-up, chopped fiberglass roving is blown into a female mold along with catalyzed resin. The mixture is then rolled by hand and allowed to cure at ambient temperatures. This type of lay-up is popular with smaller manufacturers, although the builder must control the percentages of fiberglass and resin to control strength.

Hand lay-up is generally saved for one-off fiberglass pieces. Fiberglass mat, cloth, or roving (or a combination of these) is laid in the female mold and saturated with resin. The entire surface is then rolled to ensure proper mixture and balance throughout and to remove air bubbles. Pieces formed this way are usually very strong and thick, but the process is costly.

Repair of any of these types of fiberglass parts is pretty much the same: remove the damaged material, bevel all edges, grind off any paint and the protective gel coat to reach the raw fiberglass underneath. This should be done on both sides of a repair. Then cut a piece of mat and apply to the inner surface with the resin mix. Cover the mat with a piece of resin-saturated cloth pressed firmly in place. After the repair is allowed to cure, grind the surface smooth and either re-mat or fill the remain-

Fiberglass is an ideal material for custom work because it is lightweight and very easy to work with when creating new shapes and forms. This full custom Corvette was created by mixing and matching existing aftermarket fiberglass parts.

Fiberglass Fundamentals

The fundamentals of fiberglass begin with a basic understanding of the chemical processes and some basic supplies, including 'glass mat or cloth, resins, catalysts, and safety equipment such as rubber gloves and respirator.

ing low spots with plastic body filler. Finish the filler as you would a metal repair. Remember that this process must be repeated on each side of the repair. Some repairmen claim you can repair small cracks with pure resin and filler, but for a permanent and strong repair you should always use mat or cloth for reinforcement. The process takes more time, but the repair will last many times longer when done right.

Besides using fiberglass to repair fiberglass, the material works very well as a medium for bonding fiberglass parts together. Adding fiberglass flares, spoilers, scoops, and the like, is a relatively simple process of attaching, bonding, filling, reinforcing, and finishing (see accompanying flare how-to). A fiberglass on fiberglass repair or addition can be as strong as, or stronger than, the original piece.

Tools and supplies you'll need for most fiberglass repairs or add-ons include a disc grinder, cheese-grater file, screwdrivers, small rubber body putty squeegee, small roller, sandpaper, goggles, respirator, and gloves to protect yourself, as well as some

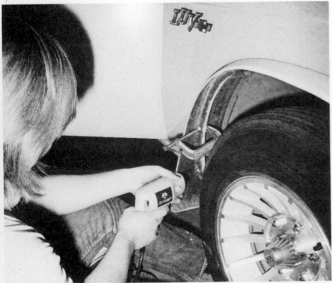

Fiberglass isn't just used for Corvettes and plastic-bodied street rods. There are many fiberglass accessories including flares, spoilers, and whale-tails that are easily riveted onto steel-bodied cars and trucks.

acetone to clean resin from you and your tools. You'll also need fiberglass mat or cloth along with resin and catalyst, all of which should be available at major paint and body supply outlets.

Fiberglass on Metal

We said at the beginning that there is very little similarity between fiberglass and sheetmetal. It should be no surprise then that the two materials don't really mix very well. The problem relates to their basic makeup. Fiberglass does not bend or stretch the way metal does. It has a rigidity that causes it to flex and expand and contract at a different rate than metal. While it is entirely possible to attach fiberglass flares, scoops, and other pieces to metal vehicles, even the best workmanship will eventually crack and deteriorate due to this unequal flexing and expansion/contraction.

The key to attaching fiberglass to metal, when the two are to be molded together rather than just riveted on (leaving a visible seam), is to prepare the metal to bare surface for maximum bonding and to attach the fiberglass part as securely as possible. This means, for example, in the case of a fiberglass hood scoop, to run rivets or screws as close as possible (every 1-2 inches) to limit flexing. Then carefully apply mat or cloth, using epoxy resin instead of polyester, as the latter will not adhere well to metal. Finish the molding with plastic body filler, being careful to avoid heavy filler buildup which is more susceptible to chipping and cracking.

Finishing and Painting

Finishing and painting fiberglass is not much different than finishing and painting metal. After you feel that the surface of the car or repair is virtually free of all imperfections and you have spot puttied in any pinholes or flaws in the plastic filler, you can proceed to priming. Most professional fiberglass repair shops recommend using a lacquer primer-surfacer. Before applying the primer, go over the 'glass with 80-grit, 100-grit and then 220-wet and 320-wet sandpaper. Apply several coats of primer, hand sanding the area with 320-wet paper between coats. Before painting with the color coats, go over the body or repaired area one more time. Fiberglass is susceptible to pinholing, caused by bubbles in the fiberglass popping through the paint. Again, fill any pinholes in the primer with putty, resand, prime, and check the body again. When you are satisfied, let the body dry out. Unlike metal, primed fiberglass needs to cure (at least two weeks is recommended). It's not only the primer that is drying, but all the chemicals underneath.

After curing, the fiberglass can be painted. Lacquer, not enamel, is again recommended because it is easier to spot in and dries faster during painting (eliminating the problem of dust and dirt getting into the paint finish). For a top-quality job, spray four or five coats of lacquer, color sand, and then spray an additional five to 10 coats. After the lacquer has been rubbed out you should have a vehicle that truly qualifies as a plastic fantastic.

Molding Fiberglass to Metal

1. Ready-made fender flares are available for many makes of vehicles. Some can be riveted right on while others require opening up of the stock wheelwells with an air chisel, as shown on this Datsun Z-car installation.

2. The fender opening is trimmed until a close fit between the sheetmetal and the flare is achieved. The front fenders on this particular application bolt right on.

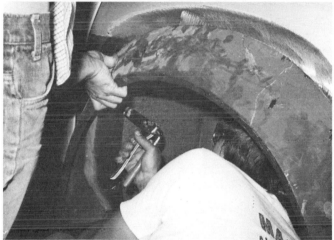

3. The quarter panel is ground bare, and the flare and body are coated with a bonding epoxy. While one person holds the flare firmly against the car, a second person drills and rivets it to the inner fenderwell sheetmetal.

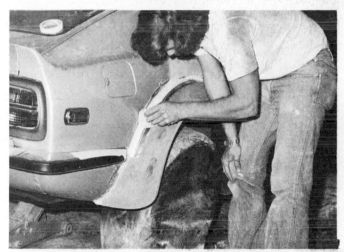

4. To provide a smooth transition from the body to the flare, a thin swipe of body filler is applied into the seam.

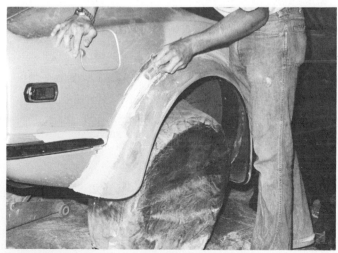

5. A smooth radius is sanded into the seam using sandpaper wrapped around a short length of heater hose.

6. The flare is finished by block-sanding and priming. After painting the flares to match the car, the job is done. Besides looking super, the flares accommodate larger-than-stock wheels and tires.

Fiberglass Repair

1. There are many ways to make a fiberglass repair—most of them wrong. A good repair starts with proper materials. For a proper fiberglass repair, you will need fiberglass mat or cloth, resin, catalyst or hardener, and plastic body filler.

2. We followed the repair of a '59 Corvette at D&D Corvette and Fiberglass Repair, San Bernardino, California. The Vette, like many, was suffering from cracks caused by a previous, poorly done repair. The first step was to remove the old panel.

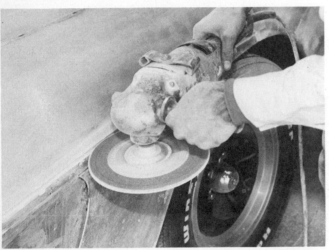

3. After locating the bonding strip on the inside of the fender, a cutting disc was used to cut through the bad panel, leaving the bonding strip underneath intact.

4. A hammer and chisel were used to pry the panel away from the strip and then from the rest of the car in one piece.

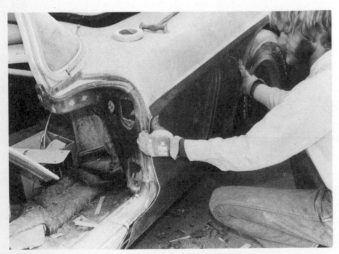

5. The new panel was test-fitted into position. A lot of grinding was necessary to make it fit properly and blend into the contour of the fender.

6. One of the tricks used by D&D is to blow the fiberglass debris away from the working area with a fan. It is also a good idea to always wear gloves, a respirator, and goggles when working with fiberglass.

7. Using a 36-grit sanding disc, all traces of the old binding adhesive were removed. The disc is coarse enough to remove the excess material without damaging the fiberglass. It leaves a textured surface on which the new bonding material can adhere.

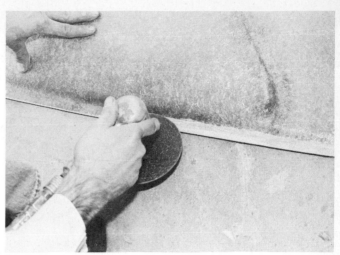

8. The areas of the new panel that would bond to the car were then roughed up using the 36-grit disc.

9. The panel was then screwed into place with special tapping screws made to work with fiberglass. They have a portion of the beginning threads removed so they won't damage the glass.

10. With the screws in place, a visual check was made of the fit. Note that the door was reinstalled to make sure the body line would flow properly from the door to the panel.

11. Eckler's Bonding Adhesive has the consistency of day-old oatmeal. It was mixed with cream hardener until the mixture took on a light red color.

12. Then the thoroughly mixed adhesive was generously applied to the points where the new panel would connect to the body.

13. With the panel loosely positioned, the screws were reinstalled and left in place until the adhesive had thoroughly dried. Once the screws were removed, the resulting holes in the panel were filled with resin and smoothed out.

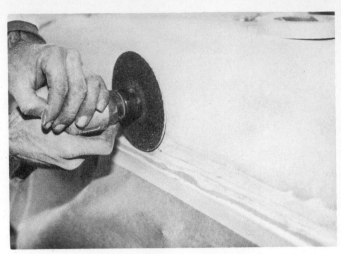

14. Using the 36-grit sanding disc, a "V"-shaped groove was cut along the point where the two panels butt together.

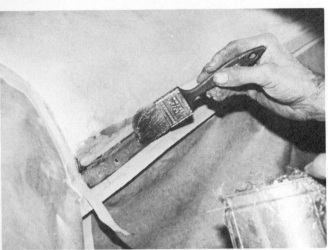

15. Masking tape was laid on both sides of the groove, marking the limits of the area to be resined. Using a paint brush, the resin/hardener mixture was brushed into the groove.

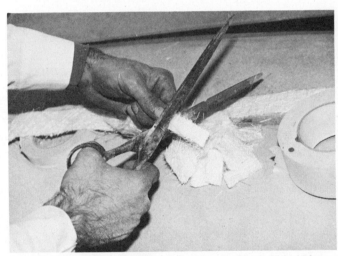

16. Fiberglass mat was first cut into ½ and 1-inch-wide strips, and then further cut down into small rectangles.

17. The rectangles were soaked in resin and placed in the groove. After the narrower rectangles were laid into position, the wider rectangles were added for a layered effect that filled the groove completely.

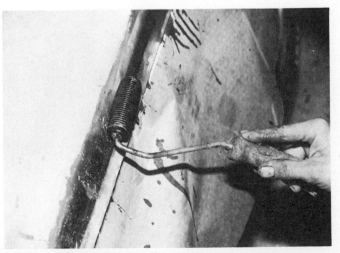

18. A roller was used to remove any air bubbles trapped in the layers of resin-soaked fiberglass mat.

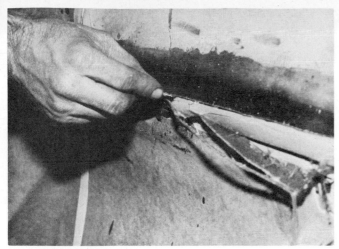

19. Once thoroughly dried, the excess mat and resin were cut away with a razor blade.

20. The disc grinder was used to smooth the panel joint so it was flush with the rest of the car. In areas where a bonding strip was not used as a backing panel, a temporary strip was used to support the panel from behind.

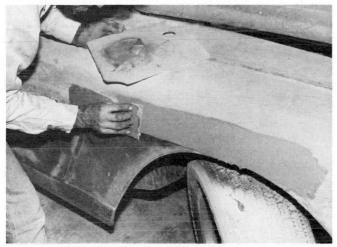

21. A thin coat of plastic body filler was then spread over the panel joint. Nowhere on the repair should filler be more than 1/16-inch thick.

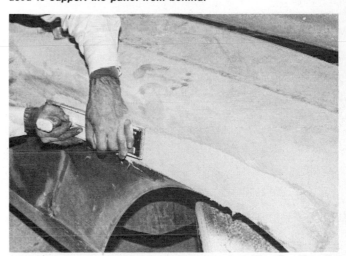

22. The filler was then sanded smooth with 40-grit paper, forming the final contour of the finished fender.

23. After sanding, gelcoat mixed with hardener was sprayed over the entire fender to fill any pinholes or nicks. D&D recommends the use of six heavy coats of gelcoat to ensure the fender is well sealed against flaws and future cracks.

24. The finished fender looks as good as new, and probably is stronger. As is, it is ready for priming and final painting.

Molding Fiberglass to Fiberglass

1. Installing fiberglass fender flares on a fiberglass body is relatively easy. Start by mounting the flare in the desired position, using the locating tabs as a guide.

2. Secure the flare to the car with sheetmetal screws, using the holes provided. Use a grease pencil to mark a line on the body along the edge of the flare. Then remove the flare.

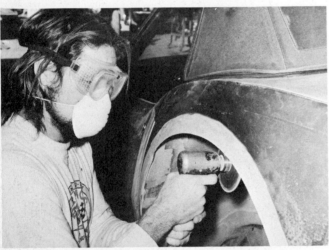

3. With a saber saw or small grinder, cut a new opening about an inch lower than the marked line, closer where you approach the doorpost. Grind the back of the flare and both sides of the body around the wheelwell.

4. Reinstall the flare with the screws, and cut off the locating tabs. Be sure the flare fits the body well before adding extra screws at 5-inch intervals.

5. Mix a small batch of adhesive and catalyst, using about 20 drops of catalyst to a golf ball-sized glob of mounting adhesive.

6. Back out the screws and pack the adhesive between the flare and the body. Then tighten the flare firmly against the body and squeegee the excess adhesive off the seam.

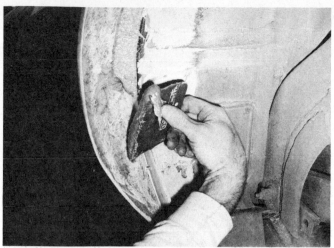

7. Fill the gap between the flare and the car body with adhesive. Pack it in solid and work out all air bubbles. Allow the adhesive to cure until fairly hard (about two hours).

8. Work the resin/catalyst mix into small mat patches. Do not soak the patch. Tear the mat apart to produce fuzzy edges for better overlapping. Cut the 'glass cloth slightly wider.

9. Mat patches should overlap the adhesive used to fill the space between the flare and body. Work out all air bubbles before applying wider cloth patches over the matted area.

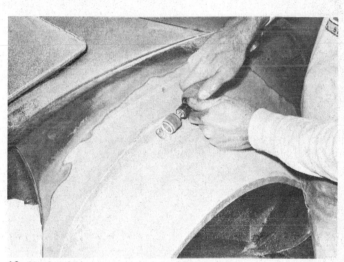

10. Next, grind out screw dimples and sand the entire surface with 80-grit paper to remove the surface gloss. Fill the dimples with adhesive and grind flush when semi-hard.

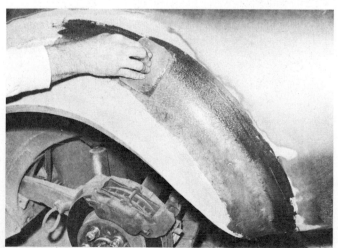

11. Slightly thin the plastic body filler with resin after adding the catalyst. Squeegee a thin coat over the seam area, filling all surface flaws. Allow this to cure.

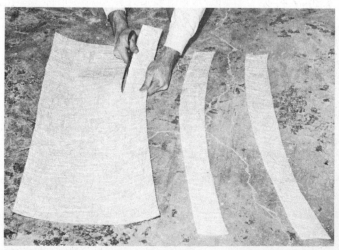

12. Then cut 3-inch-wide curved strips of mat and tear them into 6-inch lengths. Curved patches will fill the fender without wrinkling. No cloth is used here.

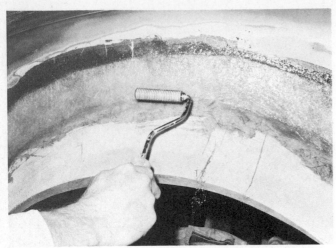

13. Using an old paint brush, work wet patches down into the seam area. Then use a roller to press out excess resin and force mat down against body and flare.

14. Use 24-grit paper with a very flexible backing pad to grind down the area to the desired finished radius. Then feather the patches into the surrounding body.

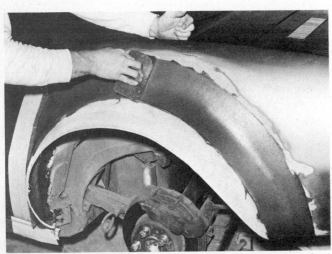

15. Use a plastic squeegee to apply a fairly heavy coat of body filler to fill any low spots. Wipe the filler on in long, smooth passes.

16. Using a piece of cardboard in the door opening keeps the edge straight. Work the body filler in against the lower edge, shaping carefully at the lower tip of the flare.

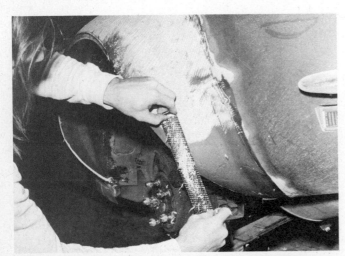

17. Once the filler has set up, work the entire area with a cheesegrater file, removing and shaping the body filler while it's still soft.

18. After sanding the filler with 40-grit paper, refill any low spots. Before priming, the flare should be sanded progressively with 80-grit, 100-grit, 220-wet, and 320-wet paper to obtain a glass-smooth finish.

Using Fiberglass with Wood

1. Fiberglass is more versatile than many people think. Here fiberglass mini-truck fenders are extended by mating them to wooden spacers. After cutting the spacers, use a grinding disc to rough up the edge of the flare.

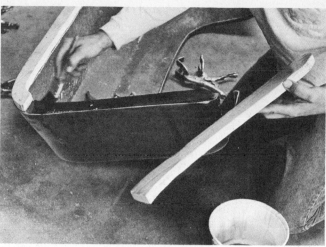

2. The fiberglass resin is then applied generously to both the wooden spacer and the fender edge. Once coated, join the two immediately and position carefully.

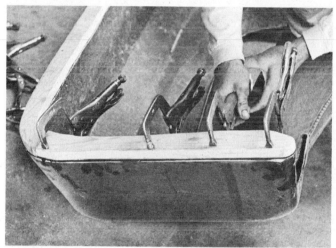

3. Use C-clamps or locking pliers to hold each section securely in place.

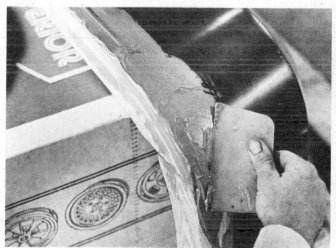

4. Fenders extended more than 1 inch should receive a strengthening layer of fiberglass cloth. Such conservation jobs can utilize body filler to enforce and smooth the bond.

5. The fenders are then finished on a workbench or 55-gallon drum. A combination of Surform file and sanding blocks are used to finish the wood, filler, and fiberglass.

6. The widened fender looks as though it came from the mold that way. The fender now covers the extra wide wheels and tire completely while retaining stock fenderwell flaring.

9
Vintage Bodywork

A visit to a local old car swap meet is the only proof needed to realize that the price of old car body parts has gone right through the ceiling. The really good parts and solid, unfinished cars are in the "if you have to ask, you can't afford it" bracket. The affordable cars and parts are the kind that even people who have been in the hobby less than 10 years categorize as "I threw away better stuff than that just a few years ago." Any crumpled, rusted old piece of sheetmetal is likely to turn up at a swap meet for sale.

Two things can be deduced from the current state of affairs at old car swap meets: the whole hobby has gone stark raving nuts, or the supply of quality vintage tin is rapidly disappearing. The situation is probably a little of the former and a lot of the latter. People no longer have the luxury of discarding dented fenders and bolting on a set of new or cherry used ones (although there are an ever increasing amount of quality reproduction steel body

parts and patch panels); so previously ignored vintage tin is now being salvaged.

It is not uncommon for several totalled old cars to be pieced back together into one good car. This is particularly true of the more desirable open cars. It seems like there are more steel '32 Ford roadsters around today than in 1932. The trend to salvage almost any old car is mixed with the trend toward flawless bodywork. Old cars are no longer jalopies used to putt around town in. Old cars of any type are valuable possessions and many once common cars are being restored to a level previously reserved for the great classics.

The desire for flawless cars and the shortage of good raw material means that the bodymen of this country are doing a great business in fixing up old cars. Hobbyist restorers are having to learn more and better skills to keep up with the state of the hobby. A person who can turn out near-perfect vintage bodywork is a person who can enjoy an in-

Really great vintage sheetmetal is getting harder and harder to find. Even seemingly good bodies can need extensive massaging once the paint is removed. Sanding this '32 Ford roadster door revealed many low spots. Also, notice how rust has started to eat away at the lower edge of the cowl.

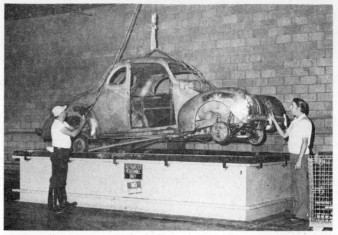

Many restorers and street rodders like to remove all traces of old paint and rust by having their cars chemically cleaned. This process will remove all old body filler so you will know exactly what repairs are in order.

triguing occupation and a healthy income.

The key to vintage bodywork is old time craftsmanship just like the care that was used to build the cars in the first place. Shortcuts and quick fixes aren't desired in vintage bodywork. Patience, and attention to detail are important traits that can bring handsome rewards.

When working on old cars, try to keep everything the way it is supposed to be. When enthusiasts crawl over and under a car, they look for bad metal in the deck lid (flat spots that run across the lid are very common), high and low spots in the metal panels directly above and below the deck lid, short vertical waves in the quarter panels above the rear fenders (also very common), and flat spots in the hood and irregular fender edges.

Typical of the special problems encountered in old cars are the problems with deck lids. Deck lids are relatively low crowned panels that normally have a curve in both directions. When flat spots appear, they usually appear as bands about 4 inches wide, from one side to another.

The lower sections of old cars are especially prone to rustout. The only sure way to cure the problem is to cut out the damaged area and replace it with a new panel.

The quick and dirty way to repair a "banded" deck lid is with large amounts of plastic filler, but this isn't the best way. The metal should be worked. Raising all the low bands can be accomplished by either picking and prying or by cutting the inner panel away and working with a hammer and dolly. The latter is preferable. When the inner panel is cut out, use tin snips or a panel cutter. Do not use the torch. This panel removal technique can also be used with doors.

With the inner panel removed, work up the low spots. Since the metal will tend to work harden during this process, the panel will hold shape better after working. Always check the progress with an adjustable body file. Since the flattened spots will have displaced the panel elsewhere, the edges of the bands will tend to be high. After a panel is perfect, the inner panel is spot-brazed back in place being careful not to use enough heat to cause external panel distortion.

The body panels directly above the deck lid on older cars are not as large as the deck lid, but often

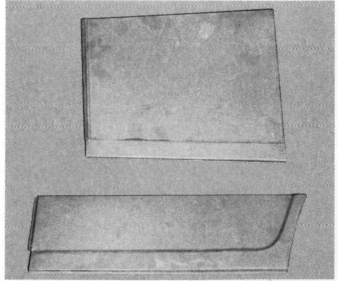

An ever increasing array of reproduction patch panels are available for rust repairs. The supply of patch panels is particularly good for early Ford products.

Vintage Bodywork

Welding tends to warp sheetmetal, unless the patch is hammer welded using a dolly behind the panel. This patch panel was hammer welded for most of its length, but lower heat brazing was used at the ends, because there is no way to get a dolly behind these areas.

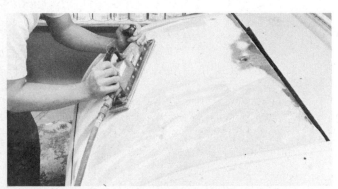

The deck lids of old cars can be full of flat spots. The deck lid should be worked up as much as possible with a hammer and dolly. A thin coat of filler can be applied and worked with a sanding board or air file to finish the deck lid.

To gain access to deck lids and doors, it is sometimes necessary to cut out the inner support structures, straighten the panel, and then weld the support section back in place.

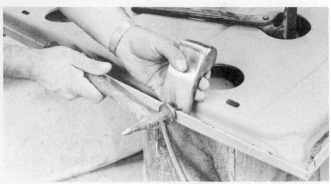

Many bodymen overlook the flange lip of deck lids. These lips get wavy over the years and should be straightened with a hammer and dolly.

cause as much trouble. The upper panel normally requires work to smooth out low spots. Again, these spots can be filled with plastic, but since the panel is easily reached it is better to work out the dents in the traditional manner. The lower panel is not so easy. This particular piece of sheetmetal is usually hemmed over a rather substantial brace.

The lower panel is one place where plastic filler is almost unavoidable. There is seldom room to get a dolly or even a pick of some kind inside the bracing. The alternative is to weld up any cracks (they usually start at the upper and lower edges where this panel is riveted via a flange to the quarter panels), grind and lead if necessary, and straighten the flanged lip along the deck lid opening. To get a perfectly smooth contour often requires the use of plastic filler. When working such a large area which has a very low crown in both directions, it is an advantage to rely primarily on large sanding files.

One area of the deck lid that is often overlooked is the flange lip itself. This should be cleaned thoroughly with a rotary wire brush, both inside and beneath. Clean out all the old paint, rubber, and cement, and then weld up the minute cracks that are sure to be present. Do not prime the lip heavily; instead use a thin coat of primer/surfacer and a thin coat of color to reduce its tendency to chip.

Quarter panels are the dead giveaway as an index to quality of bodywork on older cars. While rust is possible at the bottom edge, vertical waves are common in the area around the fender opening. These imperfections may have been caused by a rear end collision at some time, but many undamaged bodies also have them.

Fixing Fenders

Banged up fenders with cracked and split seams are one of the most common problems with vintage sheetmetal, probably because the design of old cars made the fenders vulnerable. Also, the fenders weren't supported as well as modern ones are. Vibrations also play a big part in the

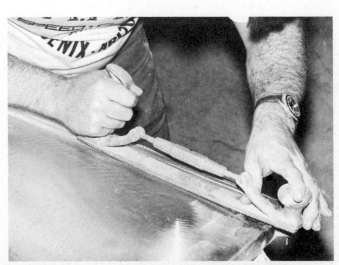

Adjustable body files are widely used to check for high and low spots when repairing vintage sheetmetal. Use the file carefully so you don't take away too much metal.

The attention paid to vintage bodywork today far exceeds the care given to the cars when they were new. Here is a Model A roadster being worked on at Customs by Eddie Paul. The entire underside and inner body areas were painted with Ditzler acrylic enamel with hardener. All of these hidden areas should be painted before the exterior of the body.

It is best to remove fenders from the body, either for repairs or painting. Very often there is a noticeable ridge of old paint buildup from previous paint jobs where the fenders were left intact. Removing the fenders also makes it easier to install new fender welting after the paint job.

Irregularities in fender edges are sometimes difficult to see. Draw a straight reference line on the floor and run a straightedge along the fender bead while holding a piece of chalk. The line on the floor indicates the fender waves.

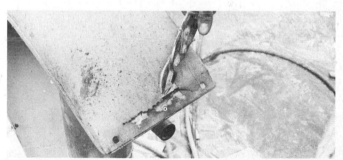

The bottom of the rear fenders, where they meet the running boards are prone to rust. The damaged area should be cut out and replaced with a patch panel.

If a commercially made patch panel isn't available, one can be made from the same gauge sheetmetal as that used on the original fender. Clamp the metal in place, trace it, and cut it out with metal snips.

downfall of old fenders.

A good way to diagnose wavy fenders is with either a plumb level or a plumb bob. Position either of these vertical plumb devices at stations down the fender edge and make chalks on the pavement below. Connect these marks with a line to determine how straight the fender edge really is.

Fender edge repair on older cars is best done with a hammer and dolly, at least until all the workable metal is straight. Because some fenders used wire in the rolled bead, it is nearly impossible to get each tiny dent out so some filler must be used.

Another very common problem with old fenders is that they are prone to rust and deterioration where the fenders join the running boards. This damage is usually out of sight, but it should be stopped before the cancer spreads up to visible areas. The common way to repair such damage is to cut out the damaged section and weld in a replacement section.

With the high cost of beautiful fenders, many restorers and street rodders are resorting to making a good fender out of two bad ones. A typical way of making two otherwise useless fenders into one good one is to take a fender that was "bobbed" (an old customizing trick consisting of cutting several inches off the rear end of a fender for a "sportier" look) and mate it to the good rear section of a fender that was hit very hard in front. Conservation projects like this can save lots of vintage tin.

Filling with Lead

One of the most common catch phrases concerning bodywork on old cars is "it was all done in lead." There is sort of a snob appeal to saying that there is no plastic filler in your old car. Leading was the accepted way of filling holes and other imperfections before plastic fillers achieved their current state. Modern plastic body fillers are quality products that are easy to use and quite durable. Still, the connotation of lead work is one of old time craftsmanship and quality.

With the current interest in high quality restora-

Vintage Bodywork

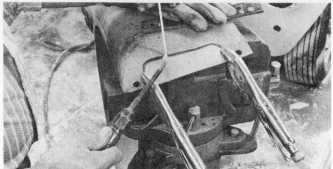

Clamp the patch panel in place and spot weld it. Use hammer welding to complete the seam. Hammer welding is necessary to control warpage.

Ditzler Alum-A-Lead is preferred by many bodymen because it is harder and less prone to shrinkage than plastic fillers. Alum-A-Lead is applied like ordinary fillers with a plastic spreader.

Gray primer should be sprayed over the fender and sanded. Then lightly spray a guide coat of darker primer or black paint.

Block sand the guide coat and low spots will still be darker than the gray primer.

tions there has been a renewed interest in working with lead. There are even companies that sell all the supplies necessary for lead work. These firms usually advertise in the old car publications like *Hemmings Motor News.*

The advantage of lead is that when it is correctly alloyed, it is especially well suited for auto body repairs. Lead can be heated and easily shaped. It bonds perfectly and permanently to sheetmetal. It is easy to finish, and it will accept paint like sheetmetal.

Lead will bond to metals because it will tin the surface with its own properties. Although tinning is often accomplished with a secondary compound, the lead itself can be used. Tinning is made possible by heating the sheetmetal to the melting point of lead, using some kind of flux to clean the metal and applying a thin coat of lead. If the metal is the right temperature and has been cleaned well, the lead will flow across the metal surface like water.

Lead that is alloyed for body and fender repair has its own peculiar melting characteristic, in that it does not melt from a solid to a liquid immediately. Most body leads start to soften about 360 degrees F. and become softer as the temperature is raised. The point at which a particular lead compound will melt is determined by the percentage of tin in the mixture. Furthermore, the body lead alloy will melt below the melting point of pure lead, 620 degrees F., and it may be below the melting point of tin at 455 degrees F. The higher the amount of tin in a compound, the lower the melting point. This should be considered when buying lead.

For all-around shop use, the 70-30 alloy is best (70 percent lead and 30 percent tin). This alloy melts just under 500 degrees F., which gives a wide latitude or plasticity for working in prolonged areas. Lead is available in a wide range of percentages, but anything other than 70-30 or 80-20 is not easy to use.

The basic steps in lead work include cleaning, tinning, filling, shaping, and finishing. An area larger than that which is to be leaded must be cleaned before leading can be done. This is because the lead

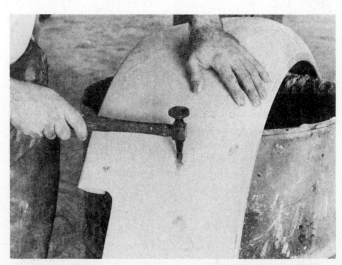

The high and low spots should be worked with a hammer and dolly until the fender is perfect. Then apply another coat of primer, finish sand, and apply the color coat.

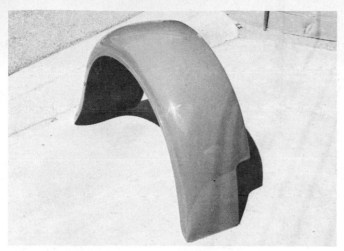

The newly painted fender is beautifully finished inside and out, making it almost better than new.

The high cost of good fenders means that many bodymen are taking two damaged fenders and mating them to form one good fender. Such was the case with this '36 Ford that had bobbed fenders. A fender that was badly crunched in front was used to supply the missing rear section of the bobbed fender.

must blend perfectly into the surrounding area.

After a thorough cleaning, tinning is necessary. The tinning flux is a chemical cleaner for steel. Tinning flux comes in a variety of types, but the kind normally associated with other forms of soldering is not acceptable in bodywork. Tinning flux is usually wiped on with a rag or brushed on the surface. Steel wool dipped in the flux can also be used to apply the product to the work surface.

When a liquid flux is used, the area to be tinned is first lightly heated then the flux is brushed on. After the area is brushed with tinning liquid, the metal should be heated with brief passes of the torch until it is hot enough to melt the lead pressed against the surface. When pressing the lead bar, just a small mound will melt; then as the metal becomes too cold, the car crumbles. A slight twisting motion of the bar will help get the correct amount. Repeat this brief heat and solder treatment to about one-third the area to be covered with lead.

To spread the lead over the surface and thereby gain the full tinning advantage, heat an area around a lead mound or two. As the lead changes appearance from the solid, grainy look to a shiny look, wipe it across the panel with a wadded clean rag. Make all the wipes in the same direction, and make sure the entire area is tinned. There will be a series of overlapping wipe strokes, and when slightly cooled, the tinned area will appear dull in contrast with the freshly sanded steel. While the lead is being wiped over the surface to get a good tin, the flux residue is being wiped away. Tinning is an alternate heat-and-wipe situation.

Be careful when using heat and the rag on a tinned area. If too much pressure is applied to the rag, the tinning film can be completely wiped away. If too much heat is used over a tinned surface, the film can burn away. If a surface will not take a complete tinning, that is, if there are some small spots of bare metal that continue to show, it means the metal is not completely clean. Don't leave small, uncleaned, and untinned spots and hope to bridge over with lead, such as craters in a welded seam. Get the metal as clean as possible.

Controlled heat is important in leading. Only a soft flame, one that is spread over a wide area, is

The patch piece was cut off the scrap fender with a saber saw. The saber saw leaves a clean edge with no metal distortion.

The patch piece was installed with widely spaced tack welds to prevent great concentrations of heat which can lead to metal warpage.

After the seam was hammer welded, a grinder was used to lightly grind scale off the seam. Standard metal finishing techniques were employed to prepare the fender for painting.

Vintage Bodywork

The hammer welding was done so expertly that no filler was needed. Several heavy coats of primer/surfacer were applied and ample time was allotted for shrinkage of the primer before the final color coats.

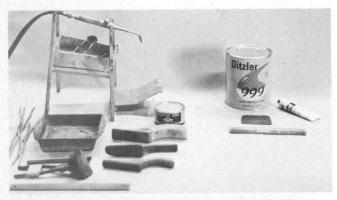

The quality and working ease of modern plastic body fillers (right) is outstanding, but many old car fanatics insist on having all filling done in lead. A lot more equipment, time, and skill is required for leading.

required. Generally a medium-size tip is selected, one that might be used for welding slightly heavier steel gauge than sheetmetal. The acetylene is turned on as with welding and the torch is lit. Next the oxygen valve is opened slightly. The idea is to get a long fuzzy flame, which is usually made up of a long, irregular blue cone with touches of yellow at the extreme tip.

When applying this flame to the metal, keep the tip well back and use just the end of the flame. Let it "lick" at the work. Use the flame on the lead as it is used with brazing; flick the flame tip onto the metal, pass it across the lead; then flick it away. Repeat this process until the desired results are achieved.

It is important to learn good torch control before the application of lead can even be considered, since merely keeping the unfinished lead on the panel will seem almost impossible at first. The secret is in keeping the lead at that particular temperature between first softening and melting.

The beginner is advised to work on horizontal flat panels at first, until some experience has been gained in learning to recognize when lead is beginning to soften and how to control the torch flame. The beginner trying to lead a vertical panel will find most of the material on the floor.

Lead can be applied in two methods: from the bar or from a mush pot. The former is the most common for smaller areas, the latter is better for large areas or for beginners who have trouble keeping the bar at the right application temperature. The lead is scooped out of the mush pot with a wooden paddle and applied to the surface like stucco on a wall.

The key to successful leading is in the cooking. When the bar begins to get shiny on one of the exposed edges, the temperature is about right for the plastic state. If the torch flame is kept on the lead, the shiny appearance will spread throughout the bar which usually means the temperature is too high. When this happens, the lead will suddenly be-

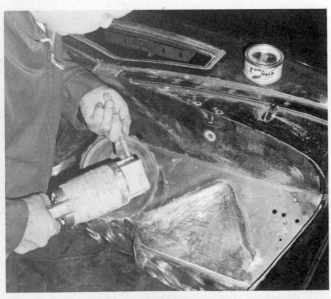

The area where leading is to be done must be completely clean and ground down to bare metal.

A lead alloy comprised of 70 percent lead and 30 percent tin is best for car bodywork. The lead is heated then spread like butter with a wooden paddle, but beeswax or oil should be on the paddle surface to keep the lead from sticking.

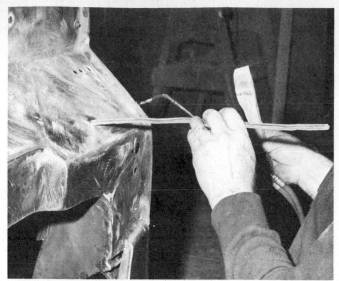

The lead stick is melted on to the firewall. The tip of the torch flame is allowed to lick over the end of the lead stick until it softens and begins to crumble.

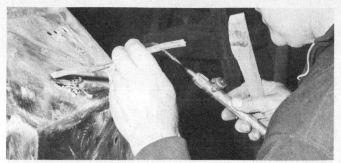

The lead stick is pushed onto the metal until a low pile of lead is deposited. All this time the torch is kept in such a position as to keep the lead pliable.

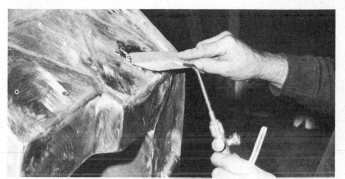

While the lead remains in a near-molten state, the wooden paddle is used to push the lead around. The flame must be applied repeatedly to keep the lead soft.

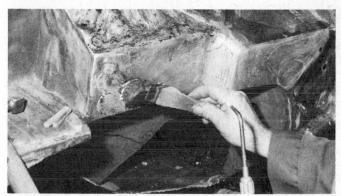

Horizontal surfaces are easier to do than vertical ones since the lead tends to melt and fall away. The lead should be allowed to build up higher than the surrounding area since a second coat is not advisable.

A fine-toothed body file should be used to bring the leaded areas down to the height of the adjoining metal. If low spots show up from filing, more lead cannot be added because it will ruin previous work. The solution is to leave the necessary filing to heavy priming and lots of block sanding.

come liquid and run off the panel. Paddling lead across a metal surface is like buttering bread. If the butter is too warm, it flows too thin; if the butter is too cold, it doesn't spread at all.

The beginner will find that not having enough lead to work will be a major problem once the paddling technique is mastered. It is difficult to go back and add lead, since the temperature must be brought up carefully. The new lead must be applied and worked without overheating the already paddled lead film, and the two areas of lead must be heated enough to flow together at the mating point. If there is too much lead for a particular spot, it can be removed with the paddle while it is still in its plastic state. Ideally the lead surface should be reasonably smooth and only slightly higher than the surrounding metal.

Lead will grind away faster than the surrounding area so care must be taken not to cut the lead too much or make gouges and scratches in the lead's surface. Use a file rather than a disc sander for final finish work because it will cut slower and the long surface of the file will level the lead with the area of the surrounding metal.

When the area is finished with the file, all the edges should blend smoothly into the metal. If there is a tiny, low spot at the edge that does not smooth out, it may be picked up slightly or filled with putty later. A large, unfilled area indicates the lead was not run into the surrounding metal far enough, or the metal has distorted. Additional lead is the usual remedy if the panel cannot be picked up with a pick hammer.

After the initial filing, the area should be block-sanded with #80-grit paper. This paper is coarse enough to cut the file marks from the lead without loading up. It is only intended to finish off the lead and not to shape it.

Lead is an invaluable aid to the bodyman and restorer, but it must be used properly. Never use lead where the spot can better be repaired or shaped; only use lead for the final finishing.

10
Customizing Tricks

Customizing isn't a fad that died with the Fifties. It is still with us and going strong. The lead sleds of yesteryear aren't as common as they once were, although there has been a noticeable resurgence of interest. Many old customs that were thought to be part of a new Toyota are finding their way out of dusty old garages. Other enthusiasts unable to find a vintage custom are making new versions of those once popular cars. Since the cost of radical bodywork like chopping, sectioning, and channeling has risen so dramatically, the current trend seems to lean toward the mild custom look.

Many of the mild customizing tricks that are so vital to a custom cruiser also work well on other types of vehicles. Almost any vehicle will look better with some of the excess trim removed and the holes filled. Many of these customizing tricks are subtle, but that is what makes them so universal.

To learn how to perform some of the most popular customizing tricks we contacted expert customizer, Eddie Paul, who operates Customs by Eddie Paul, 124 Nevada Street, El Segundo, CA 90245. Follow along as some easy customizing tricks are explained.

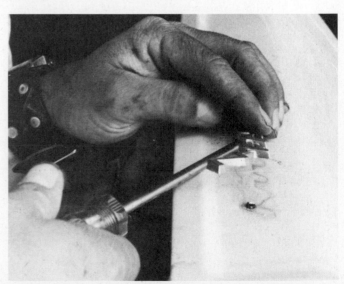

1. Filling the small holes left after emblem and trim removal is a basic customizing trick. Some emblems are fastened from the back side, but most are snap-in affairs. Use care when removing emblems so as not to make a depression with the screwdriver.

Filling Small Holes by Welding

2. To prevent warping, pack the area around the holes with lots of Moist Bastos which is available at welding supply stores.

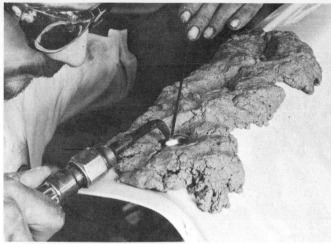

3. Fill the holes by using a 1/16-inch welding rod and an oxyacetylene torch.

4. As soon as a hole is welded, push the surrounding Moist Bastos over the weld to help cool the area. Wet rags can also be used in the cooling procedure.

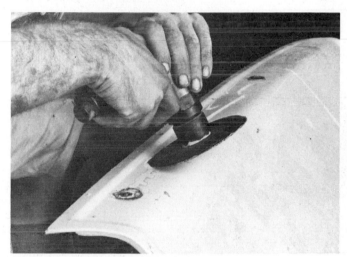

5. Grind down the welds with a disc sander.

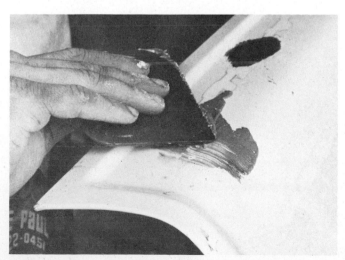

6. Fill any low spots or grinding scratches with body filler and spot putty.

7. Block sand the area until it is perfectly smooth. Cover the area with a couple of coats of primer, and it will be ready for final painting.

Filling Small Holes with Body Filler

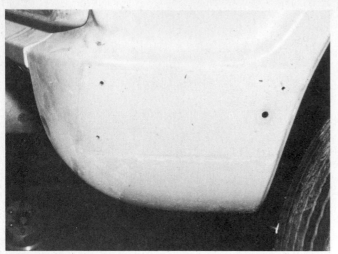

1. Little holes like these can be filled without welding, although welding is still the preferred method.

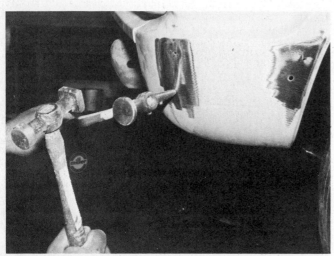

2. Plastic filler needs a clean, semi-rough surface for best adhesion. Remove old paint with coarse sandpaper. A disc sander will make the job quicker and easier.

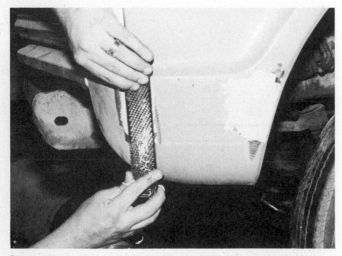

3. A slight crater will give the filler something to adhere to while bridging the hole. This recess can be made by placing the pointed end of a body hammer in the hole and hitting the flat end with another hammer.

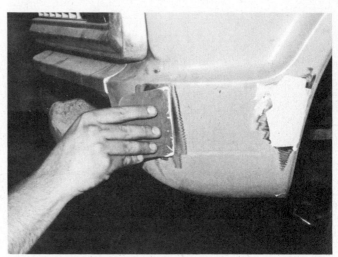

4. Cover the area around the hole with a liberal application of body filler.

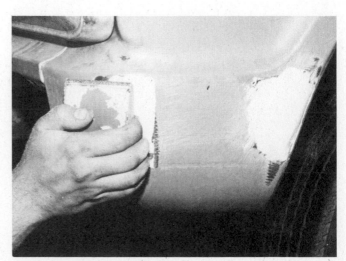

5. After the filler has dried enough so that it is no longer soft, yet is still pliable, shape the area with a cheesegrater file. The filler should come off in long strings.

6. Use a sanding block with progressively finer sheets of sandpaper to smooth the body filler.

7. When the sanding is finished, cover the area with primer.

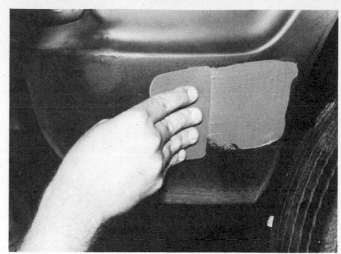

8. After the primer dries, use spot putty to fill any pinholes left by the filler.

9. After the spot putty is completely dry, wet sand the area with a sanding block using 400-grit or finer sandpaper.

10. Apply a final coat of primer, and the filled area is ready for paint.

Filling Large Holes

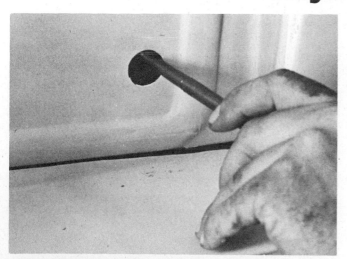

1. Holes that are too large to fill by brazing, like those left when door handles are removed, must be filled with the same gauge sheetmetal as the surrounding area. Hold a piece of sheetmetal behind the hole and mark the size of the patch.

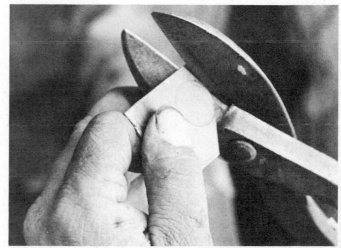

2. Trim the patch with a pair of tin snips.

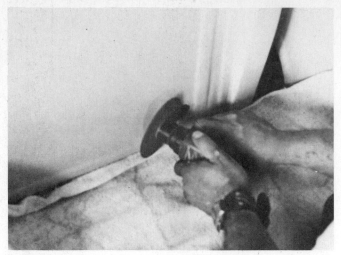

3. Grind away the paint surrounding the hole.

4. To hold the plug piece in place while welding it, tack on a piece of welding rod to act as a handle. Arc weld the patch in place. When the patch is secure, cut off the welding rod handle.

5. Finish the job by grinding down the welding slag.

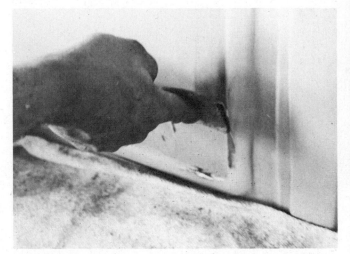

6. Make the area smooth with filler, if necessary; sand, prime, and paint.

Recessing an Antenna

1. A sunken or recessed antenna has always been a popular customizing trick. To sink the antenna, some kind of tube is needed. This tube can be made from tubular stock or an old shock absorber. The part to use is the outside collar. Cut off the mounting bracket.

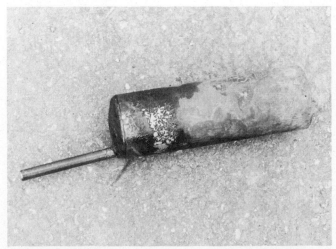

2. Drill a small hole in the bottom of the shock and weld on a small piece of tubing to act as a water drain. A rubber hose can be attached to direct the water to a convenient outlet.

3. If the antenna is sunk into a flat surface, only a hole the size of the tube needs to be cut. If the area is sloped, as it is on this van, it is necessary to use a square to figure out where the top and bottom of the opening will be. The opening will be oval shaped, but the same width as the shock tube.

4. A starting point is needed to make a hole in a sloped area. A screwdriver hit with a hammer will do the trick.

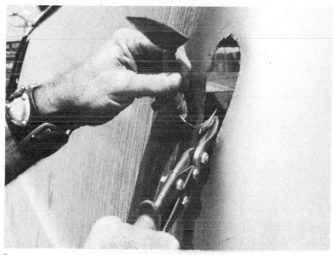

5. Use metal snips to cut the opening. Cut slightly inside your marks and trim for an exact fit around the shock tube.

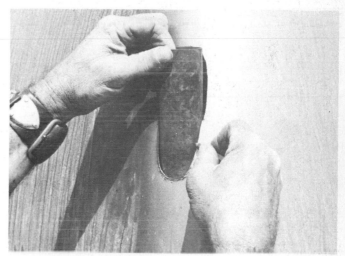

6. The shock absorber tube must be trimmed to match the slope of the body. Hold the tube in place and mark it.

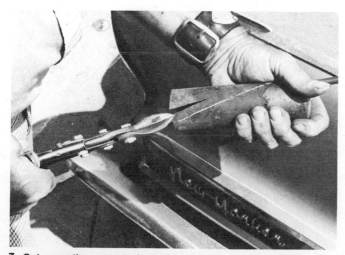

7. Cut away the unwanted part of the tube with the snips.

8. Use Vise Grip pliers to hold the tube in place and tack weld the tube to the body.

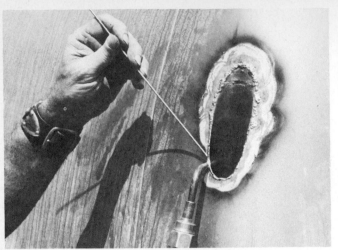

9. Finish welding the tube to the body.

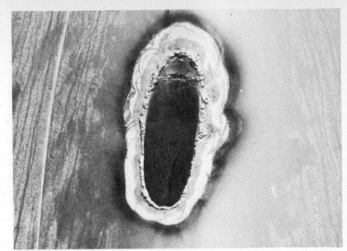

10. The sunken antenna recess is now in place, and all that remains is the finishing bodywork and the wiring of the antenna.

Truck Tailgate Filling

1. Most pickup trucks have either recessed or raised letters on the tailgates. The recessed letters can be filled rather easily. The tailgate can be ground with a disc grinder, but a sandblaster is probably quicker and easier.

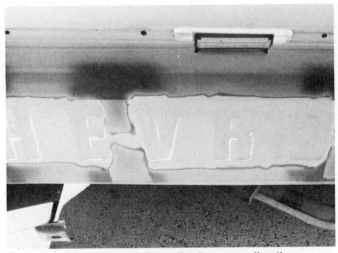

2. The letters and the area immediately surrounding them should be free of paint.

3. Body filler is spread over the recessed areas. If the recesses are deep, apply several thin coats of filler rather than one thick one.

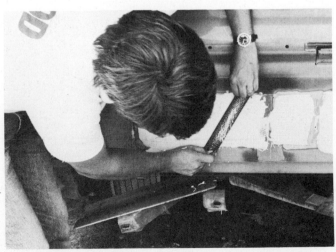

4. Shape the area with a cheesegrater file. Keep adding new filler as long as any low spots remain.

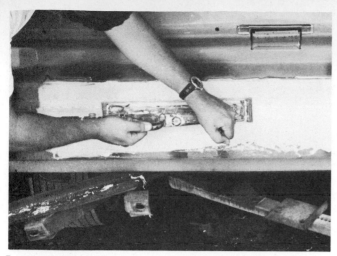

5. A big flat area like a tailgate is best sanded with a long sanding board. An air-powered sanding board can save a lot of time and energy.

6. Cover the filled area with primer. Sand the primer when it is dry.

7. Spot putty should be used wherever there are any imperfections in either the filler or primer.

8. Block sand the area with a rubber sanding block and lots of water. Use 400-grit or finer paper.

9. Apply a final coat of primer and let it dry. The longer the primer dries before final painting, the better, because primer has the tendency to shrink slightly.

10. Here is the tailgate after it was painted and reassembled.

11
Dent Repair

One of the most important steps to learning bodywork is the experience of working on a variety of dings and dents. The professional bodyman gets his never-ending supply of different dents as they roll, or are towed, in from the street. As a beginning home bodyman, you don't have that luxury of choosing what type of dent you'll learn on. You tend to take whatever the parking lots and highways have to offer in the way of damage.

To get started, you'll need to understand and practice the basics as outlined in the chapters on metalworking fundamentals and using plastic fillers. From there it's a matter of digging in and doing a little hands-on homework. The following assortment of dent how-to's are not meant to cover every metalworking situation. Use them as a guide to get started on several representative types of common collision damage. Though the vehicle or location of the dent may be different, the methods of repair should be the same.

Repairing Hood Dents

1. One of the major casualties in front end accidents is the hood. On this Chevrolet, the grille, bumper, and trim were not salvageable, so they were removed and replaced.

2. The hood, however, was not badly damaged and could be repaired. The major dents were popped out using the force of a Porto-Power unit placed between the hood and grip wrench.

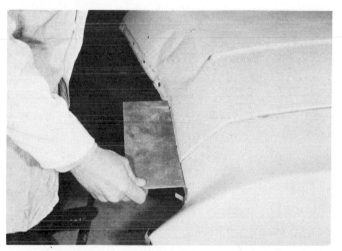

3. A piece of aluminum was used to check the panel edge line for fit. Eyeballing is not good enough on a dent like this because gaps are often deceiving.

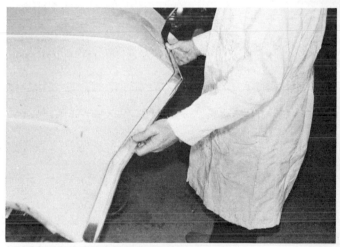

4. After further working the dents into shape, a new trim piece was fitted to the hood line to check progress. The trim piece is a good guide for creating a perfect repair.

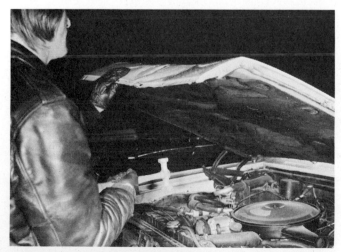

5. The trim piece indicated that a little more work was needed to bring the hood back into shape. While holding the hood, a hammer was used on the underside. Double panel construction made this a slow and tedious step.

6. The direction of hammer blows was reversed to help keep the repair uniform and to keep the creases from becoming bulges. Then the straightened hood was ground smooth and finished with body filler and primer.

Repairing a Quarter Panel

1. The problem: a 2-inch depression in a car's rear quarter panel. The dent was too deep to fill with plastic filler; it would have to be pounded out first.

2. The rear sidemarker light was easy to remove from the backside. On this vehicle, the rear fenderwell was also the inside wall of the truck, offering easy access to the repair but no protection from loose objects in the trunk shifting around.

3. The worst part of the dent was removed with a hard rubber hammer. The panel was brought close to its original shape, though care had to be taken to not put in new dents with the hammer.

4. The rubber hammer was exchanged for the flat surface of a pick hammer. The smaller and harder hammerhead flattened the wrinkles well when backed up with a flat dolly.

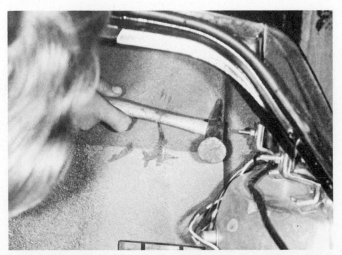

5. This operation was done with the dolly pressed firmly against the exterior of the panel, exactly opposite the area struck with the hammer.

6. The sharp end of the pick hammer was used in tight spots close to the panel corners, and the flat end was used in hard to reach areas. Great care must be taken when using the pointed pick end.

7. The hand was used instead of a dolly for this hammering operation because the sense of touch helps to avoid the creation of high spots that would have to be ground out later.

8. Once the panel is fairly smooth, it may still be a bit low. The entire area was worked slowly and evenly with a hammer and dolly to bring the damaged area back to its original shape.

9. A body file was used to remove high spots and paint. An air grinder with a coarse grit paper will also help in this case.

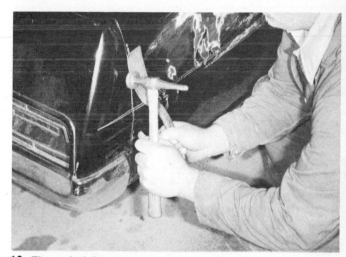

10. The end of the panel was matched with the fender cap using a spoon and hammer. Always ease into hammering steps to avoid overworking the metal.

11. The car's fender panel had a sculpture line which was redefined after pounding out the dent. A contour file was used above and below the line to get the proper effect.

12. With the hammering and contouring complete, a body grinder was used to remove all paint from the area. Filler will not stick to painted surfaces.

13. Low spots will appear quickly during grinding because they will expose old paint. A rotary brush was used to clean out all traces of old paint.

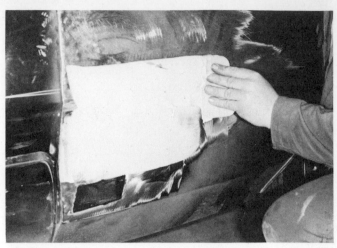

14. Because the metal was worked very close to perfection, only a very thin coating of filler was needed. Filler was applied in long, broad strokes.

15. Excess filler was removed from between the two adjacent panels with a sharp instrument while the filler was still wet.

16. Then a cheesegrater file was used to remove excess filler. Use your hand to check for smoothness and high and low spots.

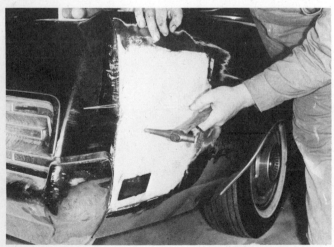

17. The grater exposed a few high spots which were hammered lightly into place. Care was used when hammering to avoid cracking off all the filler.

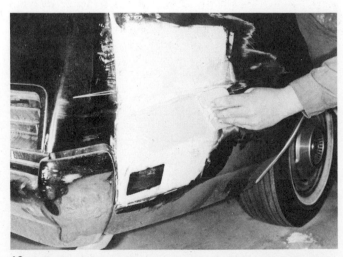

18. A final coating of filler was applied and then filed with the cheesegrater. After further sanding and smoothing, the quarter panel was ready for priming and painting.

Repairing Deck Lid Dents

1. Deck lid damage is a typical hazard of stop-and-go driving. Trim removal is always the first step in gaining access to the damaged area.

2. Deck lid repairs are often made difficult by the presence of double panels. A picking bar was inserted through holes in the inside panel and struck with a dolly to help bring the outside panel back into shape.

3. If sufficient leverage to move the deck lid panel can't be obtained from one panel, try another. The bar was used wherever it could be inserted and pressure applied.

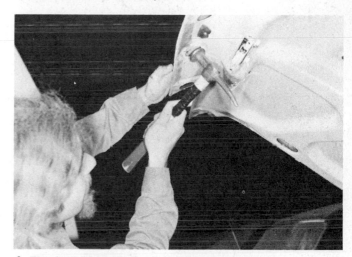

4. The deck lid was then straightened with a hammer for a perfect fit once the trim was replaced. Inner panel access holes make it possible for a pry to be inserted.

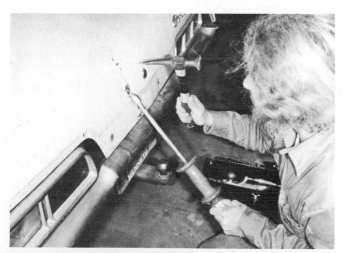

5. A slide hammer and pick hammer were used to pull out the remainder of the crease in the outer panel. As outward pull was exerted on the slide hammer, the pick hammer was used to "unlock" stresses in the metal.

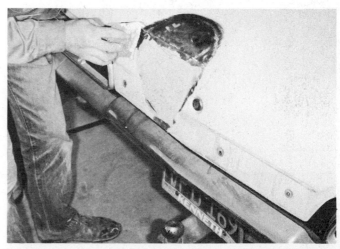

6. Then the repair area was ground down to bare metal and plastic filler applied. Once sanded and primed, the deck lid was then painted and the trim replaced.

Repairing Door Dings

1. The problem: dents high and low on this Chevy Blazer door under both chrome trim pieces. Complicating the repair is limited access to the back side of the door panel.

2. The first step, after removing the chromed trim pieces, is to "read" the dent, using a felt-tipped marking pen to denote high and low spots in the metal. The high spots (X's) will be pounded down and the low spots (O's) dollied out.

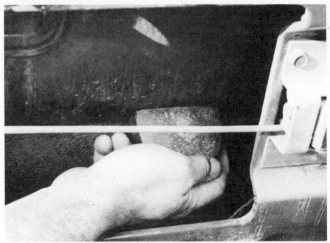

3. Because of limited access to the lower door panel from the backside, the low spots were pulled out using a body suction cup. The hammer is used to brace the metal and counteract the pulling action to prevent stretching.

4. The upper dent was accessible from the backside after removal of the interior door panel. A dolly was placed flat against the dent while the high spots were hammered on the other side.

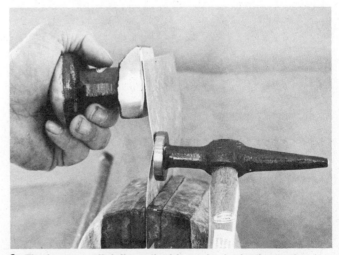

5. There are two basic methods of hammer and dollying. The hammer-on-dolly technique positions the dolly directly behind the hammer. This technique is more likely to cause harmful metal stretching than the hammer-off technique.

6. The hammer-off-dolly method is easier for beginners to master. The dolly is placed adjacent to the area of hammer impact. The hammer reduces the high spot while the rebounding of the dolly brings up the adjacent low spot.

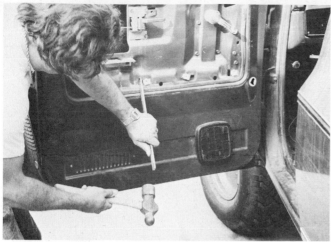

7. Additional low spots in the door were carefully forced out using a steel bar and light hammer blows. This method should be used sparingly and only in cases of restricted access since the bar can rip or stretch the metal if too much force is used.

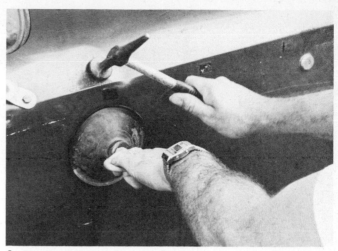

8. With the dents nearly worked out, the hammer and suction cup were used once again with good results. While some dents will often pop back into shape almost immediately, the majority of dents must be brought out in steps.

9. Further forward on the fender was another problem: a small crease in the metal. A slide hammer was used to pull out the crease, but first, a small punch was used to make holes to start the slide hammer.

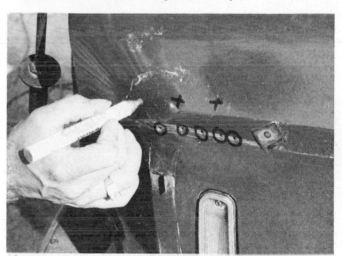

10. Before proceeding any further, the dent was marked for high and low spots. When metal is creased, the resulting low spot will usually force the surrounding sheetmetal out, creating an area of high spots.

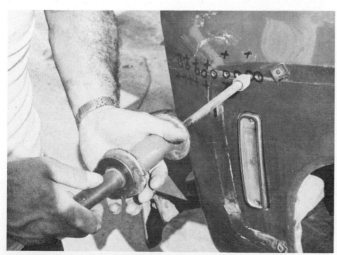

11. The tip of the slide hammer was screwed into the holes made in the crease and the sliding weight forced outward. This action pulled the sheetmetal out, a little at a time.

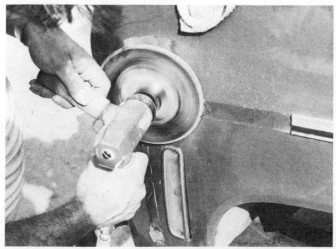

12. After the metal was worked back to normal shape, the area was prepped for final finishing. An air grinder was used to remove all traces of paint around the repair.

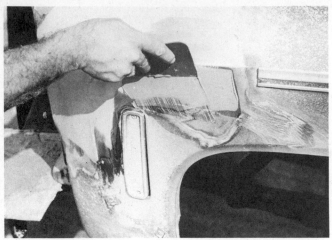

13. Then a batch of plastic body filler was mixed according to directions and carefully applied to the repair in big, smooth strokes. The smoother the filler coat, the less sanding required later.

14. When the filler became the consistency of hard rubber, a cheesegrater file was used to remove excess material. We went lightly with the file to avoid creating low spots in the surface.

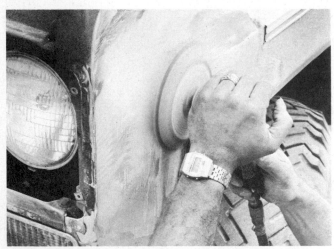

15. Working slowly and carefully, the air sander was used again to finish smoothing the fender area. A second coat of filler was applied thinly, and the area resanded.

16. Then the area was sprayed with primer. These same finishing steps were performed on the door dents as well.

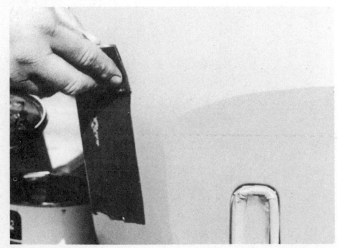

17. After the primer dried, tiny holes in the surface were filled with a thin coat of spot putty. The spot putty was allowed to dry and then lightly sanded by hand.

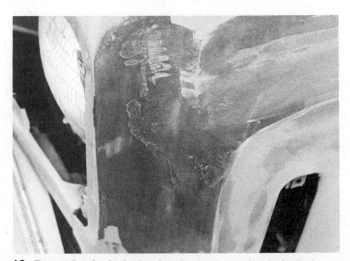

18. Except for the lack of paint, the fender and door looked as good as new.

Floorpan Replacement

1. Rusted out floorpans are a common problem for drivers living in areas where salt is used on roads during winter.

2. Though the entire floorpan shows some signs of rust, only the most severely damaged areas were replaced in this old pickup. Brazing in a new sheetmetal patch can add years of life to a rusted vehicle.

3. After removing the rust, a piece of metal was measured and cut to fit the size of the patch area. Heavy gauge metal was used for the patch.

4. Further trial fitting and trimming provided a tight, close fit that conformed well to the seat area. Note that this floor was completely rotted out.

5. The new floor was then tack welded every 4 to 6 inches with a brazing rod and torch. Additional hands or clamps were helpful when pressing the new floor into contact with the pan.

6. Once the tack welds were made on all four sides and corners, the entire seam was brazed. The seat was then positioned and new mounting holes drilled before finishing and painting the revitalized floorpan.

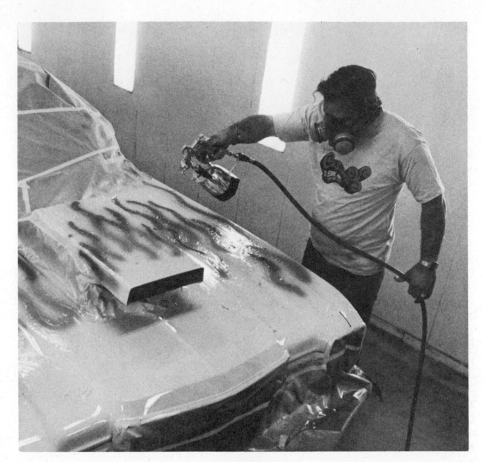

12
Painting Fundamentals

Without paint, every car on the road would look like every other—rusted. The color, or pigment, so carefully mixed and blended to give off just the right hue, is only one of three elements that make up what we know as paint. Pigments are solid material. In order to hold the pigments in solution and make them stick to whatever is being painted, binders are used. Binders are usually clear and add nothing to the paint's color. In straight form, binders are too thick when mixed with pigments to be easily applied with a spray gun. That's where the third element, solvents, comes in. Solvents, such as thinners or reducers, make the paint more fluid. When mixed in their proper proportions, the pigment, binder, and solvent should flow evenly and smoothly onto the surface being painted. Then, as the paint is applied, the solvent evaporates leaving the bound pigment which hardens into a permanent and attractive protective paint coat.

So much for the paint theory. The why it works is, however, less important than getting the right color to most painters. Since we no longer have to mix the pigments, binders, and solvents ourselves, why even bother with a chapter about paint? Simply because there's more to the subject than meets the eye. Automotive painting has come a long way from the days when every vehicle was hand brushed with a solution of varnish and lampblack. Major paint companies like Du Pont and Ditzler have advanced the science of paint chemistry so that there is a different paint for every painting need. These days when it comes to repainting an automobile, the paint is more important than the process.

Lacquers

Probably the most universally used types of paint, and the easiest to apply, are the lacquers. Made from a combination of resins, cellulose, and lac (a sticky substance deposited by tree dwelling insects), lacquers are the favorites of beginners and experienced painters alike because of their quick drying time. This quick drying time allows almost immediate correction of flaws or mistakes. You can also tape over freshly painted lacquer surfaces without fear of lifting or damaging the base coat when applying stripes or a second color. But unlike enamels, lacquers must be rubbed out (see chapter on final finish/paint detailing) to achieve a high gloss finish.

Straight lacquers have been phased out in recent years and replaced by acrylic lacquers. Acrylic lacquers differ from straight lacquers in that their base (binder) is a liquid plastic medium. Acrylic lacquers dry quickly and leave a long-lasting finish that is not subject to cracking or yellowing. Because they dry almost immediately, acrylic lacquers are ideal for use in a driveway or garage.

Acrylic lacquers should be applied in light coats for maximum gloss. As it is applied, the thinner (solvent) evaporates from the pigment and binder. As each new coat is applied, the thinner seeps into the previous coat, making that coat expand. As the two coats mix, they bond together. Then, as the thinner from the second coat evaporates, the swelling shrinks, leaving one bonded surface. Lighter coats allow more thorough bonding of pigments and binders, which in turn produce a glossier finish. For maximum coverage, six to eight coats of acrylic lacquer should be applied for the desired appearance. And while the surface of an acrylic lacquer application will feel dry immediately, many professional painters will "color sand" (lightly sand the finish coat) to open up the pores and allow the inner layers to dry more quickly. However, if the paint is not allowed to dry sufficiently before sanding or rubbing out (at least a week), the paint will shrink too much (dry too fast), leaving an uneven surface that will highlight scratches or improperly prepared surfaces underneath.

Excellent booklets are available from many major paint manufacturers. They explain in detail the uses of their products for stock and custom effects.

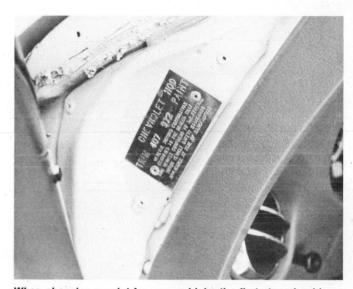

When choosing a paint for your vehicle, the first step should be to determine exactly what type of paint (lacquer or enamel) was on your car or truck originally. The body ID tag will give you the code number of the original paint's type and color.

Enamels

Enamels differ from lacquers in that their basic ingredients are varnishes mixed with alcohols, turpentines, and amyl acetates. Enamels are generally more durable than lacquers, especially when oven baked for maximum drying. Because of their slow drying time, enamels are harder to repair since application flaws must thoroughly dry before they are removed. Enamels are generally not safe for applying in a driveway or garage because every little piece of dirt or dust in the air can wind up in the paint as it dries.

The benefit of using enamels instead of lacquers is that enamels require absolutely no sanding, compounding, or rubbing out to achieve a super high-gloss finish. And the longer an enamel job is allowed to dry (heat speeds up the drying action), the tougher and more insoluble the finish becomes.

However, because of the high-gloss finish of enamels, scratches in the surface that might not be noticeable in lacquer paint jobs will be easily spotted with enamel jobs. As a result, surface preparation becomes much more important when spraying enamels.

Automotive paints have come a long way since the days when auto bodies were rubbed with felt pads and crushed pumice, and then brushed with varnish.

Painting Fundamentals

All paints must be thoroughly mixed before every use to ensure even distribution of pigments. Mixing is especially critical when using custom paints or metallics because the heavy metallic particles tend to settle.

Paints and solvents should always be strained through a filter before mixing or pouring them into the spray gun cup. Though modern paint technology has resulted in very pure and consistent paint products, you don't want to take any chances of impurities from the can or surrounding environment getting into the paint cup.

The final difference between enamels and lacquers is that while lacquers can require up to eight coats to cover a surface, enamels normally take only two coats to do the job.

Thinners and Reducers

Thinners and reducers are used in painting for a lot more than just cleaning the spray gun when the job is done. As one of the three main elements of paint, it's important to get the right thinner or reducer when selecting your paint supplies. In simplest terms, thinners are used for diluting lacquer paints and reducers are used for diluting enamel paint. The best results are always achieved when a specific paint is diluted with a thinner/reducer especially formulated for that specific paint.

But besides diluting the paint so it will pass through the spray gun, thinners and reducers control drying speed; and drying speed, as already mentioned, controls the bonding of one paint coat to another. Selection of the proper type and amount of thinner or reducer can compensate for drying problems caused by temperature and humidity. Generally speaking, thinners will take longer to evaporate on a cool or humid day. As a result, the solvent may penetrate the old paint causing problems with bleed-through. On a hot day the thinners may evaporate so fast that they won't have a chance to penetrate the paint to make a good bond with the surface. Fortunately, paint manufacturers have developed various fast and slow evaporating thinners, high gloss thinners, non-penetrating thinners, and retarder-type thinners for use in such situations.

The same sorts of problems exist with enamels and enamel reducers, so there are all-weather reducers and specific reducers. All-weather reducers typically include solvents that evaporate quickly to help the paint set up, solvents that help smooth out the enamel or solvents that help keep the surface "open" to the atmosphere to allow a thorough curing to a hard surface. All-weather reducers work in a wide range of temperatures and humidities. Specific reducers, on the other hand, include solvents formulated for specific temperature and humidity conditions. Most paint manufacturers have compensation charts specially tailored for changing weather conditions that will help you pick the right reducer or thinner for your specific spraying conditions.

Primers and Surfacers

The major job of primers is to provide that important base for the color coats of paint to grab onto. Lacquers and enamels are not formulated to adhere well to bare metal or fiberglass. Primers provide that necessary adhesion. There are various types of primers and a good paint job must always start with a good primer job.

Although primers are not designed to fill in deep scratches and gouges in the surface to be painted, they do help fill in small nicks, cracks, and imperfections, making the final color coats smoother. Primer-surfacers, on the other hand, are designed to help fill larger surface irregularities. In addition to providing a bond to the metal or fiberglass, primer-surfacers contain a higher content of solid material to provide a medium fill.

There are three different types of surfacers. The first contains a synthetic resin base and has generally slow-drying qualities. The second type is acrylic-based and has faster-drying qualities. This type is designed for use on aluminum surfaces or when acrylic urethane finish coats are used. The third type is the most commonly used, having a lacquer base and quick-drying qualities. Like regular primer, surfacers should be sanded down for a proper finish after being applied.

Primers themselves fall into two basic categories, lacquer-based and synthetic resin-based, which dry fast and slow, respectively. Some painters wait as long as a week for a primer coat to air-dry to allow for primer shrinkage and to allow ample time for any surface flaws to show themselves. Poor metal preparation or contaminants that were left on the surface might take this long to show as the primer is drying and shrinking. When applying primer you don't need to worry about running because it can always be sanded after it dries and feathered to a smooth surface.

Sealers

Sealers are simple. They are made from material specially formulated from resins which, when dry, resist the action of the solvents in the paint.

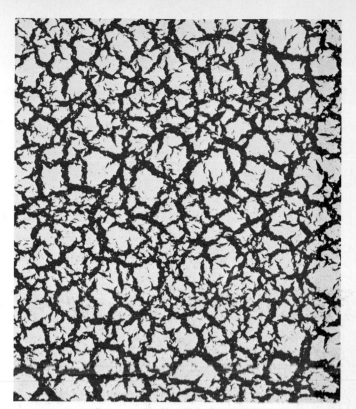

Among the most unusual of the many custom paints is Metalflake's Vreeble crackle paint. When applied, it looks much like this. The effect can be varied depending on how much Vreeble is used.

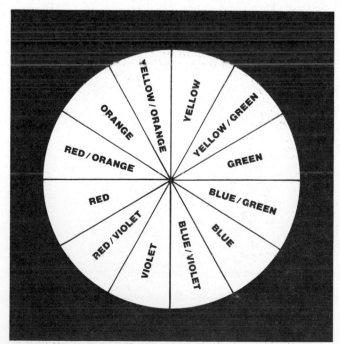

Once you've decided what kind of paint to use, you need to determine what color. A color wheel is an easy way to understand the interrelationships of differing colors. Colors which are opposite each other on the color wheel are called complementary colors and make perfect two-tone motifs. Colors neighboring each other on the wheel are called analogous colors. These colors work well with striping since they follow the natural order of the color spectrum.

In other words, they form a surface shield between the original paint and the new material. This shield keeps the old paint from bleeding through and contaminating the fresh primer and color coat. Sealers, which are sometimes referred to as primer-sealers, are also handy when spraying lacquer over enamel, eliminating the violent reaction between the two formulas of paint. Sealers also help to serve as an added base coat when covering a new light color coat over a dark base coat. Finally, they help prevent deep repair scratches from showing through the new finish much the same as surfacers do.

Custom Paints

Besides the wide variety of "standard" paints and products available for automotive refinishing, there are a seemingly endless variety of custom paints on the market today. These include such materials as epoxy paint, polyurethanes, candies, pearls, metalflakes, metallics, elastomerics, wrinkle finish, and flip-flops, just to name a few. Most of these paints, because of their special formulations, are more expensive and harder to apply than standard lacquers and enamels. However, for a truly unique paint job the expense and trouble is usually worth the price.

Epoxies and polyurethanes are classified as "two-part" paints because they utilize the addition of a catalytic hardening agent (much as epoxy glue or fiberglass resin). Unlike enamels or lacquers, they dry by a chemical reaction (between hydroxyls and polyisocyanates). Addition of the catalyst

Painting Fundamentals

starts, or ''kicks,'' the reaction that drys the paint in a short period of time. Eventually these paints become so hard that they resist chips, abrasions, gasoline, thinners, and even sandblasting. This hard finish makes them difficult to color sand if that becomes necessary because of flaws in application. These are definitely not recommended paints for beginning spray painters.

Many of the other custom paints are much less intimidating. Candies, pearls, and metallics have been the favorites of custom painters for years. Candy paints are known for their illusion of depth. They are normally applied over a base coat of silver, copper, or gold, each of which gives a different finished effect. Painting candy colors is especially difficult because mistakes cannot be easily sanded out. And because the darkness of a candy color is determined by the number of coats applied, matching a candy paint job during a repair is nearly impossible.

Pearl (pearlescent) paints are known for their iridescent appearance. They typically radiate a rainbow effect of different colors when viewed from different angles or in different lights. When applying pearl paint, the spray gun must be shaken frequently to keep the pearl particles in suspension with the binder. Otherwise those particles, which are heavier than the other pigments, tend to settle to the bottom of the paint cup. Pearls are normally sprayed over a colored base coat.

Metallics and flakes are those paints that have a fine grind of aluminum flakes mixed in with the pigment, binders, and solvents to provide a sparkling effect. Like pearls, the aluminum flakes tend to set-

tle to the bottom of the paint cup so the gun must be agitated to keep the flakes in suspension (thereby ensuring a uniform distribution of the flakes in the paint) during the entire painting process.

Elastomeric enamels are the paints used for covering surfaces such as the ''soft'' front ends and bumpers currently used on many cars. The paint film has a high degree of flexibility to permit bending without cracking.

Two other custom paints worth mentioning are the wrinkle finishes and flip-flops. Wrinkle paints are sometimes referred to as crackle paints because they contract as they dry leaving a cracked or wrinkled finish. Like some other novelty paints, a little goes a long way in a paint job and is usually confined to a small area rather than the entire vehicle. Flip-flop paints are a type of pearl developed by Metalflake, Inc. that changes color depending on how you look at it. It is applied much like any other pearl but its final effect is really startling.

Clears

Clear paints are basically just what their name implies—paint without pigment. They are primarily used as a protective top-coating, although they can also be used as a binding agent for flakes, pearls, powders, and toners. When clear paint is used as the final coat, not only is the durability of the color coat increased, but cleaning of the surface is made easier also. Generally speaking, clears should match the brand and chemical make-up of the color coats they protect, that is, e.g., clear acrylic lacquer over acrylic lacquer paint. The exception is the use of acrylic urethane clear which can be applied over regular acrylic lacquer finishes

Custom paints can create some incredible effects. This is an example of Metalflake, which uses the coarser grade of flake particles.

Automotive paints—including "trick" paints such as candies and pearls—have remained pretty fundamental. Paint manufacturers have continually made their products easier to use. But while the paints may be fundamental, what you do with them doesn't have to be, as shown by this wild door mural.

to provide an exceptionally hard "plastic" surface.

Paint Additives

The final items on the what-to-paint shelf are the preps and additives. If you are doing bodywork rather than just repainting over a good original finish, you'll have bare metal areas to contend with. When bare metal is exposed to the air for even a short time it begins to oxidize, leaving a coating of rust on the surface. Unless this coating is completely removed before painting, the rust under the paint will come back to haunt you. Bare metal should therefore be treated with a chemical etch solution to take off any oxidation and prepare the metal for paint to adhere properly.

Likewise, before painting you should remove all traces of dirt, wax, grease, and silicones from the surface of the vehicle with a wax and grease remover.

Finally, there are a number of materials that can be added to the paint cup before spraying such as retarder and fish eye eliminators. Retarders are used to slow the drying process in hot weather conditions while fish eye eliminators are used to prevent the smooth round holes often found in a paint job that are caused by trace elements of silicones.

With this knowledge of the fundamentals, you should be able to choose the paint for your car wisely and carefully.

GLOSSARY OF COMMON PAINT TERMS

ADHESION—the ability of paint to stick to the surface to which it is applied.

AIR DRY—the process of allowing paint to dry under normal atmospheric conditions.

ATOMIZATION—the process of mixing paint with air to break the paint into very small droplets.

BINDER—any substance that holds the pigments in liquid form and enables them to stick to the surface.

BLEEDING—seepage of an old color coat through the new color.

CANDY—a translucent finish with great visual depth; usually sprayed over a metallic base coat.

CLEAR—a finish, usually a cover coat, without pigment used to protect or highlight a color coat.

CURING—the final drying stage of a paint application.

DOUBLE COAT—two single coats applied as one pass followed immediately by a second reverse travel pass.

ENAMEL—a high-gloss finish that dries slowly by solvent evaporation; contains varnish, alcohol, turpentine, and amyl acetates.

EPOXY—a two-part paint which uses a catalyst hardening agent to create a very hard, high-gloss finish.

EVAPORATION—the escape of solvents from the paint during drying.

FLASH—the first stage of paint drying when some of the solvents evaporate, denoted by dulling of the applied paint coat gloss.

FLOW—the ability of a paint coat to form a smooth film.

FOG COAT—a fully thinned or reduced paint coat applied at higher than normal air pressure.

GLOSS—the shininess or reflective nature of a paint coat.

HUMIDITY—the amount of water in the air; has a direct effect on the ability of a paint coat to dry.

LACQUER—a paint finish consisting of pigments, resins, and solvents; dries rapidly by evaporation of solvents.

METAL CONDITIONER—any cleaner that removes rust or oxidation from bare metal and etches it for better paint adhesion.

METALLICS AND METALFLAKES—the presence of metallic powder or flakes in a tinted base paint.

MIST COAT—an over-thinned or reduced paint application used to blend final overlap areas.

ORIGINAL FINISH—the paint applied by the original equipment manufacturer.

OVERLAP—that part of a spray pattern that covers the previous spray pass, usually 50 percent of each stroke.

OVERSPRAY—the overlap of dried paint on surfaces adjacent to areas being painted.

OXIDATION—the combining of air with the paint film, often seen as the chalking of a painted surface as it ages.

PAINT—a protective and decorative coating consisting of pigments, binders, and solvents.

PEARLS—a paint finish that has a soft, iridescent sheen, usually sprayed over a white base coat.

PIGMENT—a solid material that is used to provide paint color.

PRIMER—a base or undercoat with low pigment content that improves the adhesion of a finish or color coat.

PRIMER-SURFACER—a heavily pigmented primer used to fill in sanding scratches and minor surface imperfections.

REDUCER—A solvent used to thin enamel paints.

RETARDER—A slow-drying solvent used to slow down the evaporation rate or drying of a paint mixture.

RUBBING OUT—a method of applying an abrasive compound to smooth and polish a paint film.

SEALER—a non-porous coating used over old paint to prevent bleeding or to prevent reactions of dissimilar types of paint applications; also prevents sandscratch swelling.

SHRINKAGE—the process of tightening of a paint coat as it dries.

SILICONE—an ingredient in automotive polishes and waxes that prevents good adhesion of new paint.

SINGLE COAT—a coat of paint, usually applied with a 50 percent overlap of the previous stroke.

SOLVENTS—any liquid that puts a paint into solution for application, such as thinners and reducers.

TACK COAT—the first coat of enamel paint, allowed to dry until quite sticky.

THINNER—a solvent used to dilute lacquers.

Painting Fundamentals

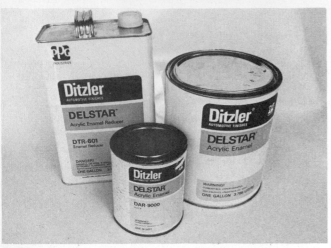

1. Enamel paints are the favorite of commercial body shops because they dry to a high-gloss finish that doesn't need sanding, compounding, or major rubbing out. However, because of their slow drying time, enamels should be sprayed in a spray booth to prevent dirt from settling into the finish.

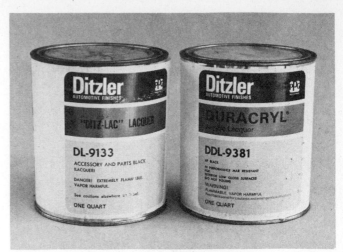

2. Lacquers and acrylic lacquers have revolutionized painting since their appearance several decades ago. Lacquers dry quickly and are ideal for backyard painting. The fast drying time also means that successive coats can be applied quickly, so you can tape over it to apply another color.

3. Regardless of the type of painting you do, you'll need a good supply of thinner or reducer. Thinners are used with lacquer paints, while reducers are used with enamels. Mixing paints with the wrong type of solvent will destroy a paint job.

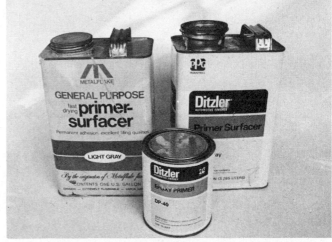

4. The major function of primers is to provide adhesion. When using primers, be sure you buy a type that is compatible with the paint being used.

5. Sealers are used to resist the action of the solvents in the paint. They form a shield between harmful chemical reactions between old and new paint coats.

6. While not really a paint, spot putties and plastic fillers are fundamental to painting because they help provide a smooth, flaw-free canvas to paint on.

7. There are many different types and brands of custom paints available in many forms. Flakes, pearls, and candies are among the most popular types.

8. Clear lacquers are one of the mainstays of the custom painting industry. They are used for mixing other custom paints and for protecting paint. It is the clear top coats that give a paint job added depth.

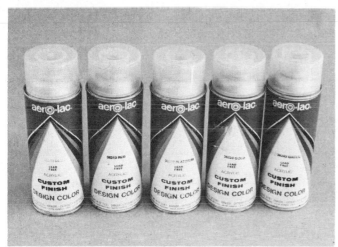

9. Many paints are available in bulk or in spray cans. This is a unique type of paint manufactured by Aero-Lac, known as Design Color. This paint is formulated so that it dries especially slow, allowing manipulation of the finish to achieve special custom effects.

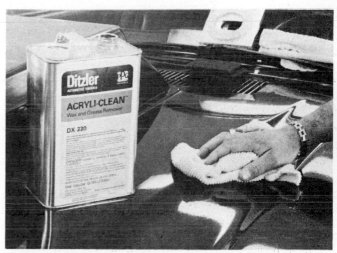

10. Not to be forgotten are the wax and grease removers. These are specially formulated to remove all traces of dirt, wax, and silicones from a surface before painting. Any of these impurities, even in trace form, will create problems in the final paint if not removed.

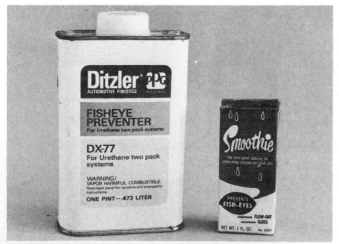

11. One of the most popular paint additives is fisheye eliminator, or preventative. When a few drops are added to paint, the eliminator prevents the appearance of those smooth, round holes in a finish known as fisheyes.

12. Pinstriping can be used to highlight both stock and custom paint jobs with outstanding results. Pinstriping paints are available in many standard and custom colors from many manufacturers.

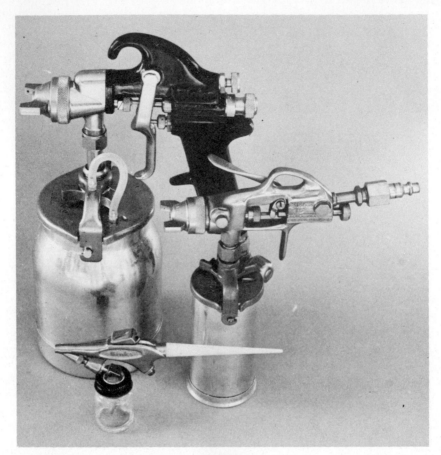

13
Spray Painting Tools

Choosing the right spray painting equipment can be a difficult and frustrating task because there are so many makes and models. If you look around any professional shop you will undoubtedly see a wide array of painting equipment. For every piece you see, there are probably several more stored in a back room. The point is that most painters go through a variety of equipment before settling on their favorite tools. And they often have a variety of spray equipment to handle all the different types of painting.

As a do-it-yourself painter, you won't need a tremendous amount of equipment to start, but you will need to choose your equipment wisely. A good way to get a feel for what type of equipment would suit you best is to rent a couple of different compressor/spray outfits.

The fact that you are painting at home will limit your equipment choices, and the biggest limitation is your compressor. Chances are that your garage

is equipped to handle only 110 volt compressors which means your compressor will have 1½ horsepower or less. Horsepower is related to air output (rated as CFM, cubic feet per minute), and spray guns and other air-powered equipment are designed to work best with specific amounts of air output. If your compressor can't put out the required amount of air for a professional quality spray gun, then your choice of spray gun is restricted.

Even if your garage is equipped with 220 volt service, the most common type of portable home compressors are rated at a maximum of 3 horsepower, which will supply enough air for most professional spray guns. However, these home compressors can't supply the *continous* demand for air encountered in professional body shops. Although you may install a 5-horsepower or bigger stationary compressor, these units are big, very difficult to move, and priced at $1,000 and up.

When buying equipment, try to be realistic about

your abilities and projected equipment use. If you only plan to paint one car, don't spend a fortune on equipment. If painting really appeals to you and you plan to be a professional, then spend a little more to get topnotch equipment. Likewise if you only want to play around with an airbrush, buy a beginner's set with the compressed air cans rather than a $500 heavy-duty compressor. Buy the best quality equipment you can afford, but don't buy equipment you don't need.

Compressors

Air power is vital to painting. Air can come from a variety of sources, but, by and large, it comes from electric compressors. There are gasoline-powered compressors but they are seldom, if ever, used in automotive painting. The tiny hobby compressors (diaphragm type) and cans of compressed air are only suited for use with airbrushes. If you are going to paint a whole car, you need a 1-horsepower or larger electric compressor.

The type of home compressors found in the catalogs of major retailers like Sears, Montgomery Ward, and J.C. Penney are excellent examples of the style of compressors best suited to home painting. Most of these firms and other local outlets such as hardware stores offer compressors larger and smaller than the 1 to 3-horsepower range, but the models in the 1 to 3-horsepower range are the best for home automobile painting. The CFM rating is more important than the horsepower rating because all 2-horsepower compressors aren't created equal. It is not uncommon for a top quality 1-horsepower compressor to put out more CFMs than a cheap 2-horsepower model. Compare the CFM ratings and match the ratings to the guns you use.

If you have a choice, a 3-horsepower 220 volt portable compressor is the best choice for home painting because it is able to power virtually all air-powered painting equipment. When your compressor has to work at its peak to match the spray gun, it can be overworked. It is preferable to have the extra reserve power of a bigger compressor.

The small diaphragm-type compressor should be used for airbrush work only. Ads may suggest that

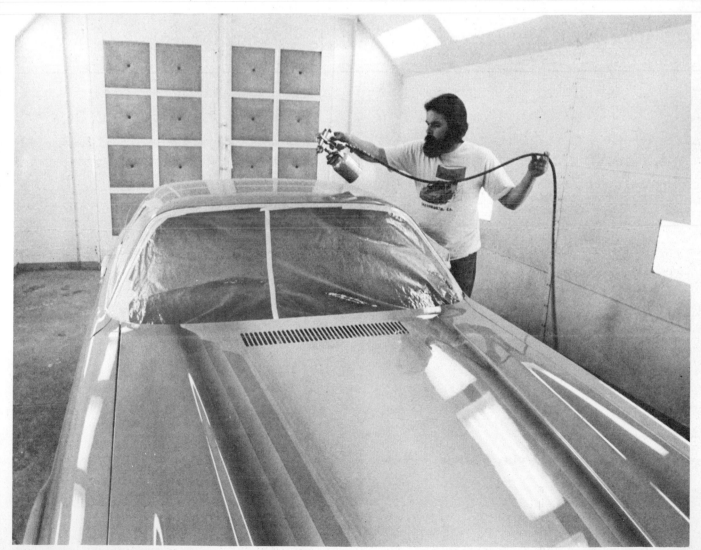

The ultimate piece of painting equipment is a professional spray booth. Spray booths offer a clean, well lighted, and ventilated environment for spraying any type of paint. The booths are expensive, but sometimes used ones can be bought for a reasonable price.

Spray Painting Tools

The heart of any do-it-yourself painter's tool collection is a quality air compressor like those marketed by Sears. A 1-horsepower electric compressor should be considered the minimum for car painting, but a 3-horsepower model is ideal.

these much cheapers ones (compared to normal compressors) are capable of painting a car, but the results can't equal the end product of a regular compressor. Also the aerosol cans of propellant cost up to $4 each, and at that price it doesn't take too many cans to equal the price of a diaphragm-type compressor.

A compressor is a big investment, but a quality unit should last a long time, and it can be used to operate a variety of tools not used for painting. If you only want to paint a single car, renting a compressor is your best move, but if you are a car enthusiast, a compressor is a virtual necessity. A compressor is very important; so choose wisely, and you will have an indispensible piece of equipment.

Spray Guns

Once you have a supply of compressed air, you need an instrument to mix the air with paint. That tool is known as a spray gun. A spray gun is a metallic canister which takes compressed air in one end, draws automotive paint from a reservoir, mixes the paint and air together inside the gun and sprays an atomized paint mixture.

How spray guns work isn't particularly of concern here; what is important is matching the spray gun to your needs, abilities, and the output of your compressor. The best spray gun in the world won't give good results if it isn't matched to the right compressor. Most spray guns are rated at a minimum CFM,

a figure that must be maintained for proper gun performance. There are special low air consumption nozzle caps which allow a professional quality gun to be used with lower output compressors. Even though the spray guns will work with these restricted nozzles, best results will be obtained if the gun receives the amount of air it was designed to use.

Even though some spray guns are designed for particular types of paint, your best bet is an all-purpose gun. Spray nozzles can be changed to make the application of different paints easier. If you can afford to have more than one spray gun, it is a good idea to only use one type of paint with a particular gun. A good spray gun will last longer and spray better if it is only used for final finishes. Use an older

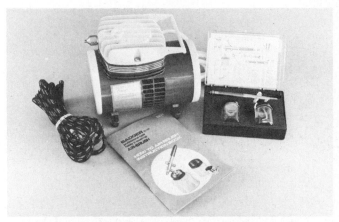

There are very compact air compressors available like this Badger Model 180-1 diaphragm-type unit which are best suited for airbrush work. This compressor also comes as a complete airbrush kit (200-4) which includes the compressor, an airbrush, air hose, and instruction booklet.

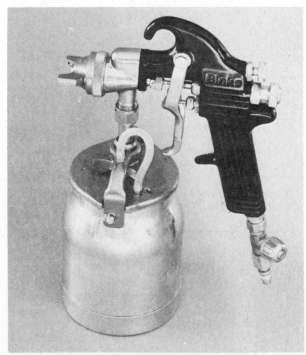

A quality spray gun like this Binks Model 18 is the second most important piece of equipment next to a good compressor. Top quality spray guns really are superior to less expensive models, but be sure to match the spray gun's air requirements to your compressor for best results.

gun or buy a less expensive model for spraying primer. Since primer can be quite thick, it can clog the precision passages of a top quality lacquer spray gun.

A top quality spray gun will last for decades if you take good care of it. Don't leave a spray gun with paint in it for any length of time. Clean the gun thoroughly after each use. Don't let the nozzle passages get clogged and *never* use any metal objects to clean a spray gun. A spray gun is a precision instrument, so treat it like one.

The standard size paint cup for spray guns is 1-quart, but there are other types of containers. There are 2-quart remote pressure paint cups and even 3-gallon models should you ever need, say, to paint a battleship.

More important than the size of the paint cup is whether or not it has a dripless venting system. All spray guns need an air vent, but when the gun is very full or tipped at certain angles, paint can run out of the vent hole onto the car. There are several types of dripless cups which should be considered mandatory equipment. There are even a couple of special paint cups for unusual situations. Some cups have built-in agitators for spraying Metalflake paints or standard paints with a very heavy metallic content, and there are heated cups for work in cold climates.

Touchup Guns

A single production spray gun is ample equipment to paint almost anything imaginable, but there is another type of spray gun that certainly is handy to have. That is a touchup gun. A touchup gun is nothing more than a miniature production gun. The basic construction and function are the same, but it is about half the size of a standard spray gun. Also, touchup guns are capable of smaller and more easily controlled spray patterns.

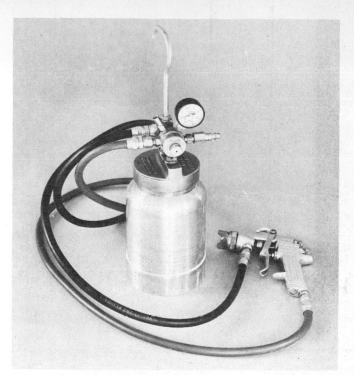

If you contemplate painting a lot of vehicles or large ones, consider the purchase of a remote pressure cup setup like this Binks Steadi-Grip Model 98-1062 outfit. Two quarts of paint are held in the remote container and since you only have to handle the nozzle, fatigue is greatly reduced and flexibility is increased (you can paint upside down with this unit).

The paint cup on most touchup guns is only 8 ounces, but there are also 1-pint cups. The smaller size makes it easier to manipulate, so it is handy in tight places or for delicate custom work.

Touchup guns don't require as much air as full-size guns, so they can be used with smaller compressors. Touchup guns are practical for painting

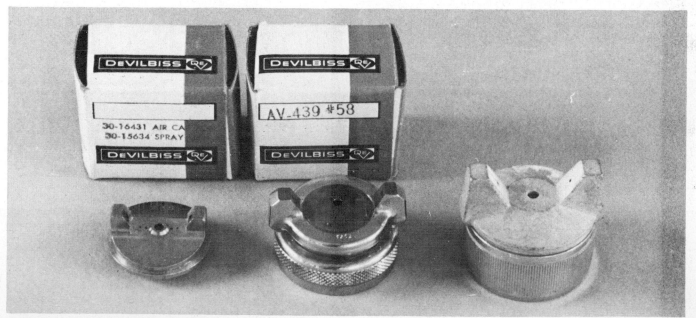

Most spray guns are available with different air caps to best match certain spraying conditions. There are low air volume caps so high capacity production spray guns can be used with smaller compressors.

Spray Painting Tools

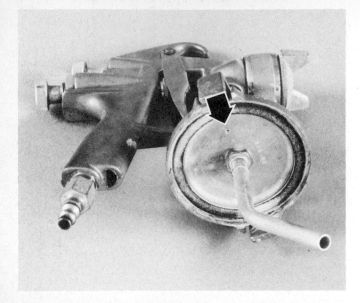

A bleed hole is necessary for siphon or suction cup spray guns. A dripless vent hole is the best. Shown here are a standard bleed hole, a Binks dripless cup that uses a plastic tube, and a Sharpe cup with an internal bleed tube.

small articles like engine parts or for painting small parking lot dents. Touchup guns are reasonably priced (most models are less than a good standard size gun), so even though they aren't a necessity, they are an inexpensive luxury.

Airbrushes

The smallest of all spray painting tools is the diminutive airbrush. Although the airbrush was invented almost one hundred years ago as a tool for artists, most automotive painters own at least one airbrush. The main automotive function of the airbrush is custom paint work like murals, lettering, and other trick painting techniques.

The airbrush also has several uses for painters not interested in custom painting. The small size of the airbrush means that there is virtually no overspray. This makes the airbrush ideal for touching up tiny scratches without a lot of taping and preparation. The airbrush is also great for detailing the interior of a car. The kind of scratches that a key chain makes on the dashboard or the scratches in the lower door panels can easily be repainted with an airbrush.

Airbrushes are available in a variety of styles and prices. The biggest difference among airbrushes is whether they are single-action or double-action units. The double-action airbrushes have a dual-function trigger. As with the single-action, the more you press down on the trigger, the more air that comes out. However, the further you pull back on the trigger of the double-action, the more paint is introduced into the airstream. The single-action has a separate needle control which regulates the amount of paint at any one time. The dual-action airbrushes offer more precise control, but the single-action units are easier for beginners to master.

Airbrushes require very little air so they can be operated by virtually any compressor. There are even adapters to run an airbrush on the air from a spare tire. Most manufacturers of airbrushes also market cans of propellant which means you can easily take your airbrush anywhere. The only catch to the canned propellant is its cost; a dozen or so cans can often equal the price of a small diaphragm compressor.

Airbrushes are available with a wide variety of paint containers and accessories. The most important accessory is a moisture trap to keep the water that forms in air hoses from getting into the paint and the airbrush. Airbrushes are very delicate instruments and require conscientious care after every use.

For a first time airbrush purchase, stick to an inexpensive model to see if you really need one. If you want to get into custom painting, consider buying a good quality dual-action model. There are many uses for airbrushes, plus they are just a lot of fun to use.

Painting Accessories

You need more than a compressor and a spray gun to paint a car; you need items like air hoses, regulators, air filters, and respirators. In addition to these necessities there are several convenience items that make painting easier and more enjoyable.

Most compressors come with an air hose but you will probably need an additional hose. Additional hoses should always be used to increase the range of a compressor. Don't use an electrical extension cord because the available current to the motor will drop and affect the output of the compressor. Remember that extra air hose also carries a performance penalty. The increased friction and distance the air must travel means that the pressure at the end of the hose will be substantially less than the pressure at the compressor. Consult an air pressure drop chart to get an idea of how hose length affects pressure at the spray gun.

A regulator is necessary to control the air as it comes from the compressor. Many of the newer compressors have built-in regulators with easy to read gauges right on the face of the compressor, but most older models require an add-on regulator. These regulators attach to the compressor air tank at the air outlet. The air hose attaches to the other side of the regulator. A regulator can be used without a gauge, but any change is only relative, so consider a gauge as a necessity. Besides the normal regulators that attach to the compressor, there are small regulators that attach to the base of spray gun handles so additional air control can be checked at the gun. These spray gun regulators also enable a painter to change the pressure at the gun without running back and forth to the compressor. There are also miniature regulators designed specifically for use with airbrushes.

The ultimate touchup gun set is this Binks Model 6-41 which contains the highly respected Model 15 touchup gun and six extra siphon cups in a handy carrying unit. This type of arrangement is ideal for busy custom painters.

Airbrushes are the most fun to use of all painting equipment because they are so versatile. An endless array of custom painting tricks can be executed with an airbrush like this Binks Wren airbrush. Airbrushes can be powered by a normal compressor or by cans of aerosol propellant.

Some regulators are combined with an air filter but if your regulator doesn't incorporate a filter, one should be added to your compressor system. An air filter or moisture trap is a must for keeping the air as clean and uncontaminated as possible. Clean air is an important part of a good paint job.

A respirator is one of the least expensive items connected with painting, but it is without a doubt the single most important piece of equipment because its sole function is to protect your health. Make no mistake, paint and paint fumes are dangerous. Some paints (like those with a catalyst) are more dangerous than others but prolonged inhalation of any paint fumes is bad for your health. Therefore, a top quality respirator should be worn during all painting operations. The best respirators are those with two replaceable filter cartridges. Replace the cartridges on a regular basis or whenever they are dirty. The little paper surgical-style masks are not an acceptable way to protect your lungs. You can cut corners on materials or other equipment, but don't skimp on safety equipment—the only loser will be you.

A touchup gun is a very handy tool to own. Touchup guns like this Stewart-Warner No. 7821 unit (which can be set up for left or right hand use) are great for custom painting as well as small repair jobs.

Spray Painting Tools

Some type of regulator and air filter is necessary for all types of spray equipment, even airbrushes. This tiny unit by Badger Airbrush Co. is especially designed for airbrushes.

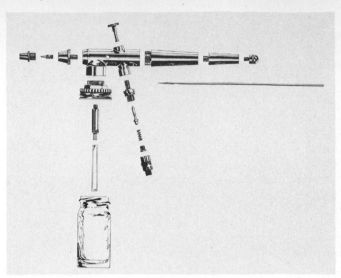

Airbrushes are precision instruments built just like a miniature spray gun. Great care is necessary whenever an airbrush is disassembled. An exploded view diagram is a good reference tool.

Besides a good respirator a couple of other safety items should be purchased. Paints and thinners are flammable, so always have a couple of quality, fully-charged fire extinguishers handy. Use adequate ventilation or fans to prevent excessive buildup of fumes in the painting area. A metal cabinet should be used to store all paint supplies, and a lock is a good idea to protect children.

If you change pieces of equipment often, you should install quick connectors on your tools and air hoses. The quick connectors feature a male and female fitting that are held together by a spring-loaded coupler. Quick connectors make refilling a paint cup quick and easy.

Another useful item is a strainer fixture. Paint should always be strained but it can be difficult to hold the paint cup, position the strainer, and pour the paint out of a heavy gallon can. Strainer fixtures are commercially available, but if you can weld, it should be a simple matter to make one out of light-weight rod. The type of adjustable stand used to hold beakers and funnels in chemistry class also makes an excellent strainer fixture.

An air nozzle or blow gun is handy when preparing a car for paint. The blow gun can be used to dust the vehicle and to get into the narrow, dirt-holding crevices that can't be reached with wax and grease remover.

It is possible to spend a large sum of money on spray painting equipment, but it is also possible to get quality equipment at a reasonable price, if you pay attention to what you buy. Buy a good basic equipment system first. Master painting and the use of your equipment before expanding your tool collection. This way you will get the best results at the most reasonable cost.

Wheel covers are very handy items if you paint often, especially if the vehicle has to be moved several times during the painting operation.

A Mahl stick or sign painter's stick is often nothing more than a piece of wood doweling with a rubber cane tip on the end. It is a handy item for steadying your hand while lettering.

Straining paint is a must, and a strainer holder makes the job easy. This unit is made by Stewart-Warner.

Masking machines come in a variety of sizes. Some models hold only one size of paper while others hold several different widths. The machines are real time savers because they put the masking tape on the paper in one smooth operation.

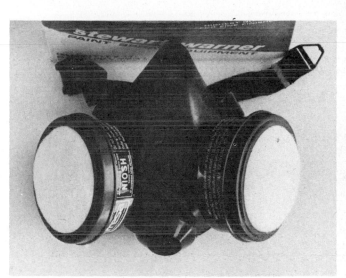

A top quality respirator should be considered mandatory equipment. The type that have dual, replaceable filter cartridges are the best.

AIR PRESSURE DROP AT SPRAY GUN

Size of Air Hose Inside Diameter	5-foot length	10-foot length	15-foot length	25-foot length	50-foot length
¼ inch	Lbs.	Lbs.	Lbs.	Lbs.	Lbs.
At 40 # pressure	6	8	9½	12¾	24
At 50 # pressure	7½	10	12	16	28
At 60 # pressure	9	12½	14½	19	31
At 70 # pressure	10¾	14½	17	22½	34
At 80 # pressure	12¼	16½	19½	25½	37
At 90 # pressure	14	18¾	22	29	39½
5/16 inch					
At 40 # pressure	2¼	2¾	3¼	4	8½
At 50 # pressure	3	3½	4	5	10
At 60 # pressure	3¾	4½	5	6	11½
At 70 # pressure	4½	5¼	6	7¼	13
At 80 # pressure	5½	6¼	7	8¾	14½
At 90 # pressure	6½	7½	8½	10½	16

This table of air pressure drop reveals the amount of air pressure drop in varying sizes and lengths of hoses. Note that your spray gun can be starved for air due to an excessive pressure drop in the atomizing air line. This is especially true where a ¼-inch hose is used, when the gun is designed for a 5/16-inch hose. Don't assume that pressure recorded at tank is the same at gun. It is not.

14
Driveway Paint Job

The beautiful '69 Camaro Z28 featured on the September 1980 cover of HOT ROD Magazine is tangible proof that a pair of amateur painters can refinish a car with a paint job that would be a credit to any professional shop. Not only was the car painted by beginners, but all the work was performed in a typical suburban driveway.

The key to a near flawless paint job at home (no paint job is perfect no matter how good the painter) is perseverance and acrylic lacquer paint. Perseverance will help you to overcome virtually any obstacle, and the acrylic lacquer will allow you to correct the flaws that are bound to crop up. Acrylic lacquer is the most forgiving and easily corrected paint, so it is a must for the home painter.

The two novice painters who painted this Camaro planned on spending a week on the job, but actually spent more like a month. Much of that time was spent undoing mistakes from an earlier custom paint job. But don't kid yourself. If you expect to achieve professional results from a driveway paint job, allow ample time.

Every inch of the Camaro was carefully scrutinized. Even the tiniest stone chips were repaired. When you aren't paying for the labor, you can afford to take care of every imperfection.

Painting a car in your driveway leaves the car vulnerable to many unwanted elements. Since you can't keep all the bugs and dirt out of fresh paint, lacquer, because of its capacity to be sanded out, comes in handy. Other problems we encountered included grass clippings and sprinkler spray from an over-zealous gardener, thick fog (the car was painted near the Pacific Ocean), three-year-old "helpers" with busy hands and a nasty screwdriver, winds that seemed just short of hurricane strength, and numerous spray gun misadjustments that sent blobs of unwanted color or clear onto the car at inopportune moments.

At times the preparatory work seemed endless. When the work got tedious, (which it often did) there was a real temptation to cut corners. The car looked poor throughout the bodywork phase, and the lacquer was very dull looking. The clear topcoat looked liked it had ruined the paint job because it was rough and dull. It wasn't until the clear was color sanded and the entire car buffed out that the shine appeared. The moment the car was completely reassembled was the moment of triumph. The sense of accomplishment made up for all the waiting and hard work. It seemed that everyone who saw the car raved about the beautiful paint job, and if that wasn't enough, the car was later selected for the cover of HOT ROD Magazine—the ultimate compliment for any professional painter, and a real ego-boost for a couple of driveway artists.

1. This is how the well-used '69 Camaro Z28 looked before the restoration.

2. The car had been repainted poorly, but the worst part was the multi-colored candy apple stripes that extended from the rear bumper to the front of the hood.

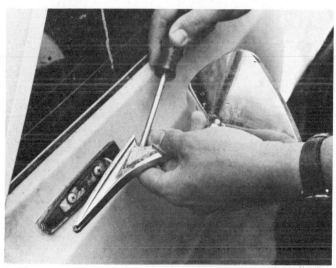

3. For a good paint job, we removed as much of the trim and accessories as possible. It is best to remove everything that won't be painted.

4. The hood was removed because it was going to be replaced with a new cowl-induction type. The hood hinges were unbolted so the inner fender panels could be completely painted. The hinges were painted before they were reinstalled.

5. The rear cowl panel was removed from the car so that the area under it (visible through the vent slats) could be painted the same color as the car, the heavy paint deposits from the previous stripes could be removed, and the new stripes could be laid out without interfering with the overhang of the cowl-induction hood.

6. The tiny fasteners that hold the windshield chrome trim in place were removed after the cowl panel was taken off.

7. All the trim around the windshield and rear window was removed. This served to protect the chrome and allow all the trapped dirt to be removed (so it didn't blow out onto the wet paint).

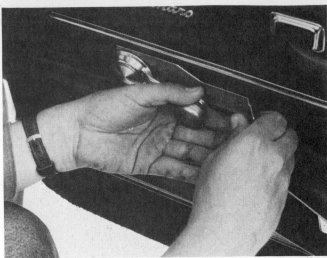

8. Rather than risk any overspray getting on the upholstery, the door panels were removed. This inexpensive door handle removal tool makes it easy.

9. All rubber weather stripping was removed. Sometimes it can be saved, but it is easier to replace the old rubber with new weather stripping.

10. The door panels are usually held in place by a combination of screws (screws hold the arm rests to the panel) and snap-in clips. The clips should be gently removed with a screwdriver. Take care not to bend the cardboard backing of the door panel.

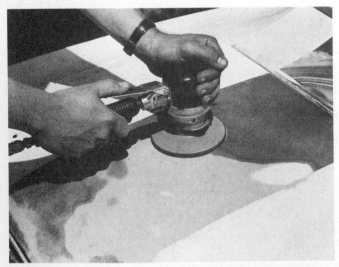

11. Removing the old stripes was really tedious because there were so many layers of paint. Several methods can be used to remove built-up areas like this. Here an air-powered dual-action (also known as a D-A) sander is being used.

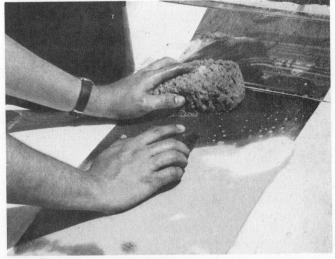

12. A rubber sanding block with coarse paper and lots of water is another good way to remove old paint.

13. After removing the old stripes, areas of bare metal often popped up. These spots should be treated with a metal prep solution like Ditzler metal conditioner to prevent rust. After applying the metal prep, cover the spots with primer.

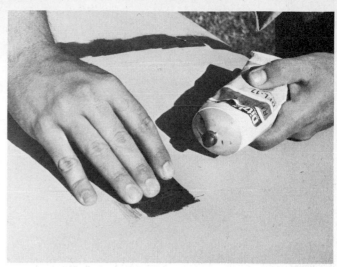

14. After all the old paint from the stripes was removed, there were many nicks and scratches left including some deep scratches that appeared to have been caused by using a razor blade to trim the old stripes. These imperfections were filled.

15. After the spot putty dried, the area was sanded with a long sanding board. Fine paper was used to avoid additional scratches.

16. The whole car required extensive wet sanding with a rubber sanding block. The surface can be kept wet either with a garden hose or a sponge and a bucket of water. Notice that the good wheels and tires were replaced with old ones.

17. Some painters like to add a little household detergent to the water when they are wet sanding. The detergent supposedly helps float away the sanding debris and makes the surface slicker.

18. Even though the Camaro's body was relatively free of damage, there were several dings and low spots that required filling. Ditzler body filler was mixed on an old plate, and the catalyst was mixed with the filler using a wooden popsicle stick.

19. Low spots like this one on the fender were sanded and then filled with a thin application of body filler. An inexpensive plastic spreader was used to apply the filler. A couple of thin coats of filler are better than one thick coat.

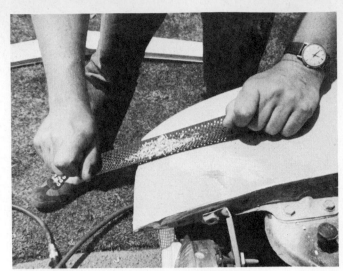

20. As soon as the filler hardens enough (not all the way) to flow through a cheesegrater file (also known as a Stanley Surform file) in cheese-like strings, start removing the excess filler.

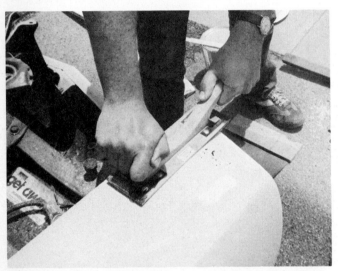

21. Use a sanding board to further shape the filled area. Start with a coarse grit like 240 and progress to a fine grit such as 400. If the area is still low, apply another coat of filler.

22. After filling a dent, cover the area with primer. After the primer dries, check for scratches or filler pinholes. Take care of any imperfections with spot putty.

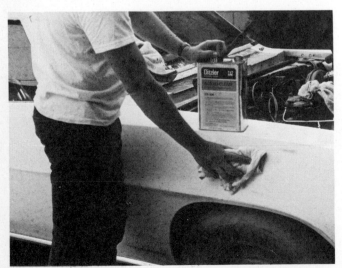

23. Prior to each application of primer or paint, the car's surface was wiped down with Ditzler Acryli-Clean to remove wax, grease, and sanding debris. A clean surface is important for a good paint job.

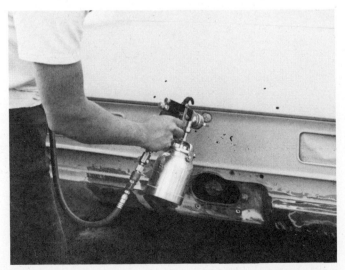

24. Many coats of primer were applied and then block sanded to make sure the body was as close to perfect as possible. Every time a flaw was found, it was repaired before continuing the painting process.

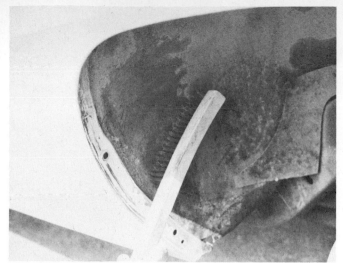

25. The areas where a do-it-yourselfer can out-perform a professional are the troublesome areas like the wheelwells. The Camaro was safely placed on jackstands, and then the wheelwells were cleaned with a wire brush.

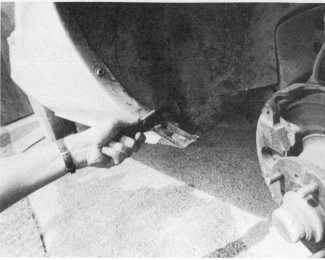

26. A putty knife was used to remove old undercoating and road tar.

27. The edges of the wheelwells require a lot of sanding to remove all the road grime so that the new paint will stick.

28. Once sanded, the wheelwells were covered with a good coat of primer.

29. Door edges are prone to chipping, so there were many places where the old paint was chipped down to bare metal. A lot of sanding and filling was required to make the door edges perfect.

30. The prime-and-sand process was repeated six times. The primer was wet sanded with 400-grit paper and lots of water. These repeated steps are dull, hard work, but they are necessary to get a perfect surface. Granted, a pro could get the surface in shape much quicker, but you must realize that as a beginner everything will take longer.

31. Fresh masking tape and paper were applied every time a new coat of primer or paint was sprayed. This ensured that the paint didn't bleed through the paper and that the tape didn't leave a gummy residue.

32. It seemed like the car was doomed to be in a perpetual state of primer because it took so long to remove every imperfection in the body surface. At times like this, you just have to keep thinking about how nice the finished car will look!

33. Before each coat of primer or paint, the car was dusted with an air hose. Particular attention was paid to all the little nooks and crannies that can harbor debris.

34. A fresh tack rag should be used prior to each coat of paint. The tack rag will pick up dust and debris that you didn't see.

35. It is a good idea to sweep your driveway several times during the painting process to keep away as many contaminants as possible. A light sprinkling of water will help hold down the dust, but you should not leave puddles as the water can evaporate into the wet paint.

36. After all the primer coats were sprayed and the body was as perfect as possible, a final coat of Ditzler Primer-Sealer was applied. This solution isn't necessary for all cars, but it was applied to the Camaro because there was some concern about the candy apple stripes bleeding through the new paint. Sealer is applied unthinned.

37. No matter what type of paint you are spraying, it should always be strained to remove any impurities. A strainer stand is a big help.

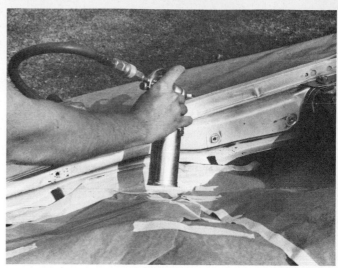

38. All the inside areas of the engine compartment, trunk, and doors were painted first. A Binks No. 15 touchup gun was used for painting these areas because with this it is easier to get into tight areas than with a standard spray gun.

39. The doors were removed and the interior securely taped before the doorjambs were painted.

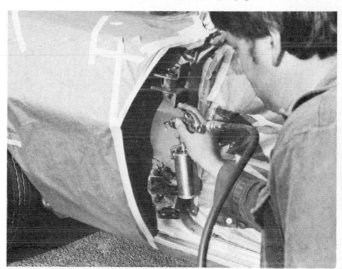

40. Paint was shot as far into the jamb/fender area as possible to cover the original color.

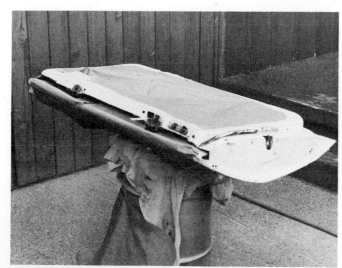

41. The doors were carefully placed on an oil drum covered with protective rags.

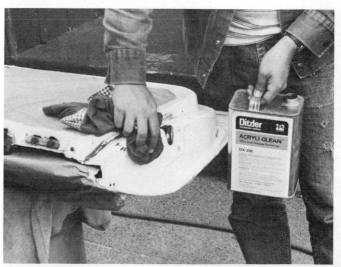

42. The doors were well cleaned with Ditzler wax and grease remover. The windows were covered with masking paper and then rolled down.

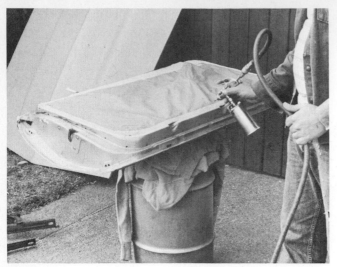

43. The color was applied to the doors with a Binks No. 15 touchup gun.

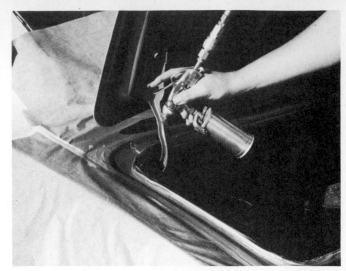

44. The touchup gun was also used to paint the inside of the trunk lid.

45. The new hood was supported on garbage cans so that the inner areas could be painted before the hood was mounted on the car.

46. After all the jambs were painted, the hood and doors were reinstalled. Then the car was put on jackstands to make it easier to get ample paint on the lower body panels.

47. A Binks Model 80 remote cup spray gun was used to paint the wheelwells because it can easily be operated in any position. The wheels and tires could have been removed since the car was on jackstands, but they were left on as an extra safety measure. Notice the dual cartridge respirator. It is extremely important to wear a top quality respirator.

48. The remote cup spray gun is also very convenient when spraying hard to reach areas like the roof. Notice that the paint hoses are draped over the painter's shoulder to keep them from being dragged across the wet paint. The painter is standing on a sturdy box so he can get a better shot at the roof.

49. Each coat of acrylic lacquer was block sanded with water using 400-grit or finer paper. The sanding seems to take forever, but that is how a smooth, flaw-free surface is obtained.

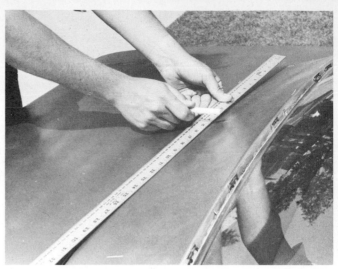

50. Trying to duplicate the factory Z28 stripes was a difficult task. Exact measurements were taken from an unaltered Z28 of the same vintage. The measurements were transferred to the car with a piece of chalk.

51. The outline of the stripes was made with ¼-inch masking tape. The tape was held tight and then set down on the chalk guide marks.

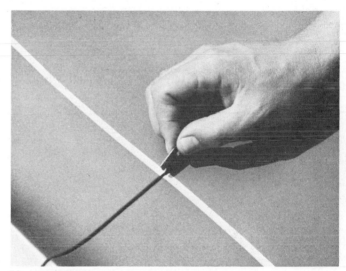

52. Where the tape crossed body separations, it was cut with a razor blade.

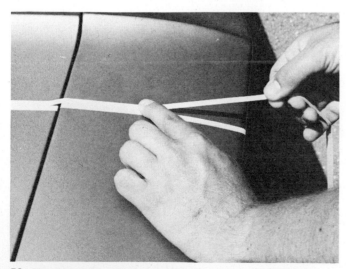

53. The Z28 stripes have a ¼-inch separation between the main panel and the bordering ¼-inch stripe, so three pieces of ¼-inch tape were laid side by side and then the middle one was removed. This left the area for the border stripe.

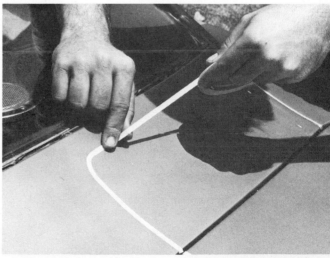

54. The top of the stripe near the back window is curved. It takes many tries with flexible ¼-inch masking tape to get the shape just right.

55. The stripe pattern was continued on the edges of all hood and trunk openings.

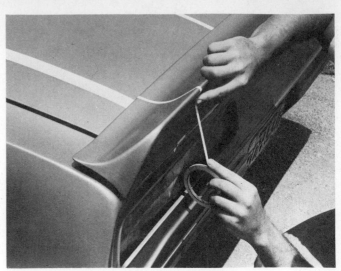

56. The rear spoiler was taped while it was on the car to ensure the stripes lined up. The spoiler was painted off the car because the stripe also goes under the spoiler.

57. All the tape edges were double-checked to make sure there weren't any loose areas. This step is very important if you want sharp, crisp edges.

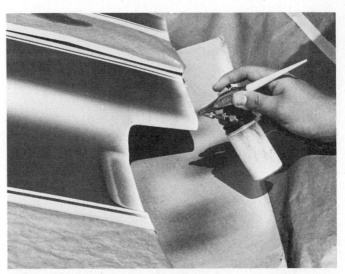

58. To make sure the edges got plenty of paint, they were painted first with a Binks Wren airbrush.

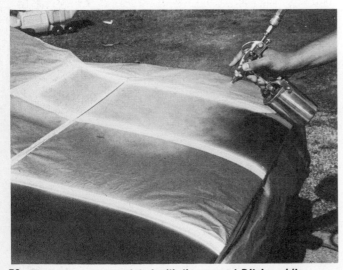

59. The stripes were painted with the correct Ditzler white paint in a Binks No. 15 touchup gun.

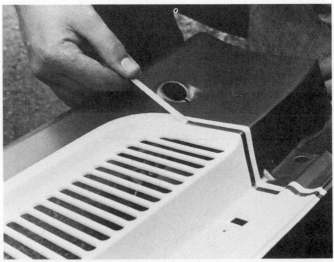

60. The piece of tape that separated the two white areas was removed very carefully to keep the edges sharp. This picture of the cowl vent shows how the striping was carried through to areas that aren't seen unless the hood is open.

61. After the stripes were finished, the car was again cleaned with wax and grease remover and wiped with a fresh tack rag. The car was then covered with approximately a dozen coats of Ditzler Hi-Performance Duracryl Clear (DCA-468).

62. The clear was allowed to cure for a week, and then wet sanded until it was perfectly smooth. The clear should first be sanded with 400-grit paper; as the surface gets smoother, continue sanding with progressively finer paper ending with 600-grit.

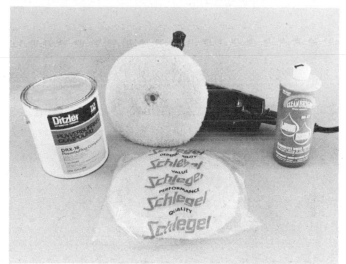

63. After the clear has been sanded smooth, it is time to rub out the paint. An electric buffer with a Schlegel cutting pad was used with Ditzler rubbing compound. A paint job can be rubbed out by hand, but hand rubbing involves considerable labor.

64. Keep the buffer moving at all times so that the paint doesn't burn. It takes a very careful touch not to cause damage with a buffer, especially along the sharp styling edges of fenders.

65. Before the paint was rubbed out it looked terribly dull, but the rubbing compound suddenly brings out a brilliant shine. The fender has been rubbed out while the door is still dull. It takes a lot of patience to reach this shiny payoff.

66. The finished '69 Z28 looks better than it did when it was brand new. The paint is unbelievably smooth and shiny. Everyone who sees the car is amazed to learn that the show-quality paint job was, in fact, performed by a couple of amateurs in their driveway. It can be done—all it takes is hard work.

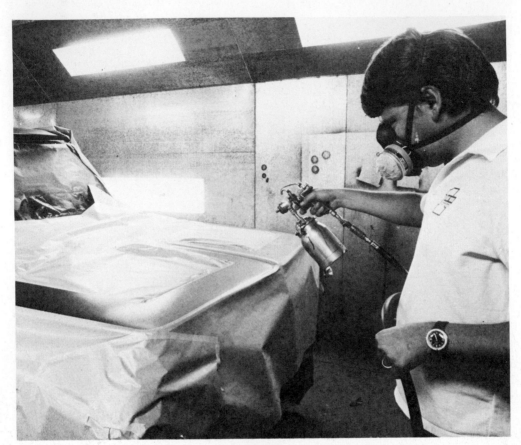

15
Paint Troubleshooting

There is an often repeated story about the famous custom painter who had a way of dealing with customers who wanted to supervise his work. He would simply exclaim, "Oops. Well, it's not my car." That kind of attitude may work well for discouraging meddlesome onlookers, but if you are painting your own vehicle, "oops" is the last word you want to hear. Mistakes do happen, although more often to the beginning painter than the professional. What separates the pro from the beginner is the ease in which the pro identifies and corrects his mistakes. There's really no reason to be intimidated or "spray gun-shy." Everybody makes mistakes when painting, and everyone can fix them.

Because of the delicate chemistry involved in the painting process, just about any variation from ideal conditions can cause problems. The most common causes of painting problems are improper paint/solvent mix, improper air/paint mix, spray gun malfunctions, temperature and humidity variations, and improperly prepared painting surfaces.

Mixes and Malfunctions

There are two important "mixes" that are vital to any good paint job. The first takes place on the mixing bench when the thinner or reducer is combined with the enamel or lacquer. The paint manufacturers help you out with this step by listing recommended proportions for varying painting conditions on the label of every paint can. When mixing paint and solvent, avoid using incompatible combinations, such as lacquer thinner with enamel paint or enamel reducer with lacquer paint. Read and follow the label instructions carefully, using a measuring cup or bucket to measure, rather than "guesstimate." Also be sure to stir all paints *thoroughly* until there are no lumps of pigment settled on the bottom of the can. Strain all paint/solvent mixtures before pouring them into the spray gun.

Once you have the proper paint mix, you can turn your attention to achieving the proper air/paint mix of the spray gun. Paint, even in its thinned or reduced form, is too thick to pass through the spray gun. It must be "atomized," or broken up into tiny droplets so it can be applied in mist, rather than liquid, form. Atomization is controlled by two knobs on the gun, the fluid feed valve, which controls the flow of paint through the gun, and the pattern control valve, which regulates the flow of air. Getting the correct adjustment of these controls is a simple matter of trial and error testing of the spray pattern. Always test the spray pattern on a piece of cardboard or scrap sheetmetal, never on the vehicle being painted. It is a good idea to retest the pattern every time you reload the spray gun and even during the actual painting if you notice any changes in how the paint is flowing onto the vehicle.

One of the biggest causes of spray gun malfunction is dirt or dried paint. Specks of dirt or dried paint can clog the gun's fluid nozzle tip, restricting the flow of atomized paint. Similarly, dried paint and dirt can clog one or both of the nozzle's air ports, causing the paint to be fanned unevenly.

A source of dirt that is often ignored is the compressor which supplies air to the gun. Dirt and water, both of which can ruin a paint job, can be thrown into the atomization process by a dirty compressor tank or air pressure regulator. The tank should be drained after every compressor use and before applying paint. The air pressure regulator should be drained and cleaned at the same time.

When shopping for spray equipment, don't overlook those items that fall into the ounce-of-prevention category, such as this Thayer & Chandler air line filter for trapping moisture and dirt and this air gauge regulator for controlling gun air pressure precisely.

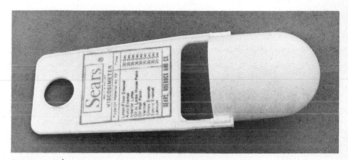

Another item that can help the beginning or professional painter tremendously is a viscosimeter. This inexpensive device lets you check the paint to see if it is properly thinned before application.

Temperature and Humidity

Unlike paint problems caused by mixture or gun malfunctions, problems caused by changes in temperature and humidity are very hard to control or correct. Most standard paints are formulated for use under average weather conditions. Variations from the average affect both paint flow and drying time. Since we can't control the weather, you can adjust the paint mixture to speed up or slow down drying time and help the paint flow. As a general rule, less solvent increases drying time (cold weather conditions) and more solvent slows down drying time (hot weather conditions.) Most major paint manufacturers make special thinners and reducers to overcome weather problems. Check with the experts at your automotive paint supply outlet for advice on which solvents to use for your regional and seasonal temperature and humidity conditions. See the accompanying troubleshooting guide for specific cures for weather problems such as blistering, blushing, crazing, orange peeling, and wrinkling.

Surface Problems

The other major cause of paint problems is improperly prepared painting surfaces. The perfect blend of paint, solvent, air, and weather won't mean a thing unless the surface you're spraying is

Two extremely important parts of your spray equipment are the pressure controls and the oil/water separator. Your spraying equipment must be free of moisture and compressor oil, and the correct air pressure is vital to proper paint application.

Paint Troubleshooting

TYPICAL SPRAY PATTERN DISTORTIONS—CAUSE AND CURE

PATTERN	CAUSE	CURE
correct pattern		
	clogged air ports or dirt on fluid tip	clean nozzle
	too high air pressure	lower air pressure
	clogged fluid tip	clean nozzle

Faulty spray gun patterns are the cause of many paint problems. These patterns are usually caused by clogged air nozzles, obstructed fluid tips, or improper air pressure.

clean and dry to begin with. An area to be painted must be cleaned before and after sanding. Sanding a dirty surface forces dirt into the surface rather than removing it. After sanding, wipe down the surface with a degreaser to remove oils and waxes. After degreasing, don't touch the cleaned area. If you are painting a vehicle in the same area where it was prepped, be sure to eliminate all sanding dust and other contaminants from both the vehicle and the surrounding area before spraying, or the dust will settle back into the fresh paint job.

Troubleshooting Guide

The following list is a guide to most of the common flaws you are likely to encounter when painting a vehicle:

BLEEDING: Commonly seen in instances where a light color is painted over a darker color, especially reds or maroons, bleeding refers to the showing through of the original paint or primer into the new finish coat. Bleeding is caused by the solvent penetration of the new paint into the old finish, usually because the old finish has not been properly sealed. To remove areas of bleeding, sand off the new finish, apply surface sealer, and recoat; or, allow the new finish to properly cure, apply surface sealer, and then recoat.

BLISTERING: This problem can show up immediately or often months after the paint has been applied. Blistering appears as bubbles in the finish, caused by pockets of air or moisture trapped under the paint. As the paint continues to cure over a period of time, these pockets expand and form blisters. Common causes of blistering are improperly cleaned or dried surfaces, improper solvent mixing, a too thick application of paint coats with not enough drying time between coats, and water or impurities in the air lines. Blistering can be repaired by sanding and refinishing.

BLUSHING: This term applies to the milky haze or mist that appears in a paint finish. It is usually caused by the trapping of moisture droplets in the paint on wet or humid days. Blushing can be avoided by using a slow-drying thinner or by lowering the gun air pressure slightly. Most blushing can be spotted during painting. To correct the problem, add retarder to the paint mixture and respray. If blushing is spotted after painting, sand to eliminate it and recoat.

CHALKING: Identified by a lack of gloss and powdery surface, chalking is caused by the weathering or oxidation of paint, lack of agitation of the paint, or poor solvent mixture resulting from use of poor quality thinners. Chalking can be prevented by mix-

Even if you get the proper paint/solvent and air/paint mixtures, you can still have problems if the spray gun is held too close, too far, or at the wrong angle from the surface being painted.

The easiest way to avoid unsightly fisheyes, those little "holes" in an otherwise smooth paint finish, is by adding a few drops of fisheye eliminator every time you mix a batch of paint.

ing the paint and solvent thoroughly before and during (agitate gun occasionally) painting and by using quality solvents for a complete chemical balance. To repair chalked surfaces, sand and repaint.

CRACKING AND CHECKING: Often found in clear cover coats, cracking and checking is usually caused by abrupt changes in temperature and humidity, excessively heavy paint coats, incompatibility of paint products, poorly mixed (weak) paint and poorly prepped paint surfaces. Careful adherence to proper paint techniques should prevent cracking and checking. If it does occur, sand down affected area and repaint.

CRAZING: This condition can be identified by the appearance of fine, irregular splits and cracks that completely cover an area. Crazing is, in effect, a shattering of the original finish, usually caused by the chemical action of the solvent on a cold paint surface. It can be overcome by either using fast-drying thinner to minimize solvent penetration, or by applying very wet (solvent heavy) paint coats to penetrate the old paint. This should melt the craze pattern and blend the new and old paint together.

DIRT IN FINISH: Dirt can be blown into the paint very easily when the painting work area and vehicle are not properly cleaned before painting. If dirt does get into the finish, it should be rubbed out with a rubbing compound or sanded out if the dirt is deep in the finish.

DULLNESS: Most lacquers appear dull until they have been allowed to dry and then color sanded and rubbed out. However, a dull finish can also be caused by poor quality solvents, poorly prepared painting surfaces, insufficient drying time between paint coats, or washing a finish with caustic cleaners. Dull finishes can usually be helped by rubbing out after the paint has been allowed to dry.

FEATHER-EDGE SPLITTING: Separating or cracking of the finish coat will sometimes appear around a repair area where it has been feather-edged into the surrounding paint. This condition is usually caused by improper curing of the primer or surfacer used on the repair. Primer and surfacers should be applied in medium to thin coats, allowing plenty of drying time between coats; otherwise, solvent trapped under the primer or surfacer can "escape" around the feather-edge when the finish coats are applied and ruin the uniform paint surface. Proper application of primers and the use of fast-drying thinners can prevent this problem. If it does occur, sand down the affected areas and repaint.

FISHEYE: A very common problem for all painters, fisheyes are the "holes" in the paint film which allow the underlying finish to be seen. Normally this problem is due to the incorrect cleaning of the surface and the presence of wax silicones. If the paint starts to fisheye while painting, either clean the paint off while wet and thoroughly clean the surface with a wax and grease remover, or, after the paint coat has set up, apply another coat containing the recommended amount of "fisheye eliminator" available from most paint manufacturers. Fisheye can be virtually eliminated before spraying by adding a

Sandscratch swelling is a paint problem that occurs when a too-rapid thinner is used in the paint, causing the soft paint to sink into cuts in the vehicle's surface.

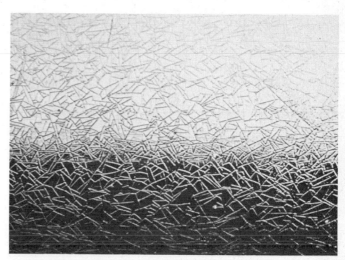

Crazing and cracking of a finish is usually caused by too many coats of paint, especially when the top coat has been overly exposed to the sun.

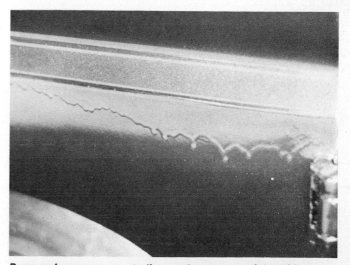

Runs and sags are among the most common paint problems. Fast-drying lacquers are less susceptible to running than enamels. Runs are caused by spraying too long in one spot, spraying too close, or not allowing enough drying time between coats. Runs must be sanded out after they dry, and the area repainted.

Paint Troubleshooting

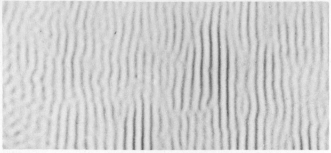

Wrinkling is caused by non-uniform drying of the paint finish, usually due to excessively thick or solvent-heavy paint coats.

Fisheyes, as shown in this extreme example, are caused by the presence of waxes or silicones on the painting surface. They can be prevented by thoroughly cleaning the surface with a wax and grease remover before painting, and by adding fisheye eliminator to the paint.

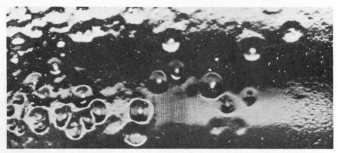

This effect could be categorized as either blushing or streaking. Blushing is caused by moisture in the atmosphere or air lines mixing with the paint before it hits the vehicle. It can be corrected by adjusting the thinner mix. Streaking can be caused by tipping the spray gun during application, instead of keeping it parallel to the surface.

The most common cure for paint bloopers is sanding and repainting. Flaws are much easier to repair in lacquer paints than in enamels, which often require repainting the entire vehicle to achieve a uniform blend.

small amount of fisheye eliminator to every paint mixture.

LIFTING: This condition appears as a shriveling of the paint surface and can be caused by insufficient drying time between coats, improper paint/solvent mix or poorly prepped surfaces. When lifting occurs, you must remove the paint and start over.

MOTTLING: This problem is characterized by a spotty or streaked appearance in a metallic paint finish. Mottling is caused by the metal flakes floating together after application due to inadequate mixing, excess solvent, or by holding the gun too close to the paint surface during spraying. If mottling occurs, allow the paint to set-up and then apply a drier coat, or increase the distance of the gun to the paint surface. Badly mottled finishes may need to be sanded down and repainted.

ORANGE PEEL: Orange peel has the appearance of a bumpy surface, much like the skin of an orange. Orange peel can be rubbed out when it appears in a lacquer job or ignored in an enamel paint job (or carefully removed with a mild polishing compound). It is caused by improper paint flow due to the wrong spray technique or air/paint mixture, high air temperature, too little solvent in the paint, or poorly mixed paint. Orange peel can be prevented by adjusting the solvent mix to compensate for high temperature or rapid drying time and by adjusting the air mixture and spray pattern. In extreme cases, paint may need to be sanded and resprayed.

PEELING AND CHIPPING: Poor adhesion of paint to surface can result in peeling and chipping. This condition usually occurs because the surface was not thoroughly cleaned or sealed, or the paint was not properly mixed. When peeling and chipping appear, remove the fresh paint and reclean the surface before repainting.

PINHOLING: Tiny holes may appear in a finish due to several different reasons such as applying paint over a moist surface, contaminants in paint or air lines, improper sealing of primer or plastic filler/putty areas, excessively heavy or wet paint coats, or poor spray technique, all of which tend to trap moisture or solvent under the paint finish. Review painting conditions and techniques if pinholing occurs during painting. Severe cases should be sanded down and repainted.

POPPING: Appearing much like blisters, popping is caused when solvents are trapped under the top coat. Solvents can be trapped by particles of dirt on the paint surface, improper paint/solvent mixture or insufficient drying time between coats. In mild cases, the blisters can be sanded out after the paint dries and then refinished. In severe cases, the entire finish must be removed and repainted.

RUNS AND SAGS: Often caused by applying too much paint at once, runs and sags may also appear when the paint contains too much solvent, when the air/paint mixture of the gun is incorrect, or when the gun is held too close to the paint surface. Runs and sags must be sanded out and the surface refinished.

SAND SCRATCHES: This condition appears as scratches showing through the finish coat. Improper surface preparation or sealing is the cause. Affected areas should be sanded down and sealed before repainting.

SHRINKING: This usually occurs in an area that has been repaired with plastic filler or body putty. The paint will sometimes separate from the repaired area due to the shrinking of the putty as it dries after repainting. If this happens, the affected area should be sanded down to bare metal and the putty or plastic reapplied in thin coats. Seal and repaint.

STREAKING: Seen as a zebra-like effect, streaking is caused by tilting the spray gun during paint application instead of keeping the gun parallel to the surface. Mild streaking can be blended into additional cover coats, but heavy streaking requires sanding and compounding and sometimes repainting.

WATER SPOTS: Much like the spots that appear on dishes when left to self-dry, water spots are caused by exposing a paint job to water before the paint is completely dry. Spots can be removed by compounding or polishing. In severe cases, sanding and refinishing is needed.

WRINKLING: This condition is caused by unequal drying of the paint finish, usually due to excessively thick or solvent-heavy paint coats, varying temperatures during paint application, or too many paint coats. Wrinkled paint must be removed and the surface repainted.

Dirt Sources in Spray Booths

Dirt has an affinity for wet paint. Here are some often-overlooked dirt sources in a *presumably* clean spray booth:

CHEESECLOTH. Paint strainers are specially made of materials that won't collect dust. Never substitute cheese-cloth which often contains lint.

DIRTY AIR LINES. Old air hoses, regulating equipment, undrained condenser chambers—all may harbor dirt, water, and/or oil. Inspect and clean regularly.

DIRTY CAR. Even though a car has been thoroughly cleaned, dust can and will blow out from under the fenders and other places where it is trapped. Steam or pressure cleaning of a car's underbody is a good investment toward a dirt-free new finish.

DIRTY PAINT. New or thoroughly cleaned containers should be used for mixing paint. Old cans and thinner which has been allowed to stand uncovered, are good dirt sources.

DIRTY YOU. Got dandruff? Wear a light fitting cap. Skin flaking off from a summer tan or other condition? Wear pants without cuffs; those cuffs are great dirt collectors.

DUCT DIRT BUILDUP. Some types of exhaust ducts may gradually become partially clogged with dirt and paint overspray. This lessens exhaust airflow, velocity, and efficiency in carrying off overspray from the present paint job.

DUSTY EQUIPMENT. Overspray dust from previous paint jobs will settle on air hoses, pressure regulators, portable heat lamps, and so forth. Keep such equipment clean at all times.

DUSTY MASKING. Never use newspaper for masking; one of the first rules a novice painter hears. Still, the practice persists. Many a non-thinker will carry a stack of old newspapers into the booth, and drop the bundle where paper lint gets onto everything.

EXCESSIVE EXHAUST. Follow the spray booth manufacturer's instructions for the *minimum* velocity of air exhaust by the fan. Excessive air agitation is conducive to dusty conditions.

EXHAUST FAN RUNNING WITH BOOTH DOOR OPEN. Spray booth exhaust fans expel air up and out a duct, but this air must be replaced. It can only enter through the filters—but if the booth door is open, the air will come through the opening of least resistance and bring in outside dirt.

PAINT VISCOSITY. Follow manufacturer's instructions for thinning paint to proper spraying consistency. Paint with too much thinner or reducer results in excessive overspray, which settles back on the car.

PAINTER'S CLOTHING. If the painter wears street clothes, or lint-catching clothing, dust will find its way onto the newly painted surface. Starched coveralls or clothing of synthetic cloth are preferred.

POOR HOUSEKEEPING. Dust will accumulate on the walls, ceiling, and floor of a spray booth. Test such areas for dirt by wiping with a facial tissue. A spray booth is no place for discarded sandpaper, masking paper, etc. These are good dirt harborers. Wet the floor with a hose before spraying a car to keep the inevitable underfoot dirt down where it belongs.

POOR TACKING. Always use as clean a tack rag as possible; they're inexpensive in relation to a repaint job. Also, after spraying the edges of doors and lids when shooting a new color, tack the car's exterior again to catch dirt that may have been blown from crevices.

SANDING IN A BOOTH. It happens more often than you'd think possible. Even wet sanding in a paint spray booth will leave dirt-filled mud, which will become dust looking for a new home when it dries.

SPRAY BOOTH FILTERS. Dirt and dust will gradually collect, and eventually clog, spray booth filters. Filters should be changed frequently.

SPRAY CAP FUZZ. Overspray may build up on the gun spray cap. If it isn't wiped off, it can blow off in gobs and cause a bad paint blemish.

STATIC ELECTRICITY. In the winter, or when humidity is low, a car may carry a small charge of static electricity that attracts dust like a magnet. After a car is in the booth, run a wire lead from the ground terminal of the car's battery to a positive ground, like a water pipe.

UNSEALED BOOTH LEAKS. It's possible air and accompanying dirt can enter a spray booth through wall or ceiling joints not properly sealed. If after following all good housekeeping measures, dirt is still a problem, carefully check all seams.

WRONG END FIRST. Some painters prefer starting at the front of a car, others at the rear. Whichever end you prefer, make sure that end is the farthest from the exhaust fan. Always spray working in the direction toward the fan.

BASED ON "DIRTY PAINT." COURTESY THE DEVILBISS COMPANY, TOLEDO, OHIO

BLOOPERS ———— Causes ————

Problems

Problems	Incorrect use of additives (type or amount)	Materials not uniformly mixed	Wrong reduction or thinning (amt. or grade)	Improper dry (tanning air, wrong force dry or bake)	Improper substrate cleaning or prep.	Flash time or recoat time between coats (too long or too short)	Effect of old finish or earlier repair	Wrong gun adjust. or technique	"Piling-on" in heavy or wet coats
Wrinkling of Enamel				■				■■	
Orange Peel		■	■		■	■	■■		
Blushing			■■	■					
Lifting			■		■	■■	■		
Crazing			■			■			
Featheredge Cracking or Splitting		■	■	■	■	■	■	■■	
Mottling		■	■		■			■■	
Adhesion Loss & Chipping		■	■	■■					
Runs or Sags			■			■		■■	
Shrinking or Splitting of Putty				■				■■	
Pinholing		■	■	■	■	■	■	■■	
Blistering	■	■	■	■■		■			
Checking	■	■					■		
Chalking	■	■	■						
Cracking	■	■							
Discoloration or Staining				■					
Sand-Scratch Swelling				■■		■			
Grease Spots				■■					
Fish Eyes				■			■		
Water Spotting			■						
"Bleeding"							■■		
Cratering				■					

Causes

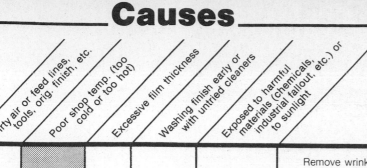

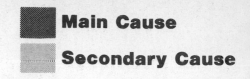

Main Cause (dark)
Secondary Cause (gray)

Remedies

Legend: ● = Main Cause, ○ = Secondary Cause

Dirty air or feed lines, tools, orig. finish, etc.	Poor shop temp. (too cold or too hot)	Excessive film thickness	Washing finish early or with untried cleaners	Exposed to harmful materials (chemicals, industrial fallout, etc.) or to sunlight	Remedies
	○				Remove wrinkled enamel and refinish.
	○				Rub with rubbing compound when thoroughly dry, or sand down to smooth surface and refinish, using a slower evaporating thinner or reducer at a lower air pressure.
	○				Add retarder to the reduced color and apply another double coat.
	○				Remove finish from the affected area and refinish.
	●				Over-reduce with thinner blended with retarder and apply wet double coats until crazing pattern disappears.
	○				Remove finish from affected area and refinish.
	○				After color coat has set up, apply another double-coat using fast evaporating thinner or reducer at high pressure.
○					Remove the finish for an area considerably larger than the affected area and refinish.
	○				When thoroughly dry, sand down to remove runs and refinish.
					Remove putty in affected areas and reapply using thin coats.
○					Sand down to a smooth finish and refinish.
○		○	○		Sand affected areas to a smooth finish, or in extreme cases remove finish down to the metal and refinish.
		○		●	If proper gloss and smoothness cannot be restored by slight rubbing or polishing, sand the affected area and refinish. In extreme cases, finish may have to be removed to primer.
				●	Rub and polish the surface to remove dead pigments and scale.
		●		○	Sand affected areas to a smooth finish, or in extreme cases remove finish down to the metal and refinish.
○			○	●	Rub with rubbing compound and polish, or in severe cases sand to primer and refinish.
					Sand down to smooth surface and apply clear or gray automotive sealer before refinishing.
					Remove finish from affected area and refinish.
●					After affected coat has set up, apply another double coat of color containing "FEE" fish eye eliminator. In severe cases, affected areas should be refinished.
○		○	●		Rub with rubbing compound and polish, or in severe cases sand affected areas and refinish.
○					Apply two medium coats of bleederseal in accordance with label directions and apply color coat.
●					Sand affected areas to a smooth finish and refinish.

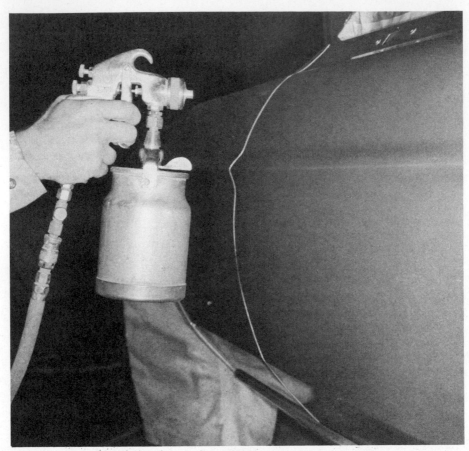

16
Paint Blending

If you go to the paint store to buy the exact color of paint that is on your car, that color should blend right in any time you repaint a portion of the car. Right? Probably not. Matching new paint to the existing paint is not as simple as it would seem. Paint companies take stringent measures to ensure the color consistency of their paints, but, even so, paint can vary slightly from batch to batch. The biggest matching problem isn't color consistency with the paint, though, it is with the fading of the paint on the car itself. Also, there is a difference of application between the factory and repaint techniques. Most factory paints are baked on at high temperatures, and the factory doesn't use as thick a coat of paint as a repainter.

Overlapping facilitates blending. The new paint needs to have ample room to interact with the old paint. The human eye will notice a disparity only if there's a reasonably sharp, clear breaking line between the old and the new. Blend the line, and even

though the difference still exists (to a lesser degree), the eye will not usually notice it.

In essence, blending a paint finish is much like feather-edging a repair spot before painting. Do it well enough, and you won't know where the damage is, once the repair is made. But if you don't feather-edge, the repair spot will catch the eye immediately, regardless of how many coats you apply over it.

If a damaged area extends over two panels, the hood and front fender as an example, the problem of blending can be completely avoided if you back-tape. Pick a high crown line beyond the damaged area and face it with masking tape so that one-half of the tape's width will form an extension of the crown line (this works best on late-model or boxy designs). If you tape the crown line in the usual manner and then paint, you'll wind up with a sharp edge, once the paint dries and the tape is removed. Blending avoids the sharp paint line but backtaping is much easier than blending and leaves no sharp line.

To backtape you simply paint to the taped crown line, and, as the paint strikes the surface under pressure, it hits the masking tape extension and bounces back, so to speak. Without the masking tape extension, the paint would just lie there and build up. When you look at a metallic paint area with a high crown line running through it, there'll be a slight difference in the appearance anyway, because of the difference in the angle of light striking it. Backtaping takes advantage of this difference and the eye can't tell that you've "cheated" a bit.

If a blend can't be easily achieved there is a trick. Begin by painting a single coat, follow with a double coat, and you're ready to blend. This blend is considered a single coat. You'll shoot color about a third of the way into the adjoining panel toward the blend area, gradually fading from the single coat to nothing. Change from color to clear and shoot a thin coat about two-thirds into that panel, again fading to nothing. Follow this with a coat of one part clear mixed with 10 parts of fast reducer and shoot it all the way to the end of the blend panel.

If you try to blend using just a color coat, you'll find it difficult to trigger the gun smoothly enough to obtain the gradual fade necessary and you might even wind up painting the entire panel. Then you'll have to start all over again and blend on another adjoining panel. When blending metallics, the possibility of ending up with a color mottle is ever pres-

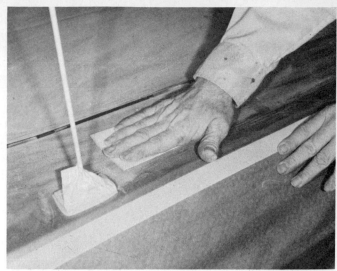

The surface closest to the backtaping should be scuffed lightly rather than sanded.

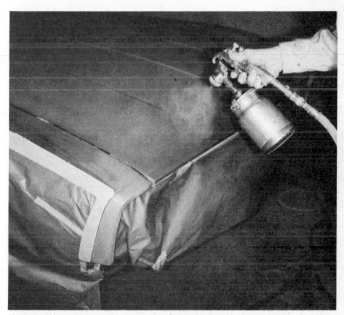

Start with a single color coat over the entire repair area. Follow this with a double coat and then the blend coat.

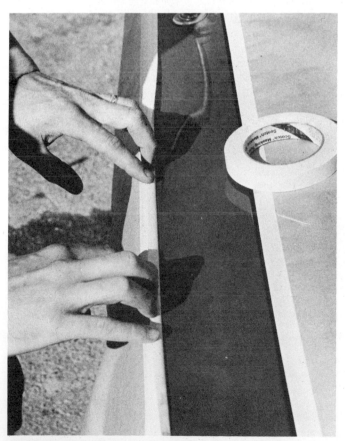

For backtaping, lift the masking tape along the entire crown line to ensure that paint can "bounce" when it is sprayed. Backtaping on high crown line of a fender can save a blending job.

ent, but extending the blend line with clear solves both problems.

Since paint reduction with metallic colors is very critical, here's another tip that influences the necessary amount of blending: follow the paint manufacturer's directions to the letter when reducing acrylic enamel for spraying. Too little reducer will give you a darker-than-desired color; too much will overlighten a metallic paint.

When using a regular color, reduction is not as critical, but the blending process is much the same. If the area to be blended is faded, your blending problem will be more difficult, but rather than tamper with the paint formulas, try buffing the old paint before you start shooting. Since buffing brings up the remaining gloss, it salvages whatever life remains in the old coat, and reduces the degree of blending that's necessary to meld the two areas so that the eye will not be disturbed by whatever slight difference remains.

Complete Dent Repair and Blending

1. This relatively small parking lot dent is a good example of the kind of everyday repair that requires paint blending. The repair and blending were handled by Customs by Eddie Paul, 124 Nevada Street, El Segundo, CA 90245.

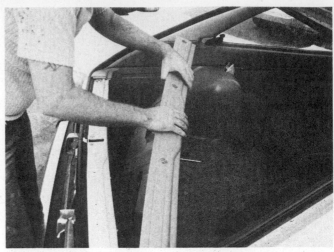

2. Access to the back of the dent is obtained by removing the interior panels. The back piece on this Accord has to be removed before the side piece can be removed.

3. The access holes allow the repairman to place a pry bar or dolly on the back side of the dent.

4. A little mounting hole for the side of the bumper allowed a slide hammer to be used in the process of working the panel back close to its original shape.

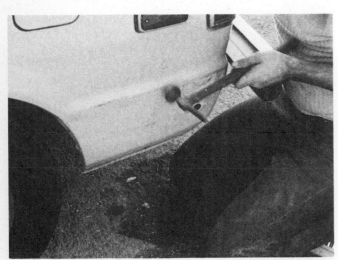

5. After the panel was brought out with a pry bar and a slide hammer, it was further straightened with a hammer and dolly.

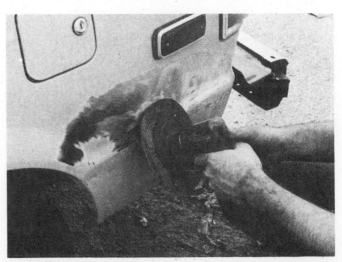

6. Grind away the paint in the repair area with a disc sander using 24-grit sanding discs.

7. Any little crevices or corners that the disc sander can't reach must be sanded by hand.

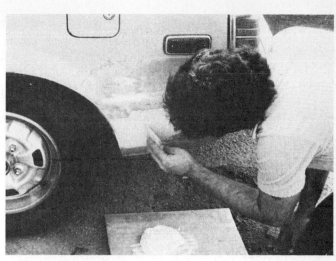

8. Apply a thin coat of body filler to the area. The first coat was mixed with red catalyst to create pink filler.

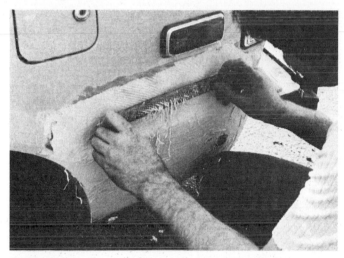

9. After it had set up, a cheesegrater file was used to shape the filler.

10. A second coat of filler was mixed with green catalyst so that any low spots would show up after the second coat was filed.

11. The taillight and side marker were removed in preparation for final sanding and painting. This step could have been performed at the start of the repair.

12. A sanding board was used to shape the filler. First, 36-grit paper was used. Then 80-grit was used to smooth the area. An air-powered sanding board was used here, but a non-power model would work just as well.

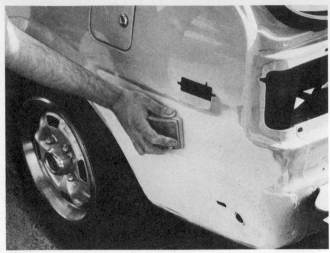

13. The final sanding was done with a rubber sanding block using 80-grit sandpaper. Any pinholes in the filler should be covered with spot putty or a very thin coat of filler that has resin added to make it "runny."

14. Use masking paper and tape to protect the surrounding areas from overspray.

15. Apply primer to the repaired area. Notice the tire covers.

16. After the primer dries sufficiently, sand the primer with 150-grit paper followed by 320-grit dry paper.

17. Use rubbing compound on a relatively large area surrounding the repair. The rubbing compound will remove any wax and get the surface down to fresh paint.

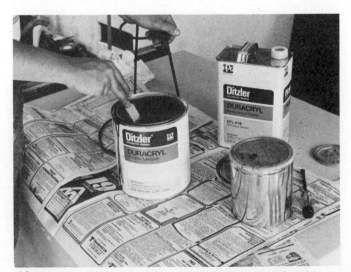

18. For best results when blending or trying to match colors, use a factory pack paint rather than one that was custom mixed. The custom mixes are helpful if the paint is badly faded.

19. The repair and surrounding area were painted with acrylic lacquer. Lacquer is favored because it is easy to rub out for better blending. Four coats of color were applied.

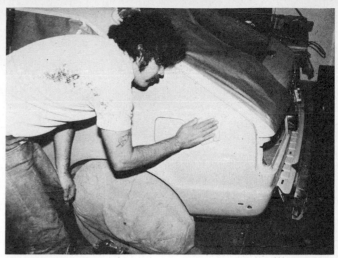

20. After the color coats were sprayed, the overspray was removed with a tack rag.

21. Four coats of clear were applied after the color coats. Both the color coats and the clear were faded toward the back edge of the door and all the way up the roof pillar to the trim strip on the roof which provided a natural break.

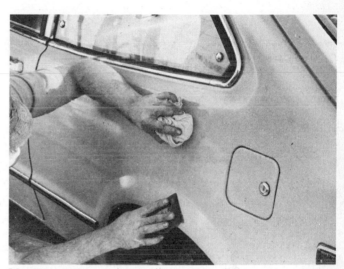

22. After a two week drying period, the area was color sanded with a sanding block and 600-grit wet paper. Sand very gently near the edge where the new paint was sprayed.

23. The area was rubbed out with rubbing compound. Rubbing by hand is the safest method for beginners.

24. The whole area was waxed and the panel looks as good as new.

17
Custom Paint Ideas

What's the big fuss about custom paint? Simple, it's pure vanity. Custom painting lets your vehicle represent what you really are, an individual. Custom paint jobs are like fingerprints, no two jobs are ever alike, even when someone is trying to duplicate a special vehicle or look. But besides letting an individual express his own tastes, talents, and identity, custom paint jobs can also greatly increase the value of a vehicle.

What is custom painting? It's many things to many people. In its most basic sense, custom painting is any paint job that is different from the one that the vehicle had when it left the factory. A custom paint job can be anything from the addition of subtle pinstriping to wild murals, flames, scallops, or special paint finishes. One of the nicest things about custom painting is the wide variety of tricks and techniques available, many of which are very easy for

the beginning painter to master. If you can lay down a line of masking tape and use a spray gun, you can learn the art of custom painting.

Custom Paint Equipment

Theoretically, custom painting can be done with a small brush and a jar of paint. In practice, however, you may need a few more tools of the trade. Equipment for custom painting can be divided into two major categories, equipment needed for painting an entire vehicle, and equipment needed for doing decorative work on just a portion of a vehicle. Items for category one, including spray guns, compressors, and the like, have been covered in the chapter on selecting spray equipment. Almost all of the equipment used for non-custom or "straight" painting can be utilized in custom painting. In addition to those items, a potential custom painter is likely to need equipment that falls into category two, including airbrushes and touchup guns.

Airbrushes are the fine-tipped fountain pens of the custom painting world. They are the most delicate instrument through which you can spray automotive paints and should be cleaned and treated very carefully. Airbrushes fall into two basic groups, single-action and double-action. Single-action models have a trigger that acts as an on/off button which affects airflow. As the trigger is depressed, airflow increases. A separate needle control regulates the amount of paint being sprayed. Dual-action models have a dual-function trigger that controls or regulates both the amount of air and the amount of paint flowing through the brush. Dual-action brushes offer more precise control, but the single-action units are easier for beginners to master.

Airbrushes are available with a wide variety of accessories including thimble-sized paint cups, several sizes of paint jars, moisture traps, and a variety of lengths and types of air hoses and compressor connectors. Because of their low air pressure requirements, airbrushes can be powered by almost any size compressor, compressed air tanks, or even cans of compressed air for very small jobs.

The other non-standard piece of spray equipment that is widely used in custom painting is the touch-up, or spot repair, gun. These versatile "junior" spray guns are sized between full-size spray guns and airbrushes. Their light weight and small size make them much easier to control than a full-size gun. Less taping and cleanup are required because these guns have less overspray and they can be adjusted for very fine spray patterns, making them ideal for custom painting applications.

Besides the guns themselves, the most important tool the custom painter has is his masking tape. High quality, fresh masking tape in a variety of widths is a must in creating clean, sharp edges between colors or areas of custom paint. Masking tape is also an ideal medium for transferring your custom designs from paper to the vehicle's body. Often what looks good in sketches just doesn't fit the actual car. By laying the design out in tape first, (before masking for painting) you can get a much better idea of the proportions of the design in relation to the overall vehicle.

That leaves the miscellaneous tools of the custom painter, stencils, sponges, pinstriping and touchup brushes, playing cards, frisket paper, and so on. For their applications see the accompanying how-to's.

A custom paint job can turn an ordinary car into a real knockout. While custom trends come and go, a colorful, perfectly executed paint job (like the Bill Carter special on this otherwise plain Camaro) will always be in style.

Custom Paint Ideas

Applying Custom Paints

While custom painting can include just about anything, there are two major approaches to custom painting. One approach involves methods, which we'll get to in a minute. The other approach involves materials. Many of the most impressive custom paint jobs are really just standard paint jobs using custom paints. The most popular custom paints are flakes, candies, and pearls. Each involves a few special techniques of application.

Flake painting was popularized through the products of the Metalflake company, the developer and major manufacturer of flake-containing paints. The basic idea behind these paints is to suspend small flakes of aluminum or Mylar in clear paint so that when the clear dries the flakes reflect light back through the top coats, resulting in a shimmering surface.

Since it is almost impossible to cover the entire vehicle with flakes, a ground or base coat is usually applied in a color complementary to the desired flake job (so primer won't show through between the flakes). Any solid color standard lacquer or acrylic lacquer can be used for the base. Next comes the flake coat. For the flake coat you can use pre-mixed (with paint) flakes or you can buy the flake powder separately and mix the flakes with any color lacquer or acrylic lacquer you want. The biggest challenge of any flake paint job is getting the tiny pieces of flake to "lay down." Static electricity can make the flakes stand vertically and therefore unreflective, especially when sprayed on fiberglass. The solution to this problem is to "ground" the car by using a steel chain with one end attached to the car's frame and the other end allowed to touch the ground. Besides being less reflective, when the flakes stand up it is very hard to get a smooth surface coat.

When spraying flakes, most custom painters thin

The van movement of the 1970s did more to bring back the art of custom painting than any custom fad before or since. Murals, special finishes, and bold graphics were among the most popular techniques. Because of their large size and unobstructed panels of sheetmetal, vans are still among the best canvases for the custom painter's art.

the paint considerably and use a lower than normal air pressure, like 25 pounds. It is important to criss-cross consecutive coats, spraying one in a vertical plane and the next in a horizontal plane. Remember to shake the paint cup often to keep the flakes from settling to the bottom. After the flake paint has dried, most painters cover the job with several coats of clear to provide a smooth, glossy surface. Clearing the flake job also protects the paint and adds depth to the finish.

Candy paint jobs are another type of custom finish with great qualities of depth and glow. Candies are translucent colors, almost like straight clear

Flames have been a staple of custom painters since the early 1950s. The owner of this classic Nomad chose traditional orange and red flames over a black base but went wild when it came to design, letting the licks engulf the entire car.

with just a little toner pigment added. They are applied over a reflective base. The number of coats applied determines the depth or density of the final color. Candy paints are probably the most admired of all custom paints but also are the most difficult to apply.

Candies get their brilliance from their reflective base coats. Traditionally the bases are gold or silver, though white can also be used. Gold bases give the "warmest" colors, silver is cooler and white is the coolest of all. The base coat must be applied very evenly over the car because flaws in the base reflect right through the candy top coats.

Generally, the metallic base coats don't have to be color sanded before the candy is applied. You should, however, lightly sand the base with #400 or #600 paper to remove any dust or minor flaws in the surface. When the base coat is perfect you can apply the acrylic lacquer candy color. Thin the lacquer according to directions and weather conditions. The hardest part of spraying candies is to keep a dead-even layer of paint over the entire car. If you stop the spray gun twice in the same spot, that spot will be darker than the rest of the car (since the more candy you spray on the darker the job gets). Vary the direction of the spray pattern and don't start your strokes in the same place every time. This will help you to avoid dark lines and streaks. You should also remember that if you run the candy coats you'll have to either live with them or start over. You can't sand runs out of a candy paint job because you can never respray it and match densities. After the candy dries you can ap-

The airbrush can be used for just about any task, from creating murals to repairing paint flaws. A close relative to the airbrush is the touchup gun. It is used here by customizer Gene Winfield to fog and shade the edges of a candy-colored flame job.

Most major paint manufacturers market their own lines of custom paint finishes. One of the specialists in custom paint is Metalflake, Inc., which offers pearls, candies, flakes, and other trick finishes in a rainbow of colors.

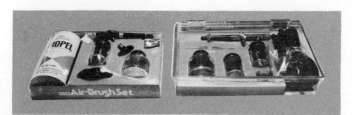

One of the custom painter's most valuable tools is the airbrush. Airbrushes are available in single or dual-action models and can be purchased separately or with a variety of accessories such as paint cups, various-sized paint bottles, and even with their own mini-compressors or compressed air cans.

ply coats of clear to protect the paint. The final clear coat can be color sanded and rubbed out after it has cured.

Another favorite custom paint material is the pearl group. Pearls give an otherwise ordinary paint job an iridescent quality. They are the subtlest of all custom paints and their effect is only noticed when light strikes the vehicle's surface in a certain way. Like flakes and candies, pearls require a base coat. You can use any color for a base, even black. The base coat is usually a non-metallic color that is close to the color of the desired final finish. After applying the base, color sand it with #400 or #600 paper (wet) until the base is flat and smooth with no orange peel (see Chapter 15). The pearl is then mixed with clear and sprayed in light, dry passes over the base.

The same cautions that apply to spraying candies apply to pearls. You cannot afford to have uneven light or dark spots and once again, a run will ruin the entire job. After a successful application of the pearl, let it dry thoroughly and then coat it with just enough clear to be able to color sand and buff without scratching through to the pearl. Pearls are available in different colors that cast different effects.

Custom Paint Tricks

Besides the custom paint materials, there are a seemingly endless variety of custom paint methods that can be used in any combination

Custom Paint Ideas

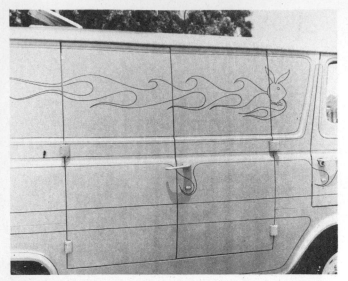

What is a custom paint job? It can be as wild as the painter's imagination or as simple as pinstriping over stock paint. Either way, a custom paint job can set you, and your vehicle, apart from every other motorist on the road.

or alone to create truly special effects. To many people custom painting encompasses all the "trick" applications like murals, flames, panels, or shading. There are also many less arduous custom tricks that work best in small areas, so a beginner can apply various designs to a vehicle without getting involved with an entire repainting project.

Probably the main thing to remember about trick applications is the importance of moderation. The same trick that looks great in a small area can be overpowering if applied to the entire car. Among the favorite custom paint tricks are:

FOGGING: Done with an airbrush, this technique is used for creating mist effects in murals or behind lettering. Adjust the air-paint mixture in favor of the air and spray as usual.

FREAK DROPS: This unusual effect is obtained by thinning the paint until it is almost watery. Hold the airbrush about 2 inches from the surface to be painted and give a short blast of paint and air. The longer the blast, the larger the amoeba-like freak drop.

CARD MASKING: Use business or playing cards to create a fan-like effect. Use the airbrush to spray along the edge of this "fan." Then move the cards slightly and spray again. This can be repeated for several different interesting effects.

ENDLESS LINE: Sometimes called spaghetti striping, this technique uses ⅛-inch wide masking tape to form abstract geometric designs. Execution requires no special skills. Just paint the desired background panel color, run a continuous line of tape and then spray the cover color. Some custom painters add a fogged accent to the endless line by spraying a third color, carefully following the tape line, before the tape is removed.

FADEAWAY: Sometimes called a "fade job," this popular custom technique is accomplished by blending one or more colors so that they overlap. Rather than having a sharp masked edge where the colors meet, the colors are blended or fogged with the spray gun or touchup gun so that a gradual transition is made from one color to the next.

The most successful custom paint jobs combine perfect technique with an eye for design. Notice how well the lines of this trick multicolored paint scheme blend with the lines of the truck.

Chrome Lettering Painting

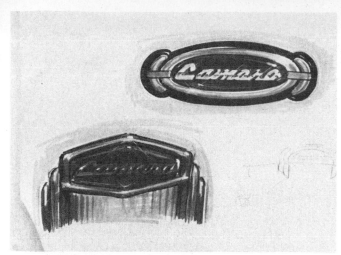

1. One of the most popular (and difficult to master) custom painting tricks is neon lettering. Glen of Glen Designs, Chatham, New Jersey, is one of the best at this technique. Glen starts with a sketch.

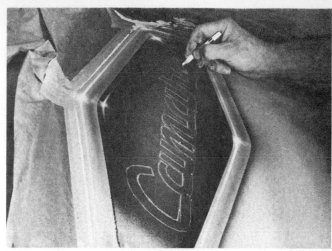

2. Then, after preparing the surface underneath, Glen covers the area to be lettered with clear adhesive shelf paper. The design is then drawn on the paper with a white grease pencil and carefully cut out with an X-acto knife.

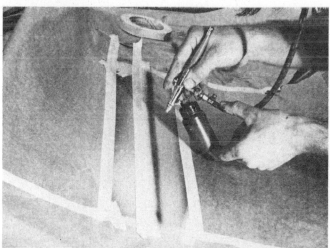

3. The chrome neon lettering was done by masking off the letters and applying straight lines of color which represent the colors reflected by the chrome. The area must be remasked for each new color.

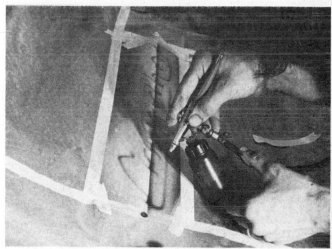

4. Black paint is used to shade and define the lettering. This part of the job takes real talent. You have to visualize the reflections before you can paint them.

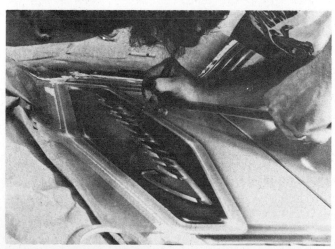

5. After removing the shelf paper, the lettering was outlined with black striping enamel. Glen uses a mahlstick to steady his hand.

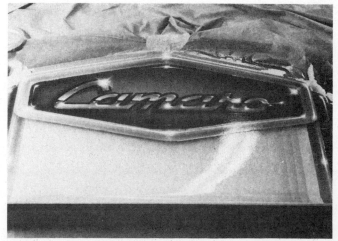

6. The finished design was covered with clear to protect it. Notice the subtle highlights and reflections that give the design luster and depth. This is custom painting at its best.

Design Panel Painting

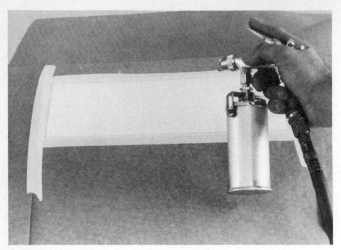

1. Design panels are one of the foundations of custom painting. We started our sample design panel by masking off a section of a trunk, then applying a candy color over white undercoating.

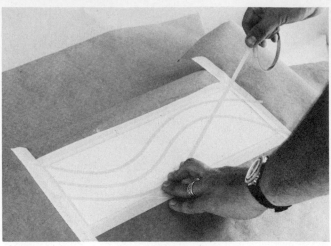

2. Next, we used ¼-inch masking tape to lay out a flowing pattern.

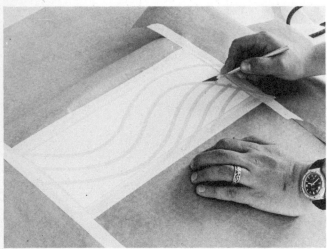

3. An X-acto knife was used to trim any loose tape ends. Only use enough pressure to cut the tape; don't cut into the paint underneath.

4. Parallel lines are best made with ⅛-inch tape placed beside the ¼-inch tape lines. When these lines are removed, the underlying paint color will be revealed.

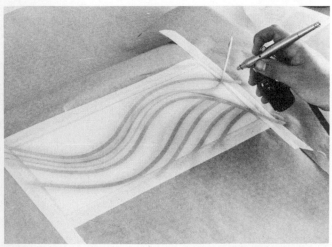

5. An airbrush was used to fog along the ¼-inch tape lines with one color. Then we switched colors and fogged the ⅛-inch tape lines.

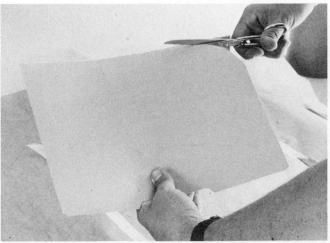

6. Masks or patterns of one type or another are a basic element of custom painting. We used an ordinary file folder to cut a curved mask.

7. The curved mask was used to apply shaded lines to a pie-shaped section of the design panel. Masking tape was applied around the area to protect it from overspray.

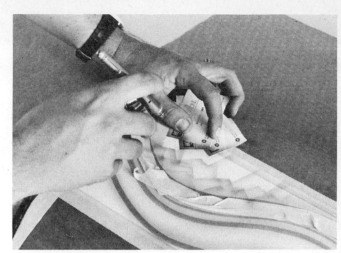

8. Card masking involves making a variety of designs by spraying the edges of a group of business or playing cards. We taped ours together at the base to keep them from shifting.

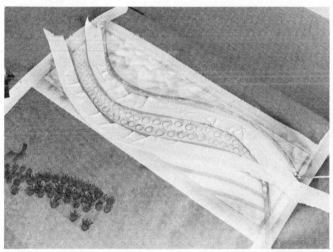

9. The area between two fogged lines was filled with small "freak drops." Freak drops are formed by holding the airbrush very close to the surface and applying short bursts of air.

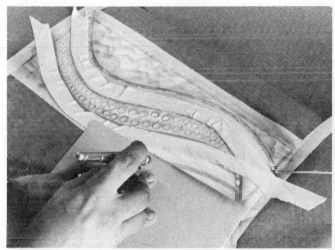

10. Next, a straight piece of file folder was used to fog some lines across the lower corner of the design.

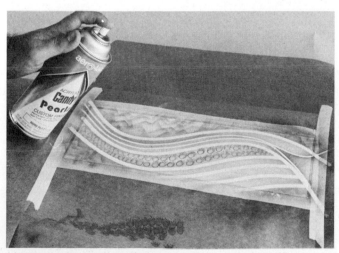

11. The whole design was topped with an application of Aero-Lac candy pearl. Some type of protective topcoat like this or clear lacquer should be used to protect the design and give it depth.

12. The black and white photo of the finished design panel lacks much of the excitement of the candy colors. But you can get an idea of how easy it is to combine a variety of easy custom paint tricks for an unusual effect.

Paint-by-Number Mural

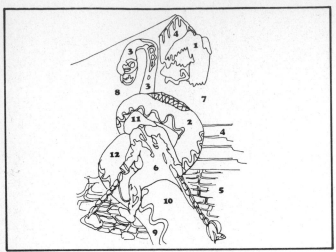

1. Creating a custom mural is basically art, only the surface is steel instead of canvas. But like the popular home paint-by-number kits, mural painting can be made much simpler if you break the design down into its basic elements.

2. Acrylic lacquer paint is a favorite of many professional muralists, such as our mural-by-numbers artist Wally Byrd, because they can reduce it with thinner to create a very short drying time.

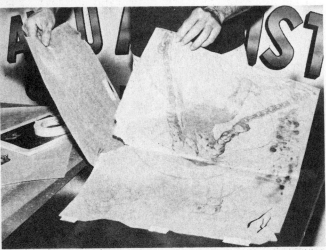

3. Wally's first step is to select a mural design and transfer it to tracing paper. After the mural is drawn, a piece of carbon paper should be placed between the traced mural and the surface to be painted.

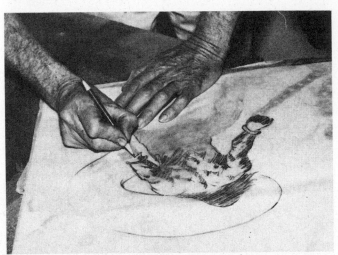

4. Using a sharp pencil or ball-point pen, re-sketch the traced mural so that the carbon paper traces a line on the surface to be painted.

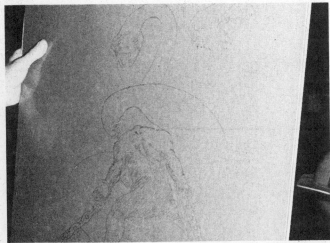

5. The surface should have a visible carbon line showing the basic outline of the mural. Don't worry about the lines showing up in the final mural because they will be painted over or erased during the painting process.

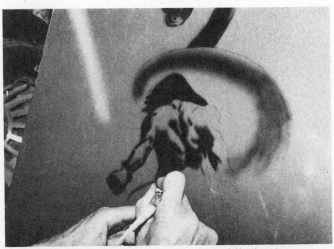

6. Next, an airbrush is used to start filling in the mural. Always test the airbrush for the desired line before painting the design. Since the base surface was a light color, Wally airbrushed the darkest colors first. Colors should be sprayed very lightly initially, and then built up to the desired shade.

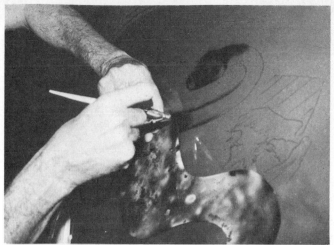

7. For making definitive line breaks between areas differing in color, use a template to block off the painted areas from those to be left unpainted.

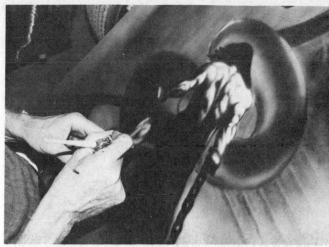

8. The lighter colors were applied after the darker colors were all in place. White does a good job of guiding your eye through a picture. The thickness of the white paint, along with its density, is what gives the mural its three-dimensional look.

9. There are no hard and fast rules about mural painting. You should choose your colors according to your own tastes. Wally traced this mural from a book of Frazetta drawings and kept the original close by as a guide.

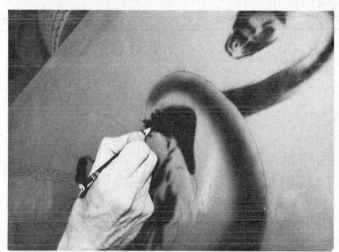

10. A trick used by Wally to make sharp lines is to use a Stabilo pencil and blending stub. The Stabilo pencil can "write" on the slick lacquer surface and then be blended into the paint.

11. After applying the finishing touches and signing his name, Wally covered the mural with several coats of clear lacquer to protect it from the elements.

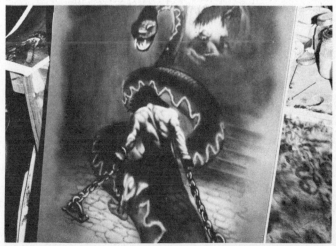

12. To say that the finished product was outstanding would be an understatement. While you might not get these results your first time out, with practice, you too can learn to paint murals by-the-numbers.

Flame Painting

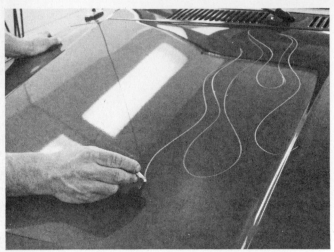

1. As with any custom paint technique, the first and most critical step is the design. After thoroughly cleaning the hood area, start laying out the flames with a grease or Stabilo pencil.

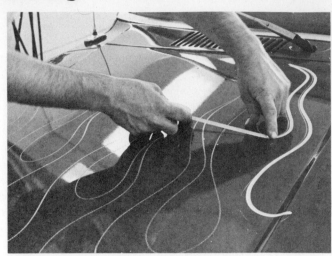

2. When you have settled on a design you like, start taping the flames. Tight corners are the toughest part of laying out flames with masking tape. While ⅛-inch tape is more flexible for curves, ¼-inch tape makes better edges.

3. A great time and effort saver when painting flames is to use clear vinyl adhesive shelf paper. Rather than mask all the areas between the flames, you simply cover everything with clear paper, applied as smoothly as possible.

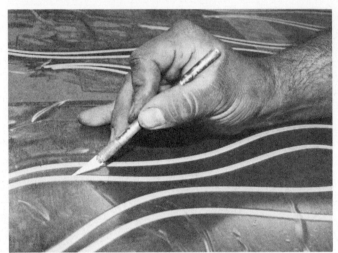

4. Use an X-acto knife or sharp razor blade to cut out the shelf paper that is over the area to be painted. Draw the knife lightly down the middle of the tape with just enough pressure to cut the shelf paper, but not the tape.

5. After the design has been cut out, carefully peel back the cutout sections. Re-check the edges to be sure they are secure. Mask off all areas of the vehicle that won't be painted, including the windshield, grille, and body.

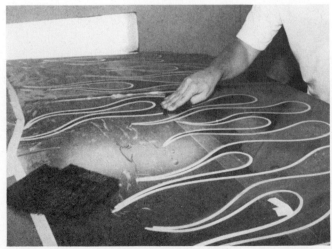

6. The surface to be flamed should be lightly scuffed with a scuff pad. (Scuff pads are also known as artificial steel wool.) Take care around the edges not to lift the tape.

7. After wiping the area down with a tack rag and wax and grease remover, the flames can be painted, using any type of spray gun. A touchup gun is much easier for beginners to handle because of its size. Fog the first application.

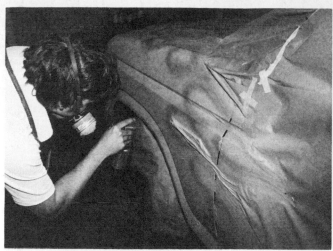

8. Be sure to apply enough paint to all areas, including the wheelwells. A touchup gun was used to fog the edges and inner curves of the flames. The base color was yellow, followed by orange fogging and red tips. Apply the fogging gradually.

9. After all the paint has been applied, let it dry thoroughly. Then cover the flames with clear, which adds gloss and protection.

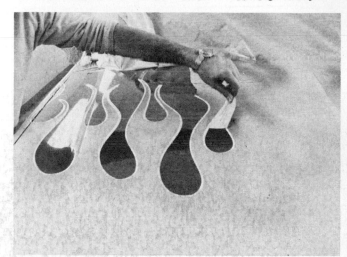

10. After the clear has dried sufficiently, carefully peel back the shelf paper. Keep a razor blade handy in case the paint needs to be cut away from the shelf paper.

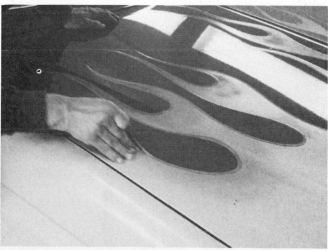

11. There will be a ridge between the vehicle's surface and the edge of the flames. This edge can be blended in by pinstriping with One Shot striping enamel. Pinstriping also highlights flames nicely and helps the flames' colors really blaze off the vehicle.

12. The finished flame job looks great and, what's more, was fast and easy to do.

Mini Mural

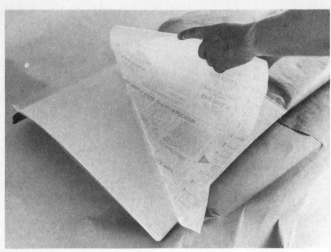

1. There are many ways for the beginning custom painter to get started, but probably none are easier than the stencil mural shown here. Use an old trunk lid to practice on. The first step is to mask off the area with a piece of clear adhesive shelf paper.

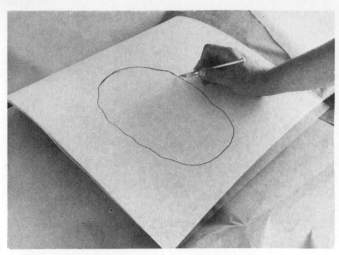

2. Next, mark off the mural border with either a pencil or grease pencil. Using very light pressure on an X-acto knife, carefully cut out the center of the circle.

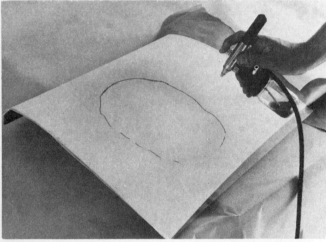

3. Use a touchup gun or airbrush to first spray the desired background color, and then fog in secondary colors. Go easy with these colors. It is easier to add more paint later than to remove it to get the desired effect.

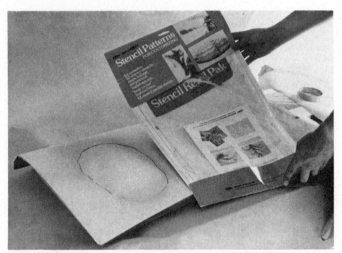

4. Several companies, such as Badger, market complete stencil pattern kits, a real aid to making a first mural.

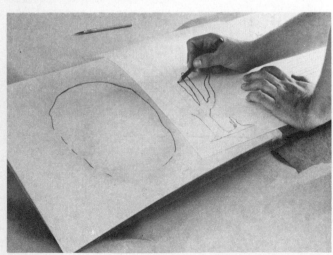

5. For our mini mural we chose a cactus as the mural's main subject. The Badger stencil paper is semi-transparent, so it is easy to trace over the patterns.

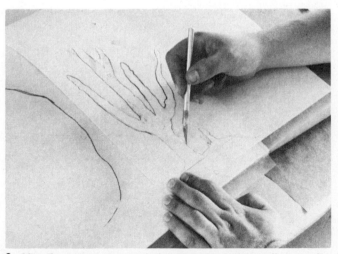

6. After the pattern was traced onto a piece of stencil paper, it was carefully cut out with a sharp X-acto knife.

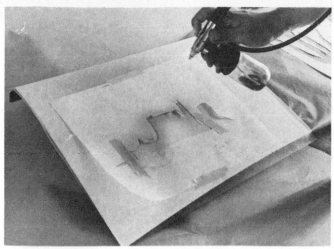

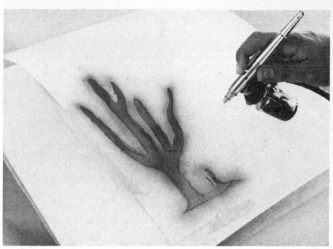

7. Before laying down the cactus, we taped a mountain stencil over the background panel and sprayed it with an appropriate color. When making a mini mural, remember to always paint the items that appear furthest away in the mural first.

8. After letting the mountain dry, the stencil was removed and replaced with the cactus stencil. Again, an airbrush was used to carefully fog in the desired color. Don't try to apply too much paint at once, or it will seep under the stencil.

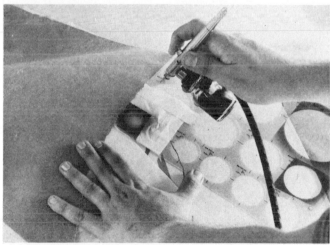

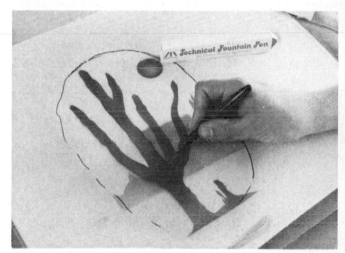

9. A drafting aid circle template was used to add the sun to the mural. The area around the circle used was taped off. To make our sun look three-dimensional, we sprayed the edges heavier than the center.

10. Details, such as the spines of the cactus and a crisp outline, were made with a Metalflake technical fountain pen. This type of pen and ink is designed to work on metal and with automotive paints.

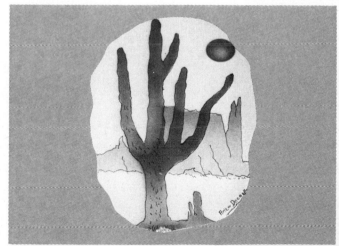

11. Aero-Lac candy pearl from a convenient spray can was used to add depth and luster to the finished mural.

12. The remaining clear shelf paper was removed to reveal the finished mini mural. While it's no masterpiece, it's not bad for a first try. A successful stencil mural should give you the confidence to move on to bigger and better things.

Blazer Bird Mural

1. When a painter turns his talents to his personal car, the result is usually outstanding. Eddie Paul chose a multi-media eagle for the hood of his custom Blazer. He began by designing the bird on a sheet of paper taped to the pre-painted hood.

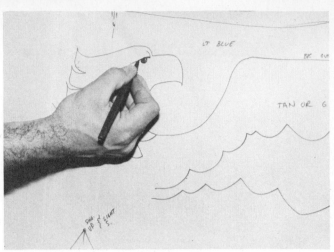

2. The eagle's head and feathers were drawn freehand and marked for the appropriate color in each area. The wings were matched by drawing one side and then reversing and tracing the pattern onto the other side of the hood.

3. The paper pattern was then set aside while the background was painted in. First, Eddie sprayed the sky in the area not covered by the eagle's wings.

4. Once the sky dried, it was masked with a piece of paper while the ground color was applied. Eddie lifted the edge of the masking paper slightly at irregular intervals to make a more realistic, uneven horizon line.

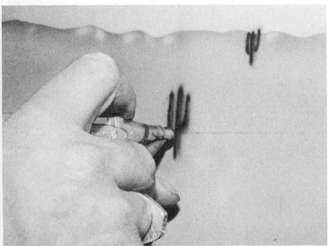

5. Then, an airbrush was used to carefully paint in a series of freehand cactuses and other details.

6. The paper pattern was laid back in place and the outline of the eagle's wings, body, and head were carefully marked.

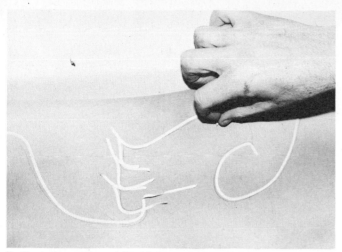

7. Next, the outline of the bird was laid out in ¼-inch masking tape, following the outline marked on the hood.

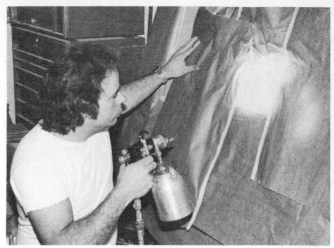

8. The head of the eagle was masked off from the rest of the design and sprayed white. The eyes and beak would be added with gold leaf and a pinstriping brush later on.

9. The head was covered, and the upper section of the wings masked off and sprayed with tan paint. Then, that section was masked, leaving the major portion of the wings exposed. Eddie then sprayed this area with an adhesive gold leaf sizing.

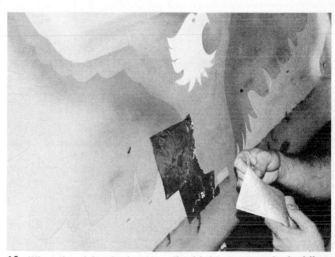

10. When the sizing had set up, the bird was unmasked while the thin sheets of gold leaf were applied to the wings. The gold leafing sticks only where the sizing was sprayed.

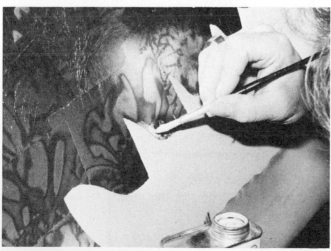

11. After the excess gold leafing was rubbed off, using a light finger touch, Eddie outlined the entire design and added details and lettering.

12. The finished hood is a real attention getter, yet is durable due to several coats of clear applied before it was installed on the Blazer. The combination of techniques, such as airbrushing, gold leafing, lettering, painting, and striping, is a good way to create really interesting effects.

18
Final Touches

It often seems like a painter's work is never done. After the sanding and filling and priming and painting, a paint job still won't look right until it's had that final finish. Adding the crowning touches to a paint job can take hours, or it can take days, depending on the vehicle and the amount of attention paid to detail. However, whether you're after a concours-quality vehicle or just a good looking grocery-getter, any time invested in the final finish pays off many times over in the appearance of your car.

There are four main steps to making the most of your repair and painting efforts—color sanding, rubbing out, touching up, and detailing. The first two are necessary to bring out the shine on newly painted vehicles (especially when lacquer, rather than enamel, is applied). The second two steps can bring out the best in any car's finish, whether it has been freshly painted or not.

Color Sanding

Color sanding sounds frightening to most beginning painters. The majority of us have been conditioned to never use anything more abrasive than soft paste wax on a car's finish so it's not surprising that the thought of sanding down the color coat, especially a freshly painted color coat, is a little hard to accept. However, rather than destroying a fresh paint job, color sanding removes any traces of orange peel or imperfections in the paint surface.

The actual technique of color sanding is simple. Using a sanding block (except on corners and edges where it is too easy to sand through to the metal, hand sand for more control) and 600-grit or higher paper, wet sand the entire painted surface. Use lots of water to keep the paper from getting clogged and to keep sanding debris off the finish. You will be sanding off several coats of paint. That's why you spray multiple coats in the first place. When the surface is uniformly smooth, stop. The paint's real shine will come up during the rubbing out procedure.

Remember that only lacquers and acrylic lacquers should be color sanded. Because of their fast drying time on application, lacquers are subject to the orange peel and overspray-grit conditions that color sanding removes. Also, because lacquers dry from the inside out, color sanding helps open up the surface of the paint for more complete drying. Enamels, on the other hand, have a hard, gloss finish on application. Color sanding enamels will remove the gloss and destroy the paint job.

Rubbing Out

Rubbing out, or compounding, a paint job can really separate a good paint job from a great looking paint job. Rubbing out works on both lacquers and enamels, though some painters recommend using only polishing, not rubbing, compound on enamel finishes.

Rubbing out paint is a procedure normally performed with a buffing machine and several types of compound. While rubbing out can be done by hand, it is tedious work and requires a lot of elbow grease. If you don't own or have access to a buffing machine, it is a good idea to rent one for the job. One important caveat, however, about the use of machine rubbing is on the style lines (such as raised body lines and edges on doors and fenders) of a vehicle. These areas generally don't retain as much paint as the flat areas of a car, so the chances of rubbing right through the fresh top coat to the primer and metal is much greater. Avoid these areas with the machine and then hand rub them when you are finished.

Rubbing compounds are available in both paste and liquid form, and contain an abrasive agent such as pumice, which actually cuts the paint's top coat to give a smoother and more level finish. This helps eliminate orange peel in enamel paint and creates a final finish on both lacquer and enamel jobs that offers an almost show car luster and brilliance. Although similar in nature, polishing compounds differ from rubbing compounds in that the abrasive particles are finer and cut less for the final phases of a rubbing out project. Both rubbing and polishing compounds are available in various abrasive strengths for both machine and hand rubbing purposes.

The first consideration when preparing to rub out a new paint job is allowing the paint to dry properly so it won't be damaged. The correct drying time varies according to the type of paint you use—and who

When it comes to detailing a car, anything goes. Some of the most valuable tools of the trade include cotton-tipped swabs, dust clothes, a variety of brushes and wisks, upholstery cleaner, carpet shampoo, and vinyl sprays.

you talk to. General consensus is, however, that enamels should be allowed to dry for at least a week and lacquers anywhere from overnight to 30-60 days. A safe compromise for lacquers would be one to two weeks.

The first step in the actual rubbing out is to carefully wash the vehicle with cool water. After drying, brush or squeeze rubbing compound over a small section of the body. Don't tackle too large an area at a time or the compound will dry before you've completely covered the area with the buffing machine. Use a compounding pad on the machine while you are using rubbing compound, and be sure to keep the pad clean at all times. Use great care when using the buffing machine, otherwise you could be rubbing your way into a second painting session. Keep the buffing machine in constant motion and take care not to apply too much pressure against the surface as this can burn the paint and possibly cut completely through the top coat. The weight of the machine alone should be all the pressure that is necessary.

After you've finished going over the entire paint surface with the rubbing compound, you can proceed with the polishing phase. Remove the compounding pad from the buffing machine and replace it with a wool bonnet. Again, just as you did with the rubbing compound, squeeze or brush the polishing compound on the car's finish and tackle a small area at a time until the entire vehicle has been polished to a super gloss.

After the rubbed out paint job has been allowed to set for at least a month, it can be waxed with a non-abrasive wax, though more for protection than shine. A properly rubbed out paint job should glisten and shine for many years.

Touching Up

At some time in every car's history, it will be a candidate for touchup paint. Often an otherwise perfect paint job, fresh from being untaped, will get nicked or scratched while the trim is being reinstalled. Other blemishes occur where the vehicle was overtaped, the tape covering body that should have been painted, or where the fresh paint

Compounding, or rubbing out, a new paint job, requires a gentle touch along with rubbing and polishing compounds and an electric buffing machine and pads.

Final Touches

The keys to getting and keeping a perfect finish on new or old paint jobs are cleanliness and protection. There are a wide variety of waxes and cleaners available to make the job easy.

lifts with the tape when it is removed. Besides new finish problems, an old finish can appear much worse than it really is due to unsightly nicks and scratches. Generally speaking, any small area where paint *isn't*, but *should* be, is a candidate for the touchup treatment.

There are a variety of touchup kits available in auto parts stores or from new car dealers. Most are available (especially from dealers) to match your vehicle's original equipment paint code. Typically they will include a small amount of paint and a brush similar to those found with fingernail polish. It is important when using these factory or aftermarket kits to prepare the surface with a light touch of sandpaper to remove any rust that might have formed on the exposed metal. You aren't going to get a show car finish with a touchup brush, but you will be saving the sheetmetal from further rusting until it is time for a total repaint. For best results, apply the paint in very thin coats until it has built up to nearly the thickness of the original paint, then carefully sand or rub the area until the edges are blended smooth.

For a more professional looking touchup, use an air brush or touchup spray gun. Obtain a small quantity of matching paint (the OEM paint code can usually be found on a metal plate under the hood or inside the doorjamb), mix it with thinner or reducer as you would if you were painting the entire car, and carefully spray the sanded and feather-edged nick or scratch with the air brush or touchup gun. To avoid getting overspray on the rest of the paint job, mask off all but the immediate problem area with masking paper or a piece of cardboard mask. When the paint has dried sufficiently, rub out and wax to blend into the original paint.

When you are touching up a fresh paint job, be sure to allow the new paint to dry thoroughly before attempting the repair. You can do more damage than good if you're trying to sand and mask an "uncured" fresh finish.

Detailing

The term "detailing" covers a lot of ground. Detailing can be anything from washing a vehicle and vacuuming the interior to preparing a car for a Concours d'Elegance competition. In either case, or any area in between, the idea is to make the vehicle look as good as you can while doing a little preventive maintenance at the same time. The exterior paint should be treated either with a good quality paste or liquid wax (after carefully removing all dirt and grit with a good washing and wiping down) or with a polymer sealant. All exterior chrome should be cleaned thoroughly (steel wool and kitchen cleanser powder remove most rust) and waxed with a quality chrome polish. This not only helps the shine but protects the chromed pieces from corrosion caused by salts, moisture, and chemical pollutants in the air. While you're on the exterior, don't forget the wheels and tires. Wheels should be cleaned or polished, depending on their makeup, and tires cleaned with a rubber cleanser/preservative. Chemical whitewall or raised white letter sidewall cleaners are available at most auto parts stores, though steel wool and kitchen cleanser will also work.

A vehicle's interior can also be easily detailed to show car quality. Rubbing compound applied by hand will bring back the shine from most painted interior areas. Scratches and nicks on the interior can be treated just like nicks and scratches on the exterior with a brush, air brush, or touchup gun. Commercial vinyl sprays are available in a wide variety of colors to match or change the color of almost any car's interior trim or seats. Several paint manufacturers market vinyl spray additives that can be mixed with acrylic lacquers and sprayed through regular spray painting equipment to touch up or change the color of any interior. These additives make the paint durable yet extremely flexible so it won't crack or peel when used on headliners or seat cushions.

Most automotive carpets can be cleaned with regular carpet shampoo and a small brush. And finally, floor mats and other rubber items such as stick shift boots can be cleaned with a rubber cleanser/preservative or re-dyed with one of the many rubber color coating sprays available at most auto parts stores.

And that's all it takes to make an old car look new or a new car look even better than when it left the showroom floor.

Before rubbing out a lacquer paint job, the surface must be carefully color sanded to remove any minute imperfections or paint flaws. Always use plenty of water when color sanding to keep the fine-grit paper from clogging and deep scratching the finish.

Repairing Paint Flaws

1. Even the most experienced painters sometimes make mistakes. Fixing flaws is relatively easy after the fact, especially with lacquer paints. On this fresh repaint job the lacquer lifted around some of the rubber window gaskets.

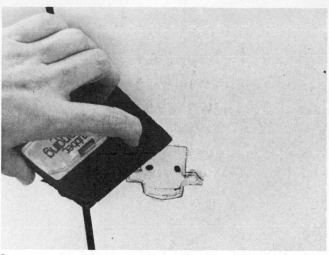

2. The flaws can be repaired by sanding down the flaking paint with 600-grit wet sandpaper. Be careful when sanding so you don't damage the surrounding paint.

3. Sand the flaw completely down to the original paint surface, making sure you feather-edge the sanded spots into the surrounding area so as not to leave a lip or harsh edge.

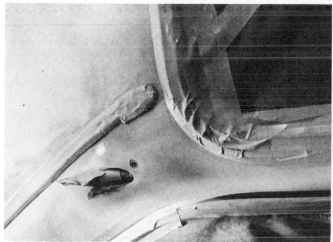

4. Carefully mask the surrounding area. If the original flaw was caused by improper masking or tape removal, take extra care not to repeat the mistake. Taping against rubber is easier if the rubber has been cleaned and lightly scuffed beforehand.

5. Then use a touchup gun to blend in the repair. Make sure the repair is well covered with color. After it dries for a few days, the repair can be color sanded and polished.

6. The finished repair is undetectable. This fix technique can be used to repair sags, runs, chips, and many other bloopers that don't require a complete repainting.

Rubbing Out Paint

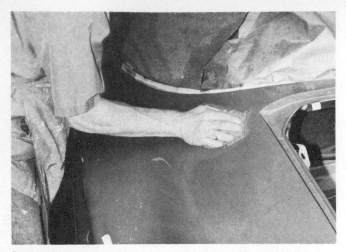

1. Rubbing out should never be attempted until the finish has been allowed adequate drying time. Begin the rubbing out process by washing the vehicle thoroughly with cool water. Then dry the car.

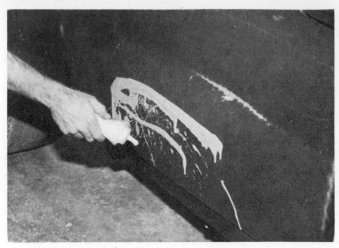

2. Abrasive rubbing compound should be either squeezed onto the finish or applied with a brush. Apply compound to a small section of the car at a time.

3. After the compound has been applied evenly on the paint surface, rub the finish out with a buffing machine. A compounding pad should be used on the machine with the rubbing compound.

4. It is very important to keep the pad clean during the rubbing procedure for maximum results. Use a screwdriver to clean particles from the pad while the pad is slowly spinning.

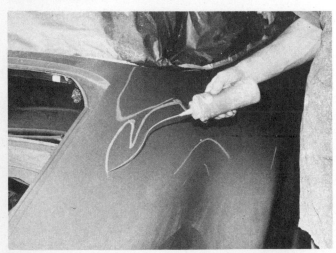

5. Then apply polishing compound to the car's finish, just as you did the rubbing compound. The polishing compound contains finer abrasive particles and cuts less than the rubbing compound.

6. Remove the compounding pad and replace it with a wool polishing bonnet. Polish the car carefully until the entire surface boasts a high-luster, show car finish.

Detailing Your Car

1. The first step in detailing·a car or truck is to wash it. Rinse the car with cold water and then go over the surface with water and a sponge. Unless the car is filthy dirty, you don't need to use a lot of soap or detergent.

2. Once a car is clean, it should be protected with a high quality wax or sealant. There are many good products available that will seal a fresh paint job and keep it shiny for months.

3. A vehicle's chrome should be well protected at all times from harmful chemical oxidation. Keeping chrome well waxed removes chemical deposits and fights further pitting or rusting.

4. Several times a year you should steam clean your engine and undercarriage, especially after trips through mud, to the ocean, or over salted winter roads. Most do-it-yourself car washes have steam cleaning sprays that work well.

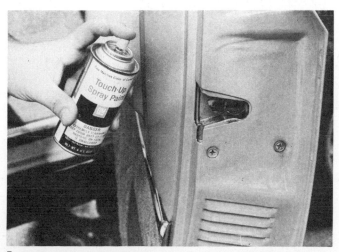

5. Don't overlook the value of a spray can for detailing areas such as the trunk, wheelwells, and engine compartment.

6. Last but not least are the wheels and tires. A light application of steel wool or wheel cleaner will shine up most rims, while tires should be treated with chemical rubber protectant.

19
Weekend Paint Job

There comes the time in almost every car owner's life when he or she must face the prospect of getting a car repainted. The economics of vehicle ownership has dictated in recent years that people hold onto vehicles much longer than they did in the past. And the older a vehicle is, the more likely the original factory paint has fallen prey to the evils of oxidation, aging, and the various chemicals floating around in the sky and on the roadways.

When it comes to an older car, the decision to fix the fading, cracking, or chipping paint is not always easy to make. Unlike a newer, more valuable vehicle, the cost of repainting an older car can often be close to what the vehicle is worth. Unfortunately, many people let this fact influence them to the extent that they ignore their vehicles' deteriorating exteriors, which in turn hastens the demise of these otherwise still useful cars. Once the protective paint coat is gone, rust won't be far behind.

Obviously then, the trick is to get some new paint

over the old without spending a lot of money (which, as we'll see, can be spent for other things). When it comes to cheap paint jobs there are two basic alternatives: the so-called "one-day" repaint shops, which promise quick service and reasonable quality, or the do-it-yourself method shown here, which promises stiff muscles, missed meals, strained friendships, and a top quality paint job for very little cash investment other than supplies.

We decided to try out method number two on a faithful but aging Honda Civic. The Honda fit the previously mentioned profile perfectly. The stock factory paint had held up well, but was beginning to show signs of rapid deterioration. Each washing produced rinse water full of oxidized paint, turning the driveway the color of the vehicle. On close inspection, tiny bubbles could be seen in the paint, indicating that rust was starting to take place underneath. In a couple of spots the rust had broken through the surface and was forming deep orange pockets in the metal. Clearly, a total repaint was in order.

Aside from badly worn tires, the car was basically mechanically sound, making it worth fixing up. However, since the car was our daily transportation, any transformation from beast back to beauty would have to be confined to the weekend.

Friday Evening

All good weekends start on Friday evening and ours was no exception. The first stop was the tire store where without much persuasion we decided on a set of 175/70 R13 Radial T/A tires from the BF Goodrich Tire Company (500 South Main St., Akron, OH 44316). We hated to think about putting that nice new rubber on the ugly stock wheels. The wheels had already been repainted once and were again showing heavy signs of rust. Rather than having the stockers sandblasted and repainted, we decided to upgrade the appearance with a set of aftermarket wheels. Custom wheels will do more than any other single item towards changing the look of a vehicle. Knowing this, we went for a set of the best, Enkei Empire gold basket wheels from Golden Wheel Corporation (22130 So. Vermont Avenue, Unit A, Torrance, CA 90502).

While we were at it, we stopped for one more special dress up item, a flexible front air dam and spoiler from P & P Products (503 Boccaccio Avenue, Venice, CA 90291). Besides nicely complementing the racy look of the wheels and tires, the front spoiler/air dam combination improves the aerodynamics of the vehicle, which helps both handling and miles per gallon of gas.

The last stop for the evening was the paint store where we picked up all the needed supplies, includ-

Normal oxidation, along with chemical pollutants, and salt from the nearby ocean, caused the paint to wear thin, especially around body edges, such as on the hood. As a transportation car, the Honda received fewer protective waxings than some of the more exciting family vehicles.

Even in a simple repaint like this, one thing can lead to another. Replacement BF Goodrich Radial T/A tires led to a new set of Enkei Empire wheels, which led to a P&P Products flexible air dam. The money saved by painting the car at home more than made up for the cost of the new wheels and spoiler.

The decision to repaint this transportation car was easier to make when we noticed the rapidly deteriorating exterior. While this was one of the largest rusted areas, we knew that once a vehicle's protective paint coating is penetrated, rust spreads very quickly under the remaining paint.

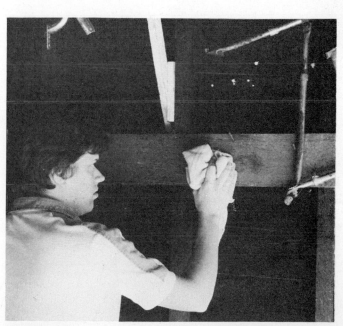

To create our own home spray booth, we first moved everything out of the garage that could be moved, and then wiped down the walls with a rag to remove as much dirt and dust as possible.

Weekend Paint Job

Then the walls were hung from ceiling to floor with the plastic drop cloths. Creating this "sterile" environment is a good idea for any type of painting, though it is especially critical when spraying enamel. However, unlike a professional spray booth that has forced ventilation, a backyard booth needs one unsealed side (an open garage door) to vent the dangerous fumes that can build up during painting.

With the garage cleaned and ready, we started stripping the car in preparation for sanding. For a quick paint job like ours, we decided to remove only major items, like bumpers, and those trim pieces that could be easily taken off.

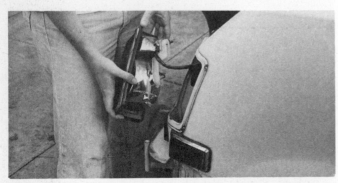

Taillights and sidemarkers on most vehicles can be easily unscrewed and unplugged. Notice the buildup of dirt around the taillight housing.

ing plastic drop cloths, sanding paper and sanding blocks, paint mixing buckets and mixing sticks, masking tapes and paper, paint strainers, tack rags, and a selection of Ditzler wax remover/degreaser, body filler and putty, lacquer thinner, and Duracryl acrylic lacquer paint.

Before going to the paint store we had a difficult decision to make regarding what type of paint to use—acrylic lacquer or acrylic enamel. Each paint has advantages and disadvantages when used for a quickie paint job such as ours. The enamel based paints are good in that they take less surface preparation (sand scratches don't tend to show through as much, since enamel is heavier and tends to fill and hide better than lacquer). Enamels also don't need to be rubbed out. Once the paint is dry, you can drive away and not worry about secondary finishing processes.

For a true "weekend" paint job then, enamel would be the choice, as it is with most one-day paint shops. However, enamel is a much harder paint to apply, due to its slow drying time. Mistakes (runs, sags, orange peel, etc.) are hard to remove without redoing the whole paint job. Also, enamel is not as well suited for garage or driveway paint jobs as lacquer, again because of its slow drying time. Any particles of dust or dirt in the air can settle into an enamel surface all too easily unless you maintain spray-booth-quality clean conditions. For these reasons we decided to use lacquer, even though it would mean an additional day of color sanding and rubbing out on a later weekend.

With our new rims and rubber, spoiler, and paint supplies in hand, we headed home to get a good night's sleep.

Saturday

The first full day of the weekend would be the toughest. We started out bright and early by getting our "paint booth" ready. Even though we

Dirt is the real enemy of a successful paint job. Besides getting rid of dust and debris from the painting area, we brushed off and wiped down the engine compartment, door seams, wheelwells, and any other place where dirt could be blown onto the car as it was painted.

Then, after washing the car to remove surface dirt, the real fun began. The more friends you can talk into helping sand the body, the more you'll see of your weekend. The entire paint surface was gone over with progressively finer sandpaper (wet) to remove grime and oxidized paint.

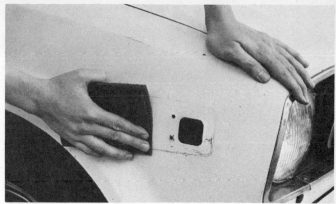

We used a painter's scuff pad to remove dirt buildup before sanding such areas. Sandpaper does not remove dirt, it only forces the particles into the paint.

The flexible scuff pads are also ideal for cleaning out tight areas such as the rain gutters. The cleaner you get the car, the better the finished job will be.

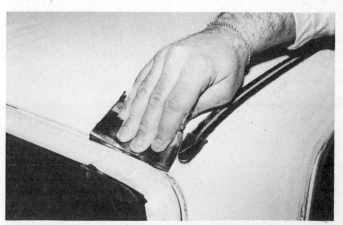

When it came time to sand around chromed pieces such as the windshield molding, we first taped off the chrome so we could work right up to the edge without damaging it.

were going to use acrylic lacquer, which can be sprayed without problem outside, we decided to do our painting inside where there would be less flying debris in the air that could get into the paint. First, we cleaned out both stalls of the garage. Even though the Honda is a relatively small car, we wanted plenty of room to move around so we would use both spaces. After straightening out as much as possible, putting loose items from the floor up onto shelves, we dusted all the walls with a rag and broom. Again, the idea was to remove any dirt that could possibly make its way into the paint job.

Next, we covered the walls of the garage with sheets of plastic, sealing the pieces together with masking tape. Hanging plastic on the wall accomplishes two things: it keeps dirt from blowing out of cracks and corners into the paint and it keeps any overspray from getting onto items stored in the garage. This "sterile" atmosphere is especially important if you are spraying enamels. We did not cover the inside of the garage door, because unlike a real spray booth that has strong fans for ventilation, our home spray booth would have only three sides, with the garage door left open for ventilation during painting. Finally, the garage floor was given the first of many thorough sweepings.

With the booth under control, we turned our attention to prepping the car itself. The first step was to wash the car to remove as much dirt, grit, and oxidized paint as possible before sanding. You should never sand a dirty surface as the sandpaper tends to work the dirt into the old paint, rather than out of it. After washing the car, we removed the bumpers and trim. Again, at this point we had to make a decision. Since the real cost of a paint job is the time and labor spent on preparing the car for painting, and not the actual spraying itself, we had to decide how thoroughly we wanted to prep the car. We knew that removing all the trim would result

Weekend Paint Job

Wet sanding helps prevent deep scratching caused by clogged sandpaper. From time to time, we used a squeegee to wipe off the body in order to check the surface's condition. Our goal was to eliminate any traces of gloss from the old paint. When the surface was uniformly dull, we stopped sanding, rather than reach bare metal.

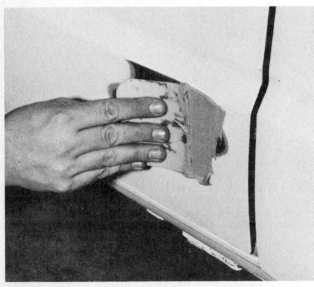

Getting a body perfectly straight is time consuming. For our weekend quickie, we decided to repair only the biggest dents. After grinding the dent down to bare metal, we filled the indentation with plastic body filler.

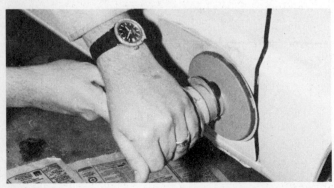

After the filler was applied, it was allowed to dry before it was filed, sanded, and spot puttied. An electric drill with sanding pad, or a dual-action pneumatic grinder will greatly speed up even little repairs.

in a better finished paint job than just taping around it, but it would also take more time and work. For our quickie job we compromised, removing all the lights, side markers, wipers, etc., that were easily reached and leaving the nameplates and such that we couldn't get to without trouble.

Then the long sanding process began. Even on a quick paint job like ours, sanding the entire surface well is critical. There is no point in applying paint if it isn't going to stick, and the best way to guarantee good paint adhesion is to properly scuff the old paint. By choosing to repaint the original factory color we saved a lot of prep time by not having to sand the doorjambs, interior, and engine compartment.

Concentrating on the body only, we started by wet sanding with 220-grit paper, using sanding blocks for the large flat areas and hand sanding around style lines and trim. After the entire surface was dulled, we switched to 320-grit wet paper and then to 400-grit wet to remove as many of our own sanding scratches as possible. In areas where there were signs of rust, we sanded down to bare metal, removing all traces of rust and then feather-edging the bare spots into the surrounding paint.

Rather than trying to remove all the little nicks and dents, which would have taken an additional day, at least, we repaired only the two largest dents. In each case we did the minimum repair possible, grinding off the paint and filling the impression with plastic body filler rather than pounding out the dent. While we compromised on the method of body repair, we made sure the plastic filler was sanded properly and free of pinholes or flaws that would show through the finished paint. These repairs were then primed carefully, as were the spots where we had sanded through to bare metal to remove the rust.

Though the prepping we had done so far had

We then covered the repair with primer. We also applied primer to any bare metal spots created when sanding out traces of rust.

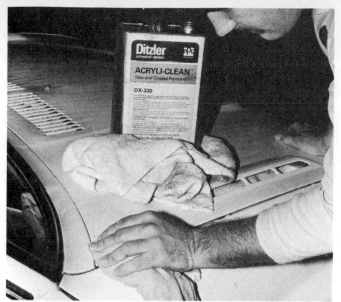

With the sanding and dent repair taken care of, we wiped down the entire surface with Ditzler Acryli-Clean degreaser to eliminate any sanding debris that would keep the masking tape from properly adhering.

Everybody joined in with the taping, speeding up the process considerably. Because we were repainting the Honda with its original factory paint color, we did not have to paint or tape off the interior, door and window jambs, or the engine compartment. With the taping complete, we decided to call it a day. Prepping a car for painting is tedious work, but it is critical to a good paint job.

been kept minimal in execution, it was time consuming. A crew of four was kept busy all day. After a break for dinner, the Honda was moved back inside where it was masked and taped. The taping went quickly on a car the size of the Honda. It also helped that we had purchased top quality masking tape that adhered easily to the chrome trim, rubber window and windshield gaskets and grille. With the taping done, we called it a night.

Sunday

With the most difficult labor out of the way, we relaxed Sunday morning. After a leisurely breakfast we rolled the car out of the garage so we could give the area one last sweeping. Once we were satisfied that the entire garage was as clean as we could make it, we rolled the car back in and got ready to paint.

Before the actual painting, we wiped down the whole vehicle with wax remover/degreaser followed by a tack rag to get off any remaining dirt or dust. Then the acrylic lacquer was thinned according to direction and strained into the spray gun. We borrowed a spray gun and 1-horsepower air compressor for the painting, though if you don't have easy access to such equipment, it can be rented from most tool rental outlets. Since this was our very first paint job, we spent extra time checking the spray pattern on a piece of scrap cardboard before putting any paint on the car. Once we were satisfied with the "wetness" and flow of the paint, as well as the pattern, the spraying began. Starting at one corner, we worked our way around the entire car making a double coat (one pass of the gun immediately followed by a second reverse pass, followed by a 50 percent overlap on the next double coat pass). Once we covered the entire car, sufficient time had passed for the lacquer to "flash" so we started the second coat. This process was continued until we

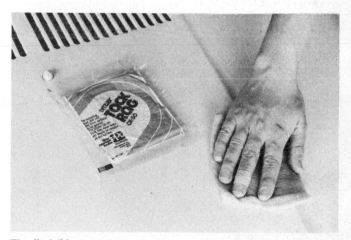

The first thing we did on Sunday was more house cleaning. After sweeping out the paint booth again, we wiped down the car one more time with degreaser before using a fresh tack rag to remove any remaining impurities on the surface.

Then we mixed the Ditzler acrylic and thinner according to directions and strained it into the spray gun's paint cup. Before applying any paint to the car, we carefully tested the spray pattern and paint flow on a piece of scrap cardboard.

Weekend Paint Job

The moment of truth arrived at last. The actual painting is one of the easiest steps in the whole process. We applied about eight coats of paint (¾ of a gallon), making sure to thoroughly cover the primed repaired sections.

After the car was covered to our satisfaction, we painted the P&P fiberglass spoiler. Prior to painting, we had scuffed the surface of the fiberglass using several grades of sandpaper.

While the paint was drying, we cleaned up the spray gun. The borrowed gun and 1-horsepower compressor did a great job. It doesn't take much equipment for a basic paint job.

had covered the car about eight times. The number of coats you put on for a quickie paint job will vary depending on the output of your spray gun. Our gun had limited output so it took a lot of separate coats. We stopped spraying when we had applied approximately ¾ of a gallon of paint.

When doing your own weekend update, remember to follow the basic rules of painting: drain the water from the compressor before using it, always test the spray pattern after reloading the spray gun, use a respirator at all times, and use a tack rag between coats (except enamel) to remove debris from the surface.

After spraying, which took about two hours, we let the paint dry for a few hours before untaping. Lacquer dries to the touch almost immediately which makes it simple to untape without worrying about marring the finish. Enamel should be allowed to dry as long as possible before untaping, even overnight. After untaping, the car looked clean, but dull. Unlike enamel, lacquer is dull on application. That good gloss finish comes after it is rubbed out. However, as soon as the lacquer dries it can be safely worked around. After untaping, we reinstalled the taillights, bumpers, and the rest so the car could be driven around while waiting for the paint to "cure" enough for rubbing out.

Had we used enamel paint, all that would have remained at this point would have been to put on the new wheels and tires and spoiler, making it a true two-day project.

Second Weekend

It's often hard to schedule two free weekends in a row to finish the painting and rubbing out combination. Fortunately, there is no rush to rub out lacquer once it has been applied. While you should leave at least a week for the paint to thoroughly

After the paint was allowed to dry for a couple of hours, the untaping began. We took our time with the untaping so as not to lift the paint from around the trim or body edges. Then the lights and bumpers were reinstalled so the car could be driven to work the next day.

After a week or two of drying, the lacquer paint job had to be color sanded to smooth out any minor flaws and to open up the pores of the paint for total drying. Enamel jobs do not need to be color sanded.

The color sanding was followed with a rub out. We used both machine and hand rubbing to bring out the shine of the paint. After rubbing out, it looked like a completely different car.

The final step was to mount the new wheels and tires and to rivet the front spoiler/air dam into place. The spoiler, which was easy to install, not only gave the Honda a racy custom appearance but improved the car's aerodynamics.

Finished! The tired old commuter car looks better than the day, years before, when it was driven off the showroom floor. And all it took was a weekend.

cure before color sanding, waiting longer doesn't affect the finished result a bit.

We waited two weeks, then started out early Saturday morning wet sanding the color coat with 600-grit paper. Color sanding is tedious, since you are using such fine-grit paper, but it is not difficult. The idea is to eliminate any traces of overspray or orange peel without damaging the paint underneath. Once the finish is uniformly smooth and even, you can bring out the paint's luster with rubbing compound.

Rubbing out, as the process is called, can be done by hand or with a buffing machine. By far the easiest method is machine buffing. Even using a machine, which can be rented at any tool rental store, you will have to spend a lot of time finishing style lines, door edges, and corners by hand.

We started out by first washing the car very carefully with cool water. After drying, we squeezed a small amount of rubbing compound over a small section of the car. Using a compounding pad on the buffer, we carefully applied the compound evenly over the section, being careful not to apply too much pressure for fear of burning through the finish. After the entire car was compounded by machine and hand, the process was repeated using polishing compound and a wool polishing bonnet. The change in the finish was amazing. What started as a bright, dull paint surface was turned into a professional looking, showroom-quality finish.

We installed the custom wheels and tires, mounted the spoiler and the transformation was complete. The tired old commuter car looked better than new.

By using our own labor (and that of a few friends), we saved enough money to justify the new dress up items. But even if your own weekend update only includes new paint, you'll get more than the price of materials back in increased life and value of your car. And all it takes is a weekend.

20
Engine Painting

People who like cars just naturally seem to appreciate a sharp engine compartment. In fact, a nice engine compartment has become so common in all types of enthusiast's cars that it would be hard to imagine a well-painted car without an equally maintained engine compartment.

Achieving a sharp engine compartment is more a matter of physical labor than exceptional painting skill. The biggest deterrent to having a nice engine compartment is the accumulation of dirt and grease. Steam cleaning is the easiest way to clean an engine compartment. A professional steam cleaner is the optimum way to go, but a couple of cans of degreaser and a fistful of quarters will get the job done at the local self-service car wash.

The best way to achieve a sparkling engine compartment is to remove the engine. If this is your plan, have the car steam cleaned before the engine is removed. Then, if it is possible, have the empty engine compartment steam cleaned again. If the engine is being rebuilt, the hot tanking process at the machine shop should do the trick. Otherwise, cleaning the engine will require a lot of hand labor with solvent, a putty knife, and a wire brush.

After the engine and engine compartment have been cleaned as well as possible, thoroughly go over them with a wax and grease remover like Ditzler's DX440. Hidden traces of grease can make it difficult for the new paint to adhere properly. For a real show car engine compartment, remove the front sheetmetal and have the inner fender panels sandblasted or chemically stripped. The front of the frame could also be sandblasted at this time.

A variety of paints will work on the engine and engine compartment. Since heat really isn't a problem with the inner fender panels and firewall, virtually any paint you desire can be used. The engine will stay sharp longer if heat-resistant paints are used. These paints are available in spray cans, and quart cans for application with a spray gun. A check of old car publications like *Hemmings Motor News* will reveal ads for companies that stock factory duplicate colors of engine enamel for almost any car ever made. For custom applications like street rods and street machines, a quality acrylic enamel with a hardener like Ditzler's Delstar acrylic enamel and Delthane hardener is available.

An engine compartment can be detailed with the engine in place, but lots of masking and careful painting is required for a good job. An airbrush is helpful in situations like this because of its limited overspray. It is also a good idea to remove or disconnect as many engine accessories as possible when painting the engine in the car.

Engine Compartment Prep

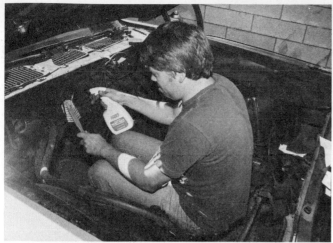

1. After a trip to the steam cleaner, pull the engine and clean up the remaining grease deposits with a liquid degreaser and a stiff brush.

2. The best way to do a super job is to completely strip the front of the car. This '37 Chevy had the sheetmetal and suspension removed so the frame and firewall could be sandblasted. The car is safely supported on jackstands.

3. Extra holes and surface pits were filled. Any imperfections in the filler should be covered with spot putty.

4. Ideally, an engine should be completely disassembled and hot tanked, but if that isn't possible, remove as many parts as you can for a thorough cleaning. The oil pan is usually the dirtiest part of the engine. It needs to be completely clean.

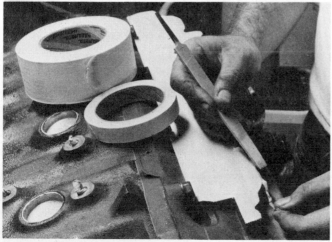

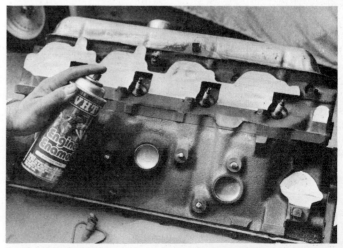

5. Mask off machined areas and other parts of an engine that shouldn't be painted. A file works well to trim the tape.

6. The masked engine was painted with cans of spray engine enamel. Aftermarket valve covers were slated for use, so the old ones were left in place to protect the valvetrain from paint.

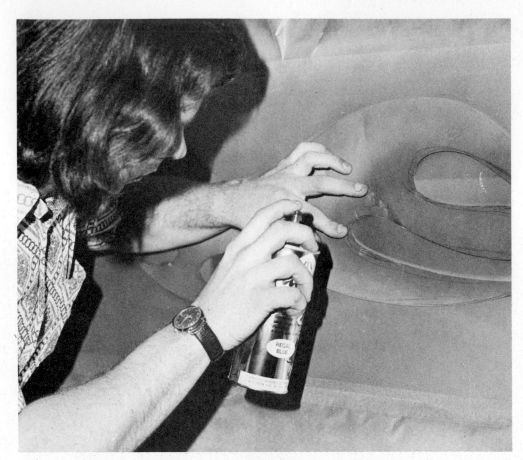

21
Spray Can Painting

Spray cans are good for much more than painting graffiti on alley walls. They can be real time savers when you are doing minor painting jobs. There are a lot of times when it just doesn't pay to haul out the compressor, mix a batch of paint, and do all the post-painting cleanup work. These are the times when it makes sense to use spray cans.

There are limitations, however, to spray can paints. The biggest limitation is cost. The average can of spray paint actually contains more propellant than paint, making it a very expensive way to buy in large quantities. Spray cans are, therefore, best suited for small jobs. The availability of colors is another limiting factor, although color selection is much greater than it was 10 years ago. Mixing is virtually impossible, although you could spray two cans simultaneously in an attempt to mix colors. Finally, the inability to control the spray pattern is one more reason spray cans are not as versatile as regular painting equipment.

There are a wide variety of paints available in spray can form. One of the most commonly used is the factory touchup paint cans. These spray cans are sold by new car parts departments and general automotive parts stores. The colors are usually quite close to the original, but the manufacturers can't make any allowances for fading that may have occurred to your paint. The most common use for factory touchup paints is to repair small scratches and dings.

Before painting the scratch, clean the area. Many times there will be paint left by the offending car. This paint can be removed with rubbing compound. Start the repair by sanding the scratch with 400-grit wet/dry sandpaper to remove any rust and to give the new paint something to grip. Clean the scratch and surrounding area with wax and grease remover. If bare metal is exposed, it must be covered with primer. To avoid overspray, tape off all but the bare metal area before spraying the primer. Shake the touchup paint can vigorously to ensure that the paint is well mixed. As with the primer, tape off the area around the scratch, or make a mask out of a manilla file folder to control overspray. Spray several light coats rather than one heavy coat to avoid runs. Let each application flash (surface dry) before applying the next coat. Leave the scratch alone for two weeks to allow ample drying time. After the drying period, the repaired area can be rubbed with rubbing compound to make it blend into the surrounding area.

Another common use of spray cans is for engine and engine compartment painting. All factory engine colors and many custom ones are available in spray cans. There are even special heat-resistant paints for use on exhaust systems.

Even custom paint work can be accomplished with spray cans. Several manufacturers make custom paints in aerosol cans. SEM Products in Belmont, California, makes a wide array of custom spray paints marketed under their Aero-Lac label. These paints include candy, pearl, and flake colors plus wild Design Colors. Design Colors are pearl paints with mineral spirits. The mineral spirits make the paint dry slowly so that it can be manipulated for some wild custom effects. Base coats and clear top coats are also available in aerosol cans.

A big asset in successful spray can painting is patience. If a run occurs, wait until it dries and then lightly sand it out. Reprime if necessary and apply more paint. A run is most likely caused by holding the can too close to the surface or not allowing enough time for the previous coat to flash before applying another coat.

To operate a spray can properly, depress the finger spray valve tip and move across the surface in a sweeping motion, letting up on the valve after each pass. Make the passes evenly from side to side, with slightly overlapping spray strokes, until the area displays an even, solid coating of paint. Each pass should be allowed to flash dry before the next coat is applied. When covering large areas, it can help to alternate the direction of the strokes. If one coat is laid on using horizontal strokes, the following coat should be applied utilizing vertical strokes. If a run occurs, wait an hour or so before trying to sand it out. Surface mistakes can be corrected when you are using opaque colors, but mistakes with candy paints have to be repaired all the way down to the base coat. Take extra care with custom finishes. We mentioned that runs are caused by holding the can too close to the surface. A reverse problem can occur if the can is held too far from the surface. Orange peel or pebbling is the result of holding the can too far away. Practice on a piece of scrap metal to find the ideal distance for each type of spray paint.

Spray can finishes can be final finished just like spray gun applied finishes. Clear acrylic can be applied over the paint for added gloss and protection. Allow the paint to dry for several days (preferably a week or more) and then lightly color sand with 600-grit wet sandpaper and lots of water. After wet sanding, the paint can be rubbed to a final gloss with rubbing compound and lots of elbow grease.

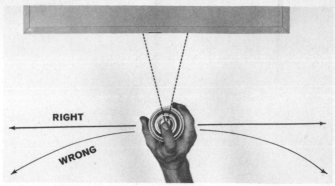

To ensure uniform paint thickness, the nozzle should be moved parallel to the surface. The only exception is when painting very long panels.

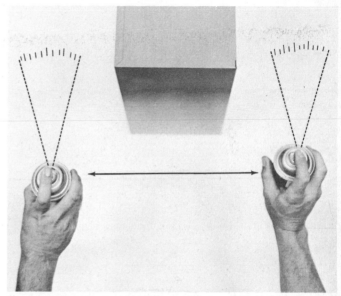

When painting long panels that can't be covered in one sweep, arc away from the surface at the end of each sweep to avoid a double thickness of paint where the sweeps overlap.

This cutaway shows how most spray cans have curved siphon tubes. If a near empty can fails to spray when tilted, turn the nozzle 90 degrees or 180 degrees, and try again. The end of the curved tube may not be down in the paint.

Repairing Parking Lot Scratches

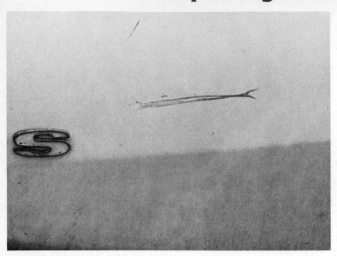

1. Common, garden-variety parking lot scratches and dings can be repaired with spray can paints.

2. Paint left from another car can be removed with rubbing compound.

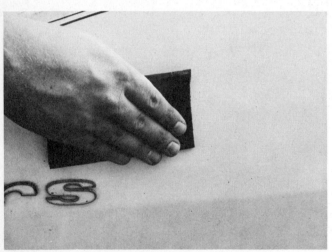

3. Prepare the area with 400-grit wet/dry sandpaper to remove any rust. The sanding also gives the new paint something to grip. Wipe the scratch and surrounding area with a good wax and grease remover to clean the surface.

4. Primer must be applied if the scratch exposes bare metal. Use masking tape to control primer overspray.

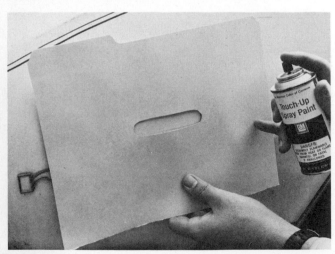

5. Apply the factory-matched touchup paint in several light coats. A mask can be used to control overspray.

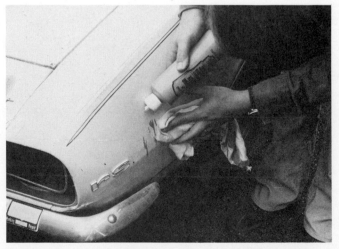

6. Blend the repair into the rest of the car by rubbing out the new paint with rubbing compound. Allow two weeks of drying time before applying the rubbing compound.

Color Panel Painting

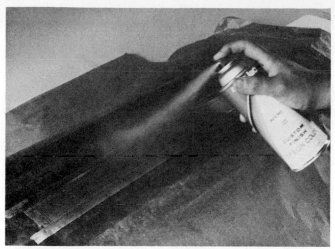

1. Custom painting tricks can be achieved with spray cans. This is a Design Color panel made with Aero-Lac Design Color. The effect works best when applied to a dark colored base.

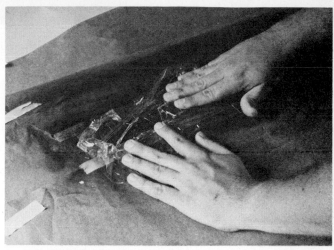

2. Both plastic food wrap and aluminum foil work well for creating designs with Design Colors. Stretch the plastic wrap so that it wrinkles, and pat it down on the still-wet Design Color.

3. When the plastic wrap is peeled away, it takes some of the Design Color with it, giving the area a novel pattern.

4. A strip of wrinkled aluminum foil also works well with Design Colors.

5. Design Colors dry slowly, so you have plenty of time to create your design.

6. A variety of objects can be used to "paint" on wet Design Colors. Here some freehand squiggles were applied with a cotton swab. Sponges and paint brushes also work well with Design Colors. The custom effects are only limited by your imagination.

22
Vinyl Top Replacement

Vinyl tops have been a popular option on new cars for a long time. Many used car owners also had vinyl tops installed on their cars. A vinyl roof in good condition can be a handsome addition to any car. Vinyl roofs were meant to impart a feeling of luxury, which they do, until the vinyl gets ragged. Worn out vinyl tops look far worse than a plain roof. A frayed vinyl top marks a car as a loser that hasn't been well maintained.

One solution to a worn out vinyl top is to have it replaced with new vinyl. There are times, though, when it is desirable to replace the vinyl top with a painted roof. Such was the case with a Camaro Rally Sport that was being refurbished at Customs by Eddie Paul, 124 Nevada Street, El Segundo, CA 90245.

Removing a vinyl top can be more involved than simply peeling back the vinyl and applying some new paint. This is especially true if the top has been in a deteriorated state for a long time. There is a very good possibility that under the tattered vinyl is severe rusting. Vinyl roofs are much more prone to rust damage than non-padded roofs because they can trap moisture. If you have a bad vinyl top, take care of it as soon as possible. The longer you wait, the greater the chance of rust.

The subject Camaro sat outside for three or four years with a bad top. There were areas around the back window where the vinyl appeared "puffy." This, coupled with the fact that the trunk filled with water during the slightest rain storm, was a symptom that should have been spotted sooner. The diagnosis was terminal rustout.

When faced with areas of complete metal deterioration and rustout, the problem can be approached better if the area is sandblasted. Luckily, A-1 Sandblasting is right across the street from Customs by Eddie Paul. The sandblasting exposed the good metal so the repairs could be made easier and would last longer.

Even if you only have a bad vinyl roof with no rustout, repainting the area can be more involved than repainting a non-vinyl roof. If the vinyl roof was installed by the factory, chances are good that the roof is less than perfect. Since most roofs are welded to the lower body panels, there is always some bodywork around the seams. It makes sense for the factory to use the bodies that need more than average work as the basis for vinyl roof equipped cars. The lack of final finishing on the subject Camaro was quite obvious when the old vinyl was removed.

1. One well-worn early Camaro, a victim of too many years in the California smog and salty ocean air.

2. The factory installed vinyl top was badly blistered. There were ominous "puffy" sections around the bottom of the rear window. These signs hinted at rustout.

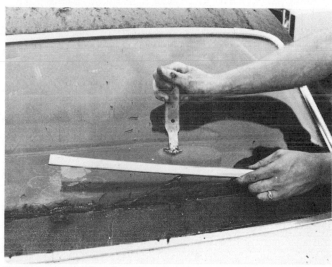

3. The chrome trim was removed using an inexpensive trim removal tool to loosen the clips under the trim. A tool like this is a must if you don't want to damage the fragile trim pieces.

4. Since the lower trim piece that separates the vinyl roof from the painted part of the body won't be needed any longer, you needn't exercise much care in its removal.

5. The belt line trim pieces often have a couple of nuts holding them in place. These nuts are located inside the trunk area.

6. Any type of stiff putty knife can be used to remove the old vinyl. Here, a wood-working chisel is being used because of its rigid blade and sloping leading edge.

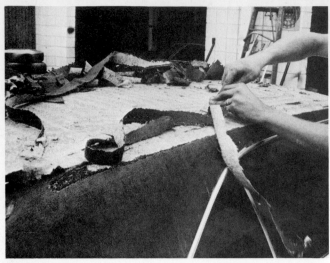

7. Peel back the vinyl and don't worry about the rough surface left by the old adhesive. Don't push the blade too hard or deep or you will risk gouging the metal.

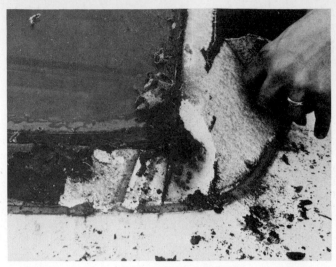

8. Underneath the "puffy" sections around the rear window was rustout. This can be a real problem since this section of metal holds the rear window in place.

9. A dual-action air sander should be used to remove the old glue residue after the vinyl has been removed.

10. Notice the difference between the sanded metal and the areas where the glue residue remains.

11. An attempt was made to grind away the rust around the rear window with a disc grinder, but the damage was too severe.

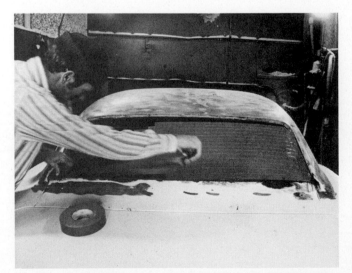

12. The car was taken to A-1 Sandblasting in El Segundo, CA where the rustout areas were blasted clean. Heavy duct tape (or racer's tape) was used to cover the glass.

13. Multiple layers of tape should be applied over the glass nearest the damaged areas since sandblasting can permanently etch glass.

14. Since the metal was quite deteriorated, lower pressure than normal was used during the sandblasting process. The "spaceman" outfit is really protective equipment with a breathing system used in commercial sandblasting.

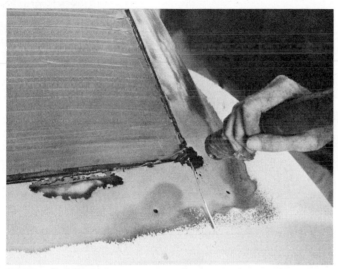

15. The sandblasting removed all the paint and rust. The border area was blasted just in case there was any hidden rust. Notice the size of the rustout holes.

16. To properly repair this extensive damage, a new piece of metal should be installed. It would be costly. Rather than use this method, it was decided to fill the area. Use a body hammer to lower the area to be built up with body filler.

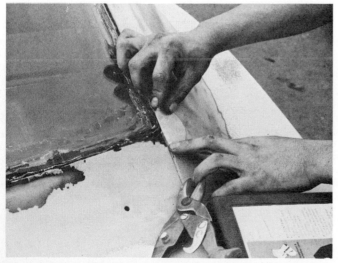

17. A piece of sheetmetal was cut and fitted to each rusted out hole.

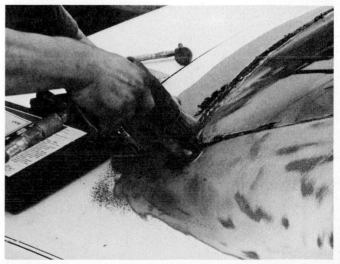

18. Drill holes through both the patch and the underlying metal.

19. Rivet the patch piece in place.

20. Grind the edges of the patch panel smooth, and also make sure that the areas surrounding the repair are cleaned to the bare metal in preparation for the body filler.

21. Ditzler Alum-A-Lead filler was used because it is superior to plastic fillers in hardness and durability. (It is also more expensive.)

22. The Alum-A-Lead comes in powder form and must be mixed with a special resin before it is applied to the car.

23. Apply the Alum-A-Lead as you would any other filler. Be sure that the patch pieces are slightly below the final surface so that the filler will bring the area back to normal.

24. After the Alum-A-Lead is dry, it is sanded or filed to the desired shape. (The filler isn't worked with a cheesegrater file like plastic body filler.)

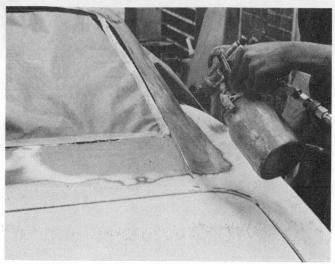

25. The filled areas should be primed and checked for additional low spots. Finish the area with sanding and spot putty.

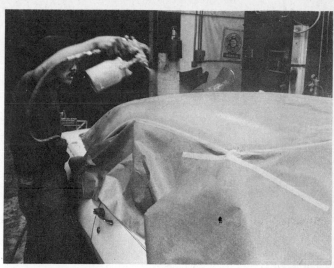

26. After the repaired areas are satisfactory, tape and prime the entire roof.

27. Silicone sealer should be used around the rear window to help seal out moisture.

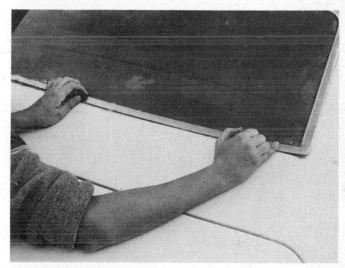

28. Reinstall the window trim.

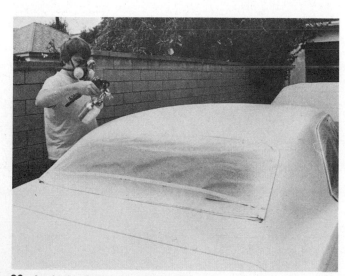

29. Apply the final color after making sure that the entire roof is ready for paint.

30. The finished product. The rest of the car still needs work, but the top looks great.

23
Pinstriping

Pinstriping, in one form or another, has been around since before the invention of the automobile. It was one of the few embellishments on early cars and trucks. After the 1930s, pinstriping faded from use by the major automotive manufacturers, but at the same time it emerged as a popular art form for hot rodders. Pinstriping was immensely popular in the 1950s. In the 1960s, Detroit rediscovered it in the form of adhesive pinstriping and it's been around ever since, adding a tasteful highlight to new and modified cars alike.

The idea of pinstriping is to make a vehicle look better. While the experienced hobby or professional pinstriper can go wild with scrolls and freeform designs, the beginning striper should start with learning the basic skills of simple lines before attempting the fancy stuff. This will give you a solid base of experience from which to develop a judgement about what line is best for a particular vehicle. Learning to pinstripe is really nothing more than learning to develop your powers of concentration. Pinstriping takes maximum concentration and a lot of practice. Both these items are more important than a steady hand. Once you've learned how to hold a brush and proper bracing techniques, you'll be surprised at how easy striping really is.

Equipment

A striper's most important tool is his brush, usually referred to as a sword or dagger, because the long hairs of the brush are shaped like a blade. There are several popular brands, available at most art supply stores, and they come in several thicknesses or sizes. Generally speaking, sizes 00, 0, and 1 are the best for striping.

When it comes to paint, a good oil-based enamel works best. Most professional stripers use a type of sign painter's paint known as Bulletin, because of its good flow and coverage qualities. Use lacquer-based paint only to stripe a lacquer-painted car, because lacquer eats away enamel paint. A retarder or castor oil is used with lacquer paint to slow down the drying time. Oil-base paint is okay for striping over all types of paint; when in doubt use oil-base. Check the directions on the can for exact use.

The other items you'll need are some rags, thinner, or turpentine (for oil-base paints) to achieve the right consistency of paint, a wax remover/degreaser to wipe down the car before striping, and an old phone book or magazine to work the paint out on.

Striping Techniques

The number one trick to striping is the paint preparation. It is also the hardest thing to describe. The paint must flow but also must have a certain amount of drag to give the brush its rudder action. On a clean surface, such as a phone book or magazine page, set up your can of paint next to a container of thinner. Dip the brush into the paint and then into the thinner. On the page, work the brush on both sides of the blade, evenly distributing the paint into the brush. This must be repeated each time a line is started, even if the lines are short. Practice and experimentation will tell you when you have the paint consistency down right. When you do, the paint flow will be even and smooth.

There is a wide variety of pinstriping tools available at paint supply shops or through mail order, including brushes, striping tape, and striping wheels. Striping tapes come in many widths and colors and give the appearance of real striping without the fuss of paint.

Books detailing types of lettering and designs can be very helpful to the beginning striper. Most professional stripers have developed "trademark" designs that started as variations on existing scrollwork patterns.

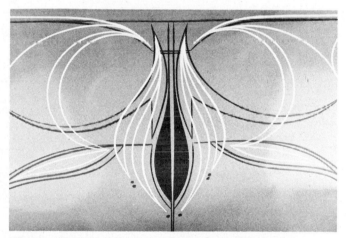
What is pinstriping? It can be anything as simple as one straight line, or as wild and intricate as this multicolored design. Good pinstriping should always enhance, but never overpower, a stock or custom paint job.

Pinstriping brushes, otherwise known as swords or daggers, come in a wide variety of sizes, though sizes 00, 0, and 1 are the best for average width lines. Properly cared for, a quality striping brush can last for months or sometimes years.

Striping brushes are available with either round or flat handles. It is easier to make straight pulls (lines) with a flat handle and curves with a round handle because you have to be able to twirl the brush when making tight circles. The normal grip is to hold the brush between thumb and forefinger, leaving the other fingers free to guide.

The first technique you should practice is pulling lines. Find the easiest line width for you to make; then practice making parallel lines of the same thickness. Next, try thicker and thinner lines. It is more difficult to maintain a constant thick line over a long surface than it is to maintain a thin one.

Once you have some confidence in the control of thickness, try pulling a line as long as you can in one continuous stroke. Once you have interrupted a line, it is difficult to start it up again and keep the same thickness. This is something that you can improve with practice.

Start practicing curves by drawing a circle with your striping brush. First try drawing the circle clockwise, then counterclockwise. Whichever way works out best for you, stick to it. In making a curve, the brush must be revolved into the curve during the stroke. The revolution starts as the brush touches the surface. This applies to all curves, even

Pinstriping

The most commonly used pinstriping paint is a type of sign painter's enamel known as Bulletin, available from many manufacturers, such as Dagger Lac, in many pre-mixed colors.

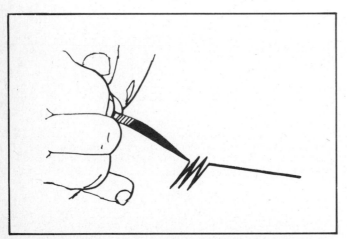

The keys to mastering pinstriping are patience, practice, and smoothness. When pulling a long continuous line, set your body to allow maximum arm reach.

gradual ones. One of the toughest things to do in one stroke is the letter "s." Practice this, and the other curves will be easy.

During the curve, the consistency of the paint is most critical, because the hairs will want to spring out. The paint must therefore be a little bit heavier than normal. It's easier to start the curve low and go up than the other way around, which seems unlikely, but it's because the paint is trying to "gravitate" out of the brush.

Once you're familiar with curves, you can move onto corners. Practice rectangles, outside curves, inside curves, and diamonds, all of which can be used at a corner point on the body of a car.

The central idea of striping should be forward motion. Striping ties different parts of the car together, making the vehicle unified. But striping should also impart a sense of purpose and direction. Senseless squiggles detract from the car's basic character, rather than enhance it. Every line has a direction, and it should correspond with the direction of the car—forward. When you want to highlight or outline objects that are protruding out of the car, such as mirrors or door handles, think of the object as sticking up out of a liquid, and moving forward toward

the front of the car. The lines that you paint around that object should record the wake of its movement through the fluid.

Always respect your pinstriping equipment. If your brushes are properly cared for they will actually get better with age. When you are finished painting, wash your brush out completely with thinner. Then saturate it with normal automotive oil (motor oil is used because it does not decompose the natural materials of the brush). Form the hairs into the blade shape. Lay it on a clean flat surface and stroke the brush flat so that the upper edge is straight and the lower edge is an even curve. Store it in a place where it will not be disturbed and the brush will take on a "set."

Before you start to stripe a car, make sure the surface is clean. Remove any wax, grease, or dirt with a degreaser or thinner. Make it easy on yourself with your first striping jobs. Pick a car that has definite character lines you can use to guide your hand. If you've done enough practice on garbage cans, old sheetmetal, and the like, you may be surprised at how nice a stripe you can draw with a body line to guide you. Part of the preparation is picking a good place to stripe—free of breeze, dust, and insects. Stripe inside a garage if possible and allow at least two days for the striping to dry before washing and waxing over it.

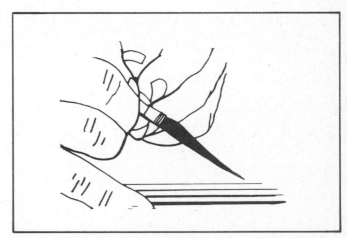

Before tackling your first striping job, practice pulling straight lines until you can control straightness and thickness. Thick lines are harder to master than thin ones.

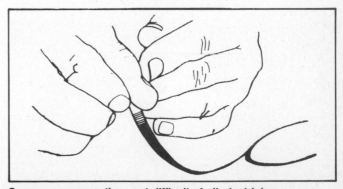

Curves are among the most difficult of all pinstriping techniques, but they're great fun once you've mastered them. Practice making the letter "s" and circles. The constant rotation of the brush into the curve is the factor that controls the width.

Tapes and Tools

While most custom painters prefer to use only a paint and brush, there are a couple of alternative methods of pinstriping. One is to use any of the various striping tapes on the market today. These tapes generally come in a selection of widths and colors. To apply the tape, put the vehicle in a warm, well lighted garage (not in the sun because the heat might bake the lines on quickly and make it hard to rearrange them during application.) Wipe the vehicle down with degreaser. Then stick one end of the tape in place where you desire. Then carefully unroll or peel the backing off the tape, depending on the type of tape used, and lay out the line, sighting down the tape often to ensure straightness and smoothness of application. If you make a mistake, simply lift up the back end of the tape and reposition it. Once the tape is where you want it, burnish it with a soft, clean, dry rag.

Handle sharp corners by crisscrossing the two pieces of tape from the different directions and then cut away the excess with a sharp knife. When you run across gaps in the sheetmetal, such as a door edge, leave a little extra tape after you cross the gap so you have enough to open the door (or hood, trunk, and so forth) and wrap the tape around to the underside edge. Be sure to clean these underside areas, too, for good tape adhesion.

Besides tape, there are several types of pinstriping tools that can be used instead of a brush. One of the most common is the Beugler Striping Tool, which is available in a variety of sizes and a large selection of interchangeable heads. The heads have a wheel that rolls out the paint, which is stored in a pressure-fed cylinder. The heads are available in single and dual-wheel designs for single and parallel striping. Another tool is the Paasche Airbrush Company's FP Flow Pencil. The flow pencil is smaller than the Beugler striping tools and has a smaller paint reservoir. The flow pencil is not much bigger than a fountain pen and as such is very easy to manipulate. It comes with a choice of four different thickness lines; however, it does not have the dual-line capabilities of the Beugler tools.

Striping tools and tapes will not make you a great artist like some of the legendary pinstripers, but they are a viable alternative to the long hours of practice required in traditional pinstriping.

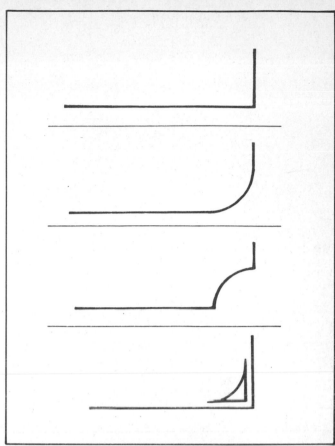

Here are four variations of striping a corner. Once you establish a motif, stick to it. Too many designs on a single vehicle are confusing.

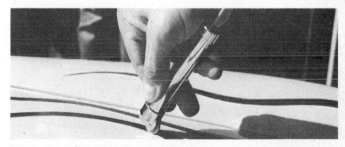

Striping tools like this Beugler "Professional" model are a good alternative to using brushes. The precision tool controls the line thickness, which varies according to which of the many interchangeable heads is used.

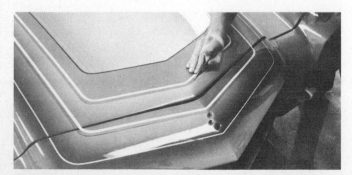

Even the best stripers will use masking tape as a guideline during the striping process, as demonstrated by Glen of Glen Designs. With the brush braced in proper position, the tape will lead your hand, leaving you free to concentrate on paint flow and line thickness.

Once you've learned the basic techniques, you can combine pinstriping with lettering or freehand painting to make many outstanding and unusual effects, such as this cartoon cowboy.

Pinstriping a Jeep

1. When well-known striper Herb Martinez tackles a pinstriping job, such as on this Jeep, he always begins by thoroughly cleaning the area to be striped with grease remover. Thinner is kept on hand to clean up paint flaws and bad surface edges.

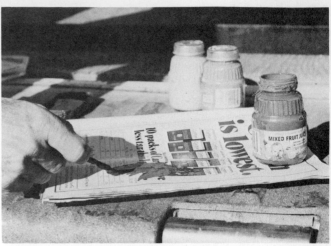

2. Using the pages of a magazine as his palate, Herb "loads" the striping brush by dipping it into the paint and then working it broadside across the magazine.

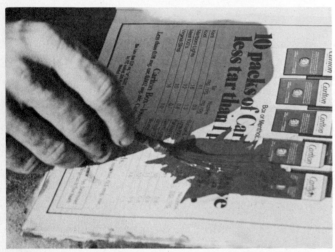

3. Next, the brush is flopped back and forth until the paint is distributed evenly throughout the bristles. Once the paint is loaded, the brush is turned or "worked" until the bristles form the dagger-like edge or blade needed for pulling stripe lines.

4. Herb then starts his first line, working from the inside of the paint design so he will never reach across his own stripes. Notice that even with simple lines Herb keeps his hand well braced, using his fingers to support his hand.

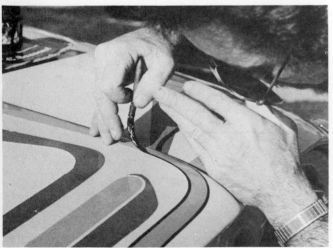

5. Turning corners with the brush is one of the hardest techniques to master. Herb uses both hands to brace the brush as it rotates through the curve.

6. Don't be afraid to pick up the brush and approach the line from a more comfortable position. The direction for pulling a corner depends on which way you feel most comfortable, or can get the most support.

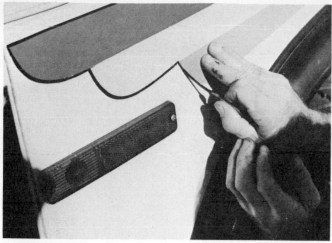

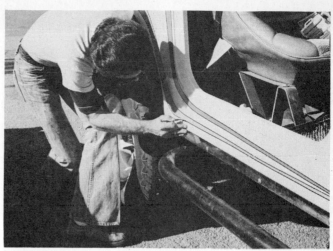

7. Common sense plays a big part in pinstriping. Look at the design you are outlining. A clean simple paint scheme should have clean, simple striping lines, including corners. Getting your lines stopped and started uniformly comes with practice.

8. When you have to move beyond arm reach to pull a continuous line, keep your movements smooth and simple. Watching a good striper maneuver around a vehicle is like watching a professional dancer.

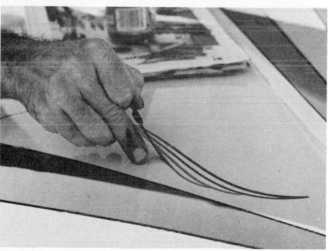

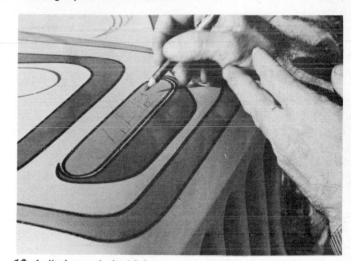

9. After completing the outlining of the Jeep's paint stripes, Herb added a few multicolored scrolls. He again starts with the lines furthest away from his body and works towards himself.

10. Lettering and pinstriping are very similar and can be combined for good effect. Herb uses a crayon marker to outline the word "Jeep" on the vehicle's hood.

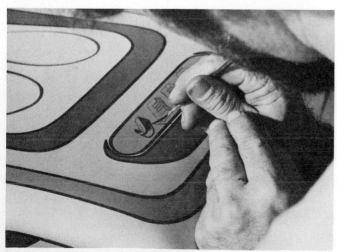

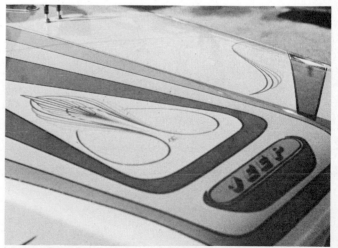

11. Using his striping paint and a fine-tipped brush, the lettering is carefully filled in. Lettering can be drawn freehand or copied from a type or design book, as Herb did for this shadowbox-style lettering.

12. The finished product demonstrates how well different techniques, such as outlining, freehand scrollwork, and lettering can combine for a really special overall effect.

24
Lettering

G old leaf lettering is one of the most popular
forms of automotive decoration. It is just a
variation of plain paint lettering, except that
the gold leaf adds extra class and sparkle. Some artistic ability is needed because the letter outlines
must be drawn before the gold leaf can be applied
inside the outlines.

There are several different types of gold leaf
(plain, variegated, etc.), but the kind used for most
automotive lettering comes on flat sheets in little
booklets about the size of a scratch pad. Gold leaf
is fragile, so care needs to be taken during application, and steps must be taken to preserve the gold
leaf once it is on the vehicle. Some type of clear
should be sprayed over the gold leaf to protect it.

Follow along as Tom Kelly of The Crazy Painters
in Bellflower, California, shows what is involved in a
gold leaf lettering project.

*1. After cleaning off the wax and polish, which could prevent
the gold leaf from adhering properly, the location of the
lettering is chosen and guidelines are made with a Stabilo
pencil.*

2. Gold powder is mixed with oil base sizing (tarnishing is no problem since variegated imitation gold leaf is used), and the flowing script is painted freehand on the surface.

3. Guidelines in white Stabilo pencil can be painted over without any harm. Skill as a sign painter, though, is what determines how the finished job will look when gold leafed.

4. An outline of each letter is done first, then brush loaded again with paint and the center portion filled in. Oil base sizing, like regular enamel, will level out after a while.

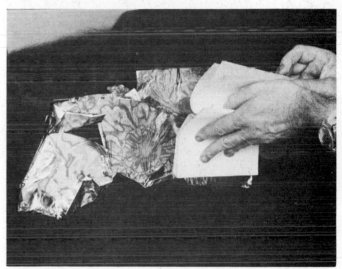

5. Sheets of gold leaf are loose in the booklet so be careful when peeling back the cover paper and applying it to the sizing. Use your fingers to push the leaf against the sizing.

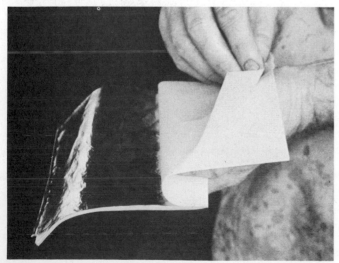

6. Thumb over the top edge of the booklet to ensure that the sheets of variegated gold leaf don't drop out. If possible, center variegated pattern on the gold-tinted sizing for the best look.

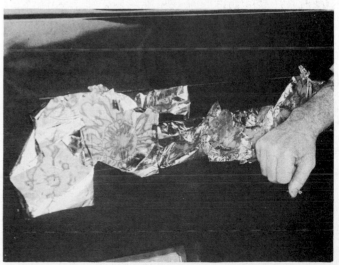

7. Use the side of the hand to gently press the sheets of gold leaf against the sizing. Be extremely careful not to twist your hand or the fragile sheets will tear and wrinkle.

8. Rubbing with a soft cloth or gently with the thumb will remove any excess left around the edges of the lettering. This excess can be used to fill in uncovered areas if necessary.

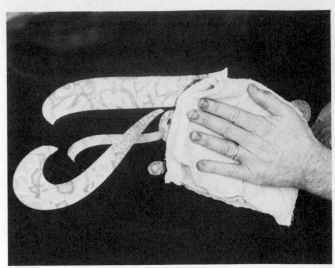

9. Burnishing gently with a cloth will get rid of tatty little whisps of leaf clinging to the edges and will sharpen up the logo. The proper placement of sheets strengthens the variegated effect.

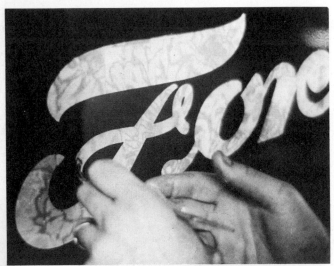

10. A sealer (clear enamel) is immediately brushed on to bring out the beautiful color and to help seal the leaf against the weather. Clear enamel is also self-leveling.

11. The lettering outline on the black vehicle is done in yellow-orange One Shot Bulletin Enamel, which is very resistant to weathering. Blue would also look nice with gold leafing.

12. Shadowing is added next and first-class results require an artist's sense of perspective. An imaginary light source is put at upper right so the letters will cast a uniform shadow to the lower left.

13. The color is darkened a little and deeper shadows added with an airbrush. Bulletin Enamel is thinned to a 60/40 paint-to-thinner ratio and the pressure regulator is set at 40 psi.

14. A yellow-orange outline is highly visible against shadows added with an airbrush. White highlights are added to create a 3-D look. Don't overdo the highlights.

15. The completed masterpiece needs only one final touch, the artist's signature. The finished gold leaf lettering is really trick although a beginner could do it with less shadowing.

For people who want some custom lettering but feel a little deficient in their freehand artistic ability, prism tape lettering is a good alternative. Prism tape is available in a variety of styles, colors, and brands but its purpose is all the same. The reflective foil comes in rolls of varying widths or in sheets. There is a paper backing which, when removed, exposes the adhesive used to stick the prism tape to the surface of a car.

Designs can be drawn freehand with Stabilo pencil or grease pencil. Mistakes can easily be wiped off the slick prism tape surface. Designs can also be traced from already existing artwork. Tom Kelly of The Crazy Painters demonstrates how he makes custom lettering with prism tape.

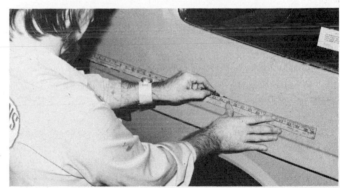

1. After deciding the size and location of the lettering, the area is wiped clean with wax and grease remover. A base line is drawn for positioning the letters.

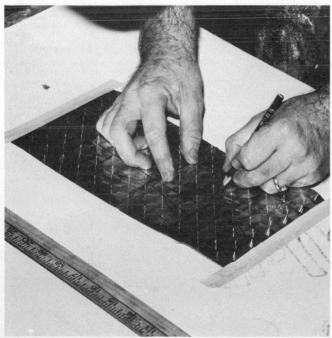

2. A sheet of prism tape is affixed to a table with tape, and guide lines are drawn to establish letter size. A Stabilo pencil is used for drawing.

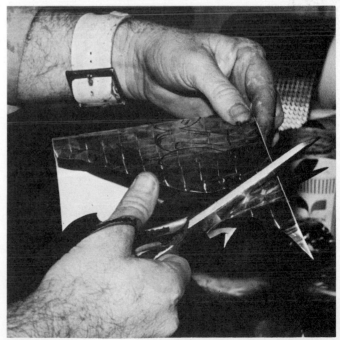

3. Once the design is set, it is cut out with a pair of scissors. The centers of the letters don't have to be cut out because they can be painted.

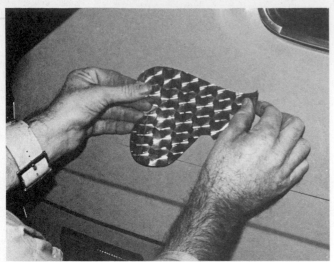

4. The first letter is easily positioned on the base line because the guidelines drawn in step 2 are still visible. Simply peel off the protective backing and carefully affix the letter.

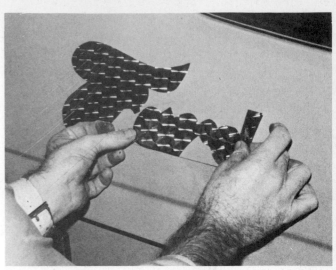

5. The remaining letters are affixed in the same manner. Take care when aligning the letters because once the adhesive touches the paint, it's stuck.

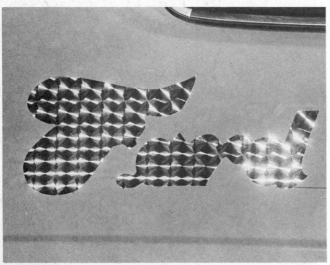

6. A soft rag with wax and grease remover is used to remove the guidelines and prepare the tape surface for paint. The logo looks incomplete, but the paint will fix that.

7. Paint is used to outline the lettering and to seal the edges so that moisture can't creep in and lift the tape. The mass of tape is filled in with paint and the letter "F" takes shape.

8. After outlining and filling in, the logo is given a 3-D look by thickening the outline. There are many styles that can be used for shadowing letters, too.

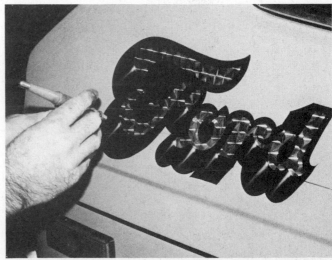

9. Adding a few highlight streaks to the shadowing with white paint really makes the lettering stand out. An airbrush is used to add the highlights.